OECD Multi-level Governance Studies

Towards Balanced Regional Development in Croatia

FROM STRATEGY DESIGN TO IMPLEMENTATION

OECD

BETTER POLICIES FOR BETTER LIVES

This document was produced with financial assistance from Norway Grants. The views expressed herein can in no way be taken to reflect the official opinion of Norway Grants or the Financial Mechanism Office.

Please cite this publication as:
OECD (2024), *Towards Balanced Regional Development in Croatia: From Strategy Design to Implementation*, OECD Multi-level Governance Studies, OECD Publishing, Paris, https://doi.org/10.1787/3c0779cf-en.

ISBN 978-92-64-76775-1 (print)
ISBN 978-92-64-49316-2 (PDF)
ISBN 978-92-64-61340-9 (HTML)
ISBN 978-92-64-42288-9 (epub)

OECD Multi-level Governance Studies
ISSN 2414-6781 (print)
ISSN 2414-679X (online)

Photo credits: Cover © xbrchx, Wlad74 iStock/Getty Images Plus.

Corrigenda to OECD publications may be found on line at: www.oecd.org/about/publishing/corrigenda.htm.

Foreword

Building on Croatia's decade-long efforts to create a legislative, regulatory and governance framework that supports regional and local development planning, implementation, monitoring and evaluation, Croatia adopted, in 2021, its National Development Strategy 2030 with the clear goal of delivering balanced regional development. To assist in meeting that objective, and in response to a request from the Government of Croatia and its Ministry of Regional Development and EU Funds (MRDEUF), this report reviews Croatia's multi-level governance and strategic planning arrangements supporting regional development. It is part of the "Enhanced Strategic Planning at Regional and Local Levels in Croatia" project, funded by Norway Grants.

The report starts by analysing Croatia's regional development trends, highlighting where territorial disparities have narrowed, stabilised or even widened across a broad range of areas over the past decade. From there, the report explores how Croatia's multi-level governance framework supporting regional development works in practice. Finally, it identifies a series of challenges that Croatia should address, in order to ensure that national and subnational governments have the necessary human and financial resources and tools to contribute to increased regional competitiveness and well-being across its territories.

The report builds on a number of activities undertaken as part of the project. First, the OECD and MRDEUF organised a series of knowledge-sharing fora bringing together representatives from Croatia's national and subnational governments to facilitate learning and peer-to-peer exchange on topics such as funding and financing, and monitoring and evaluating regional development plans. Second, the OECD organised capacity building events for staff from the MRDEUF and Croatia's 21 regional development agencies (RDAs), covering issues such as stakeholder engagement and vision-setting. Third, the OECD organised two study tours for MRDEUF and RDA staff to meet with regional development agencies in Andalucía, Spain and Wallonia, Belgium, in order to learn from international good practices.

This report was developed as part of the Programme of Work of the OECD's Regional Development Policy Committee (RDPC), a leading international forum in the fields of regional, urban, and rural development policy and multi-level governance, which is served by the Centre for Entrepreneurship, SMEs, Regions and Cities (CFE).

The RDPC emphasises the importance of multi-level governance and place-based approaches that are tailored to regional and local needs. To support the RDPC's leadership in this area, the OECD created the Multi-level Governance Studies series in 2016. This report contributes to the body of knowledge contained in this series. The report was approved by the RDPC through written procedure on 18 April 2024 (CFE/RDPC(2024)10).

Acknowledgements

The report was prepared by the OECD Centre for Entrepreneurship, SMEs, Regions and Cities (CFE), led by Lamia Kamal-Chaoui. It was produced as part of the programme of work of the Regional Development Policy Committee. The project was implemented in the context of the OECD "Enhanced Strategic Planning at Regional and Local Levels in Croatia" project. It was made possible thanks to the financial contributions of Norway Grants.

The report was co-ordinated by Stephan Visser, under the supervision of Maria Varinia Michalun, Head of the Governance and Strategic Planning Unit in the Regional Development and Multi-level Governance Division, which is part of CFE, led by Dorothée Allain-Dupré.

Chapter 1 (Assessment and recommendations) was drafted by Geoff Upton and Stephan Visser (CFE). Josh Wood (CFE) drafted Chapter 2 (Setting the scene: Regional development trends in Croatia). Chapter 3 (Croatia's regional development governance framework) was prepared by Geoff Upton and Stephan Visser. Chapter 4 (Regional development planning instruments and practices) was developed by Geoff Upton and Stephan Visser, as well as Silvia Picalarga and Claire Salama (GOV). Chapter 5 (Regional development funding and financing) was prepared by Miquel Vidal-Bover (CFE), in collaboration with Geoff Upton and Stephan Visser, under the supervision of Isabelle Chatry.

The full report benefited from valuable input and comments provided by Nadim Ahmad, Deputy Director of CFE; by Dorothée Allain-Dupré, Isabelle Chatry, and Antti Moisio in the CFE Regional Development and Multi-level Governance Division; and by external contributors Helen Creighton and Meghan Hennessy. Thanks are also due to Marc Bournisien de Valmont, Betty-Ann Bryce, Delphine Clavreul (CFE) for their support throughout the project.

The OECD wishes to express its gratitude to Dubravko Ćuk, Danijela Grizelj, Iva Novak, Luka Novosel, Spomenka Đurić and Tomislav Belovari (Ministry of Regional Development and EU Funds of Croatia) for their support of the project and for the input provided throughout the project implementation process.

The OECD also warmly thanks representatives from Croatia's central government bodies, subnational government associations, counties and regional development agencies, cities and municipalities, and academia that met with the OECD team during fact-finding missions, international knowledge-sharing fora and capacity building activities, which were organised as part of the project.

Finally, thanks are extended to Pilar Philip and Jack Waters (CFE) who provided guidance on preparing the publication, to Roxie Glavanov (CFE) for the cover art, to external editor Andrew Brenner who edited the final manuscript, and to Leslie Greenhow, Elena Arcones Sanjuan and Evangelia Thanasi (CFE) for their administrative and logistical support throughout the project implementation process.

Table of contents

Tables

Figures

Boxes

Abbreviations and acronyms

BARDA	Bulgarian Association of Regional Development Agencies
COVID-19	Coronavirus disease of 2019
EBRD	European Bank for Reconstruction and Development
EFDF	Equalisation Fund for Decentralised Functions
EIB	European Investment Bank
EU	European Union
EUR	Euro (currency)
FEF	Fiscal Equalisation Fund
GDP	Gross Domestic Product
GVA	Gross Value Added
HBOR	Croatian Bank for Reconstruction and Development
HRK	Croatian kuna (currency)
IBEROAM	Ibero-American Association of RDAs
IDETA	Regional Development Agency of Picardy Wallonia
IFI	International Financial Institutions
IMF	International Monetary Fund
IGRETEC	Regional Development Agency Charleroi and South Hainaut
IT	Information Technology
ITI	Integrated Territorial Investment
ITP	Integrated Territorial Programme
LDA	Local Development Agency
MRDEUF	Ministry of Regional Development and EU Funds
Mbps	Megabytes per second
NARDA	National Association of Regional Development Agencies of Ukraine

NDS	National Development Strategy 2030
NUTS	Nomenclature of Territorial Units for Statistics
OECD	Organisation for Economic Co-operation and Development
PIT	Personal Income Tax
PPP	Public-Private Partnership
PPS	Purchasing Power Standard
RDA	Regional Development Agency
RDPC	Regional Development Policy Committee
ROREG	Romanian Association of Regional Development Agencies
SWOT	Strengths, weaknesses, opportunities and challenges
TL	Territorial Level
UNDP	United Nations Development Program
VAT	Value Added Tax

Executive Summary

Since joining the EU in 2013, Croatia's macroeconomic performance has improved significantly. With average annual real GDP growth of 2.8% between 2013 and 2022, Croatia's GDP per capita gap with the OECD average has narrowed by 11.5 percentage points. However, this growth has not been uniform across the country, with large and sometimes growing disparities across Croatian regions including in other areas driving well-being, such as educational attainment.

These trends provide the backdrop against which Croatia has reformed its legislative and planning framework for regional development. The reform process has culminated in the adoption of the National Development Strategy 2030, which includes balanced regional development among its main long-term objectives. It has also led to the design of territorial development strategies at the county and local levels, and the creation of new funding mechanisms, many of which are tailored to the needs of specific territories.

To make sure that the regional development reforms deliver concrete results for citizens and businesses across the country however, action is needed to address a series of challenges. These relate to Croatia's relatively high level of territorial fragmentation, and small territorial scale at which regional development plans are designed and implemented. Another key challenge is the fact that monitoring and evaluation systems, so far, primarily serve as accountability tools, rather than instruments for policy learning. This report helps to identify ways in which these and other challenges can be effectively addressed.

Key findings

- **At the subnational level, development indicators point to significant disparities across Croatian territories.** In terms of economic performance, the gap between the country's most and least economically developed regions (Zagreb City and Pannonian Croatia, respectively) has widened. In 2013, GDP per capita in Pannonian Croatia was 63% lower than that of Zagreb City. This had increased to 66% in 2021. In 2022, Varaždin County's unemployment rate (3.2%) was almost five times lower than that of Virovitica-Podravina County (15.7%). Moreover, while all counties reported population shrinkage between 2011 and 2021, there were vast differences in the scale of the decline (e.g. -5.7% in Dubrovnik-Neretva County compared to -20.3% in Vukovar-Srijem County).
- **The extensive legislative and planning framework for regional development set up in 2014 established a clear hierarchy of national-, county- and local-level plans.** The government also developed comprehensive regulations and guidelines for the design, monitoring and evaluation of regional development planning documents. To ensure their effective implementation, however, there are a number of actions that Croatia is recommended to take:
  - Consider adopting a regional development strategy that can serve as a bridge between the high-level National Development Strategy, and county and local development plans. The strategy would help to ensure that the government's regional development policy is clear and well-co-ordinated among national and subnational government levels.
  - Invest in capacity-building support for local government officials, particularly in areas related to strategy design and implementation (e.g. stakeholder engagement, procurement). The

government should also deliver an outreach campaign to county officials to enhance their understanding of the purpose of regional development planning, and their responsibilities in terms of implementing, monitoring and evaluating their development plans.

- Establish performance dialogues (e.g. between regional development agencies [RDA] and the Ministry of Regional Development and EU Funds) to help ensure that monitoring evidence is not only used for upward accountability, but also to improve policy implementation.

- **A relatively high level of territorial fragmentation in Croatia undermines the capacity of subnational governments to support the implementation of the country's regional development policy.** The average local-level population in Croatia is nearly a third lower than the OECD average, with some having a population that is as small as 0.03% of the OECD average. As a result, many local governments have limited financial and human resource capacity to carry out strategic planning tasks and manage investment. Enhancing co-operation across subnational governments could help them to improve the delivery of public services that particularly benefit from economies of scale (e.g. education, healthcare). It could also increase the coherence with which development resources are deployed.
  - At the regional level, Croatia could expand the use of macro-regional development agreements between county governments, along with joint investment strategies. This could help them to more effectively mobilise and deploy financing to address shared development challenges, and reduce the country's territorial disparities.
- **Croatia's 21 RDAs have become essential to the country's regional development efforts.** They are responsible for designing development plans, supporting their implementation and reporting on progress to the national government. They also help to identify and mobilise EU funding for counties, cities and municipalities. The ability of the RDAs to carry out these tasks however, is challenged by two elements. First, by December 2025, EU Technical Assistance funding, which has accounted for 75% of RDA revenues, will end. Second, the relatively small territorial scale at which the RDAs operate (TL3) compared to many of their OECD peers risks limiting their effectiveness in driving regional development. For instance, operating at a smaller territorial scale can result in high levels of spending on basic administrative functions. It also increases the co-ordination costs of addressing macro-regional development challenges.
  - In order to ensure that the RDAs can continue to guide regional development efforts and help subnational governments mobilise funding to implement their development plans, Croatia should explore ways to ensure sufficient RDA funding post-2025, e.g. by providing core funding for the agencies through the national budget.
  - Simultaneously, Croatia should conduct an analysis of the costs, benefits, as well as legal and political obstacles to establishing RDAs at the TL2 level in the medium to long term.
- **Over the past decade, the capacity of Croatia's subnational governments to fund and finance regional development initiatives has increased.** Driven by the influx of EU funding, between 2010 and 2021, investment spending by subnational governments rose by 82.7% in real terms. In order to enhance subnational fiscal autonomy, in 2023, Croatia granted cities and municipalities additional flexibility to set their PIT rates, within a nationally determined band. However, there are concerns that the reform could lead to a 'race to the bottom', in which local governments consecutively and aggressively lower PIT rates to attract investment and talent, thereby undermining their fiscal capacity. This could hamper their ability to deliver quality public services, and make strategic investments.
  - Closely monitoring the effects of the reforms on local budgets could help Croatia to ensure that the new rate-setting powers of cities and municipalities do not lead to large fiscal disparities, and or take mitigating action should this eventuality occur.

1 Assessment and recommendations

Regional development trends in Croatia

Since its accession to the European Union (EU) in 2013, Croatia's macroeconomic performance at the national level has been impressive. Between 2013 and 2022, Croatian real GDP per capita grew by an average of 3.8%, more than double the average in the EU (1.6%) and in the OECD (1.3%) (OECD, 2023[1]). In tandem, Croatian living standards have begun to converge towards EU standards, with the country's GDP per capita only 27.1% below the EU average in 2022, as compared with 38.6% a decade earlier (Eurostat, 2023[2]; World Bank, 2024[3]). Other positive economic trends over the period have included rapid export growth, a sharp and sustained fall in long-term unemployment, rising labour productivity and stable inflation rates.

Over the same period, however, Croatia has faced significant demographic decline. Its population contracted by 9.4% between 2013 and 2022, driven by lower fertility rates and net outward migration (especially to other European counties, e.g. Germany) (Eurostat, 2023[4]). In addition, the population is ageing, with the proportion of Croatia's residents aged 64 and over having increased to 22.5% in 2021 (from 17.7% in 2011) (Eurostat, 2023[4]). Sustained demographic decline can have wide-ranging effects on public finances, service delivery and socio-economic development, which need to be considered by policy makers. For example, population decline can lead to lower tax revenues, thereby limiting local government capacity to maintain vital infrastructure. Population decline can also lead to the closure of schools and healthcare centres.

National-level well-being indicators for Croatia, meanwhile, paint a picture of modest progress in some areas, and stagnation in others. For example, the share of the population at risk of poverty fell 2.7 percentage points between 2013 and 2022 (Eurostat, 2023[5]). At the same time, in 2022, the average Croatian could expect to live 77.7 years at birth, a minor decrease compared to the 77.8 estimated in 2013, and below the EU average of 80.4 (Eurostat, 2023[5]).

At the subnational level, Croatia's economic performance since 2013 has not been uniform, with large and sometimes growing disparities among the country's four statistical regions—Adriatic Croatia, Northern Croatia, Pannonian Croatia and Zagreb City. Recent subnational-level data show that Zagreb City's productivity, employment and average income were twice the levels of all other Croatian TL2 (NUTS 2) regions (Eurostat, 2023[6]; Eurostat, 2023[7]; Eurostat, 2023[8]). Furthermore, across different metrics, the gap between Zagreb City and less economically developed regions (e.g. Pannonian Croatia) appears to have widened over time. For example, in 2013, GDP per capita in Pannonian Croatia was 63% lower than that of Zagreb City. This had increased to 66% by 2021(Eurostat, 2023[8]).

Subnational well-being data track with the economic divergences across Croatian regions. In comparison with the national average, Zagreb City performs better than other regions in terms of life expectancy, suicide rates, infant mortality and risk of poverty (Eurostat, 2023[9]; Eurostat, 2023[10]; Eurostat, 2023[11]; Eurostat, 2023[12]). By contrast, Northern Croatia and Pannonian Croatia perform below the national average for each of these metrics. In 2021, Zagreb City also reported a significantly higher share of working-age adults with tertiary qualifications than other Croatian regions; e.g. 42.7% in Zagreb City, as compared with 20.3% in Northern Croatia and 17.6% in Pannonian Croatia (Eurostat, 2023[13]). The heavy concentration of highly-skilled individuals in Zagreb City risks concentrating investment and entrepreneurial activity in the capital region, potentially exacerbating existing territorial disparities.

Subnational indicators also point to a stark territorial cleavage at the county level (TL3) in Croatia, with demographic, economic and well-being data often, albeit not always, showing a more positive snapshot in Zagreb City and neighbouring areas, as well as coastal counties. For instance, in 2020, GDP per capita was highest in Zagreb City and the coastal counties of Istria and Primorjie-Gorski Kotor, and lowest in the five counties of Pannonian Croatia (Eurostat, 2023[14]). Moreover, while all counties reported population shrinkage between 2011 and 2021, there were vast differences in the scale of the decline (e.g. -5.7% in Dubrovnik-Neretva County compared to -20.3% in Vukovar-Srijem County) (Croatian Bureau of Statistics, 2023[15]). The sharp drop of skilled and working-age residents in some counties is of particular concern, as it threatens the economic potential of such counties and jeopardizes public service delivery (e.g. to keep schools open).

These trends provide the backdrop against which Croatia has reformed its legislative and planning framework for regional development since 2014. In fact, faced with wide-ranging territorial disparities, Croatia has set balanced regional development as one of its main long-term objectives.

Croatia's governance framework for regional development

Since joining the EU, Croatia has taken significant strides to establish and strengthen its legislative and policy framework for regional and local development. First, the adoption of the 2014 Law on Regional Development established a legal foundation for place-based regional development policy making. In particular, it regulates the governmental bodies involved in supporting policy making at all levels of government. This includes the Ministry of Regional Development and EU Funds (MRDEUF), which is the key body responsible for developing and co-ordinating the implementation of Croatia's regional development policy.

In 2017, the government took further legislative action to improve the coherence with which strategic planning for regional development is conducted among levels of government. In particular it sought to address three challenges: i) an excess of overlapping planning documents at the national level, which created uncertainty regarding sectoral and multi-sectoral development aims; ii) a process for designing national and subnational planning documents that was not co-ordinated among levels of government; and iii) limited clarity regarding the assignment of responsibilities for implementation and whether development objectives could, in fact, be achieved.

To address these planning and implementation challenges, in 2017 the government amended the Law on Regional Development. Based on the new law, Croatia's 21 regional development agencies (RDAs) were reconfigured as public regional co-ordinators responsible for regional development planning. Prior to this, they had existed as limited liability companies predominantly focused on providing paid consulting services. In parallel, the government adopted a new 2017 Law on the System of Strategic Planning and Development Management. The law created a comprehensive framework for strategic planning among levels of government, with a clear set of long-, medium- and short-term national- and subnational-level planning documents. It also clarified the actors responsible for the design, implementation, monitoring and evaluation of development plans.

In tandem, the government established various horizontal and vertical co-ordination mechanisms to support regional development policy design and implementation. These included the Council for Regional Development, which was created to support multi-level dialogue for the implementation of regional development policy. It also included the network of RDAs that supports communication between the

MRDEUF and RDAs on legislative and financial developments that are relevant to the county and local levels of government.

Notwithstanding the progress made through the above-mentioned reforms, there are a number of areas that Croatia could strengthen in order to further improve the effectiveness of its regional development governance framework. First, the government should update the Law on Regional Development to eliminate obsolete planning obligations. Despite the adoption of the Law on the System of Strategic Planning and Development Management in 2017, which streamlined planning requirements, the Law on Regional Development was not adjusted to reflect these changes. As such, it still mandates the development of some planning documents that are no longer developed and/or have replaced by other planning requirements (e.g. urban development strategies having been replaced by Integrated Territorial Investment Strategies). This creates uncertainty regarding the planning responsibilities of relevant actors. In parallel to updating the Law, the government could map existing planning responsibilities at national and subnational levels, in order to identify possible areas where requirements could be further streamlined and ensure they match subnational planning and implementation capacities.

Second, between 2018 and 2023, the total number of RDA employees increased from 360 to 545 between 2018 and 2023, with staffing levels in several RDAs rising by more than 75% (OECD, 2022[16]; MRDEUF, 2023[17]). Despite this increase, there is a need to address skills gaps reported by RDAs in areas such as public procurement, monitoring and evaluation, and advancing the green and digital transitions (OECD, 2023[18]). Strengthening these skills is essential to help RDAs support the implementation, monitoring and evaluation of county development plans, and design competitive project proposals for EU funding and financing opportunities (e.g. those related to renewable energy and digital innovation). One way to address this issue would be for the MRDEUF and RDAs to conduct an annual training needs assessment, on the basis of which a capacity building plan could be developed, and training modules could be designed and delivered (e.g. by the MRDEUF and the State School for Public Administration).

Third, the legal, functional and financial ties that RDAs have to both the county administrations and the national government, whose responsibilities and interests do not always align, creates accountability challenges. For instance, while RDAs are *de jure* accountable to county administrations, which are typically their sole founder, they are also formally accredited by and accountable to the MRDEUF (e.g. for EU Technical Assistance funding that the Ministry channels to the RDAs). This creates tension over which strategic and operational tasks the RDAs should prioritise: those coming from the MRDEUF or those coming from the county administration? (OECD, 2023[18]). The government could address this issue by amending the Law on Regional Development to provide additional clarity on RDA tasks coming from the county and the national government. This could be accompanied by developing briefing materials and an outreach campaign, aimed at county governments, to ensure they acquire a more robust understanding of their strategic planning responsibilities and the mandate of the RDAs.

Fourth, the effectiveness of Croatia's RDAs could be hampered by the limited territorial scale at which they operate. Unlike many OECD Member countries (e.g. Netherlands, Romania, Spain), Croatia's RDAs operate at the county (TL3) level and not the TL2 level. Operating at a smaller territorial scale usually entails smaller pools of funding for individual RDAs, which could affect their ability to attract and retain highly-skilled professionals. Moreover, having 21 TL3-level RDAs may also imply disproportionate levels of spending on basic administrative functions. To address these challenges, Croatia could consider conducting an analysis of costs, benefits, and legal and political obstacles to establishing RDAs at the higher TL2 level. Such a reconfiguration could involve reducing the number of RDAs from 21 to four, one for each TL2 area. The assessment should also consider intermediate alternatives that might help to achieve the benefits of scale without a full reconfiguration of RDAs.

Fifth, existing co-ordination bodies for regional development should be strengthened, in order to improve the coherence of cross-government strategic planning. For instance, the Council for Regional Development, which was established in 2019, has never been operationalised. In its stead, periodic meetings between the Prime Minister and different ministries, county prefects and representatives from the association of local governments have been used to discuss Croatia's regional development policy. However, this ad hoc co-ordination body lacks clearly formulated objectives and does not guarantee the participation of several actors responsible for implementing regional development policy across government, including RDAs. These shortcomings risk limiting the mechanism's effectiveness as a forum to discuss Croatia's regional development policy, assess the extent to which the country's regional development objectives are being met, and what actions are needed to improve performance. In addition to extending the list of actors that can participate in the body's meetings, Croatia could consider reorganising the body into two chambers: one to support inter-ministerial co-ordination of regional development policy and the other to support the policy's vertical co-ordination among different levels of government. Good practices that Croatia could look to for inspiration, in particular to support policy dialogue among levels of governments, include Poland's Joint Central Government and Local Government Committee and Sweden's Forum for Sustainable Regional Development (OECD, 2020[19]; Government of Poland, n.d.[20]; Government of Poland, n.d.[21]; Lublinska, 2017[22]; OECD, 2023[23]).

Sixth and finally, co-ordination and exchange between RDAs needs to be further institutionalised, in order to support peer-to-peer learning. The Croatian Association of Counties, in which the RDAs can participate, could help to address this issue, for instance by setting up a dedicated RDA forum, which supports opportunities for peer-to-peer learning on topics that are relevant to RDAs' daily activities. An alternative could involve establishing a separate national RDA association, following the example of several OECD Member countries (e.g. Bulgaria, Romania, Spain).

Croatia's regional development planning instruments and practices

The 2017 Law on the System of Strategic Planning and Development Management has provided the impetus for significant cross-government strategic planning efforts in support of regional development. After the law was passed, a National Development Strategy 2030 (NDS) was adopted in 2021, which articulates a high-level, long-term vision for Croatia's economic development. Supporting balanced regional development is identified as one of its key priorities. In tandem, all county and some local governments in Croatia have produced development plans to support their planning efforts.

Croatia's system of strategic planning for regional development has several strengths. In particular, the legislative framework helps to ensure policy coherence by establishing a clear hierarchy among national-, county- and local-level plans. Moreover, RDAs are responsible for verifying that subnational plans align with the NDS priorities. In addition, the MRDEUF has developed comprehensive guidelines and regulations, as well as instruction manuals, to help policy makers design, monitor and evaluate strategic planning documents. Furthermore, strategic planning documents at all levels of government are developed through extensive consultation with different governmental and non-governmental stakeholders, which helps to ensure that they reflect stakeholder needs and priorities. Legislation has also embedded monitoring and evaluation activities in strategic planning processes at all levels of government, while clear processes have been established for upward reporting on the implementation of county- and local-level development plans.

At the same time, Croatia's regional development planning instruments and practices face a number of challenges that will need to be addressed to ensure the effective implementation of its regional development policy. First, at the national level, the government's territorial priorities need to be articulated better. A core aim of the NDS was to raise the profile of regional development policies across and among levels of government. At the same time, however, the document does not fully embed balanced regional development as a cross-cutting priority. The government should consider updating the document so that all relevant strategic objectives indicate how they will contribute to balanced regional development. Moreover, to clarify Croatia's regional development policy and help subnational policy makers design development plans that better align with national priorities, Croatia should design a national strategy for regional development, as required by law. Developing such a national-level strategy would enable the government to articulate its vision, strategic objectives and priorities for balanced territorial development in greater detail, and could serve as a bridge between the NDS and other national and subnational planning documents.

Second, at the county level, there are several areas for improvement in the design of county development plans. In particular, these plans currently lack clarity regarding the actors involved in their implementation, and the contributions (e.g. financial, expertise, or material resources) that they are expected to make. This means that stakeholders may not fully understand their responsibilities, which could result in a lack of ownership or commitment among involved parties, as unclear responsibilities can lead to disengagement. The government could address this issue by amending the guidelines for designing county development plans and requiring them to include an implementation feasibility plan. This plan could include: i) a mapping of actors contributing to the implementation of each strategic objective; ii) the nature of their contribution; and iii) the implementation mechanisms (e.g. co-ordination).

Third, Croatia's relatively high degree of territorial fragmentation constrains the design and implementation of local development plans. The average local-level population in Croatia is nearly a third lower (30.3%) than in the OECD, with some having a population that is as small as 0.03% of the OECD average. Moreover, 37% of municipalities have fewer than 2 000 inhabitants and only 5% have with more than 20 000 (OECD, 2023[24]; Croatian Bureau of Statistics, 2023[25]). As a result, many local administrations often lack the necessary human resource capacity to design a local development plan and support its implementation. To address this challenge, Croatia could consider taking additional steps to promote inter-municipal co-operation. For instance, the government could mandate small local governments that meet certain criteria (e.g. have less than 1 500 inhabitants) to collaborate with neighbouring cities and/or municipalities to develop a joint local development plan. Further to this, the MRDEUF, in collaboration with the RDAs, could support the strategic planning capacity of local governments in other ways, including by: i) organising targeted training sessions for local civil servants; and ii) creating an online strategic planning toolbox to enable local civil servants to learn at their own pace.

Fourth, there is a need to improve access to high-quality and timely data during the design stage of development plans. For example, 95% of RDAs surveyed by the OECD indicated that a lack of data was a challenge for designing county development plans. In particular, a majority of RDAs felt that their decision making (e.g. on development priorities) could be improved through additional economic data (81%), innovation data (62%) and investment data (57%) (OECD, 2022[26]). Currently, a lack of data at the TL3 level and lower, coupled with a limited awareness of existing datasets by subnational actors, hampers their ability to develop diagnostics of territorial development challenges and conduct thorough and accurate monitoring and evaluation exercises. To address the lack of data, the MRDEUF should consider organising regular discussions between the RDAs and subnational government associations on the one hand, and the Croatian Bureau of Statistics on the other, in order to help identify subnational data needs. To increase awareness about existing datasets, the government could consider different measures adopted by governments across the OECD (e.g. in the Netherlands), including launching a newsletter with periodic updates on relevant subnational data or building a subnational data portal.

Fifth and finally, the quality and impact of monitoring and evaluation exercises on regional development policy making should be improved. The value of such activities lies not in their occurrence as a procedural requirement, but rather as substantive exercises that can help to improve the implementation of subnational development plans. Currently, monitoring reports on county and local development plans are primarily used for upward accountability (i.e. to comply with monitoring and evaluation regulations) and are rarely discussed by relevant stakeholders (e.g. RDAs, county leaderships and the MRDEUF) to assess implementation progress and challenges. For monitoring and evaluation evidence to serve as a management tool, Croatia should ensure such evidence is embedded in a performance dialogue that is conducted regularly and frequently. Such performance dialogues should ideally consist of regular meetings between the subnational executives (e.g. prefects or mayors) and their strategic planning teams. To support this practice, the MRDEUF could develop guidelines to suggest how performance dialogues should be organised. It could also hold annual meetings with RDAs to identify region-specific implementation challenges that may require national-level support.

Funding and financing of regional development in Croatia

Over the past decade, the capacity of Croatia's subnational governments to fund and finance regional and local development has gradually improved. Between 2016 and 2022, for instance, Croatia recorded a 26% increase in subnational revenue in real terms, while subnational expenditure increased 19%. The larger increase in revenue compared to expenditure suggests a consolidation of fiscal capacity at the subnational level. Despite this improvement, subnational government revenue now accounts for 27.5% of total revenue in Croatia, which is significantly lower than the OECD average (44.9%) (OECD, 2023[27]; OECD, 2023[24]).

The composition of subnational budget revenue has been weighted towards inter-governmental transfers. In 2022, grants and subsidies accounted for 53.6% of total Croatian subnational revenues (up 3.4% compared to 2010), which is on par with the OECD average (52.8%) (OECD, 2023[24]). A reliance on transfers, which are often earmarked for specific functions, risks limiting the ability of subnational governments to allocate spending to meet specific local needs. At the same time, levels of subnational tax autonomy have slowly increased, with city and municipal governments (but not county governments) able to set rates on a number of taxes levied by subnational governments.

Croatia's accession to the EU in 2013 proved to be an important development in its system of subnational government financing. New-found access to EU financing opportunities helped drive an 82.7% increase in subnational government investment in real terms between 2010 and 2021, thereby supporting the implementation of regional and local development projects across the country (OECD/UCLG, 2022[28]; Eurostat, 2023[29]; OECD, 2023[24]).

Moreover, supported by EU funding and financing, Croatia has created several mechanisms to fund development projects that consider the specific needs and capacities of its counties, cities and municipalities. These include the MRDEUF-led Co-funding Programme, which helps subnational governments meet the EU's co-funding requirement for project calls, and funding for 'assisted areas' (i.e. the subnational governments whose performance on a series of development indicators sits below the national average). The latter element is determined through the Regional Development Index, a weighted indicator made up of various demographic, economic and social indicators.

At the same time, there are a number of areas for improvement related to Croatia's funding and financing arrangements for regional development. First, Croatia should ensure that increased access to and use of EU funding by its subnational governments is being utilised to help tackle regional and local development needs and priorities. While in 2014 Croatia reported that subnational governments did not receive revenue from EU grants, by 2020 close to 8% of subnational revenue came from the EU (Ministry of Finance, 2023[30]). EU grants have provided an important opportunity for subnational governments to invest in physical infrastructure and address their regional development priorities. Moreover, increased access to and better use of EU funding has helped subnational governments strengthen their strategic planning and investment skills and expertise (e.g. to identify funding opportunities, prepare competitive proposals and conduct monitoring and evaluation activities). This improvement could, however, make them vulnerable to potential changes in EU funding priorities. To prevent this, Croatia could explore options to further diversify the revenue streams of subnational governments. This could entail adopting new measures to boost subnational fiscal autonomy, for instance by devolving existing national taxes to lower levels of government (e.g. green taxes or fees).

Relatedly, there is a need to ensure that recent reforms to increase the fiscal autonomy of subnational governments do not add to inter-regional or intra-municipal inequalities. In October 2023, the government amended the Income Tax Act, empowering cities and municipalities to set Personal Income Tax (PIT) rates within a nationally determined band. This provides them with greater control over their revenue base, and could lead to improved financial stability and reduced dependence on central government transfers. However, the government should closely monitor the effects of the reform on subnational budgets. In particular, it should ensure that the additional powers afforded to local governments to reduce PIT rates do not lead to a 'race to the bottom' through aggressive and repeated reductions in the tax burden. Such an outcome could add to disparities in the fiscal capacity of local governments, and would be particularly damaging to smaller cities and municipalities, given that larger cities enjoy greater fiscal space to absorb tax cuts (e.g. through revenue from user charges and fees).

A second area for improvement relates to the effectiveness of the Regional Development Index. There are fears that some subnational governments attempt to 'game' their Index score and underperform on certain indicators in order to keep their 'assisted area' classification and benefit from associated funding support. To address this issue, the government could consider gradually phasing out financial support to subnational governments that are no longer classified as assisted areas. This would reduce incentives for local leaders to deliberately seek an 'assisted area' designation, while also providing them with funding to consolidate recent development gains.

A third area for improvement concerns the funding and financing-related challenges associated with territorial fragmentation at the subnational level in Croatia. In particular, the high level of fragmentation creates inefficiencies as the impact of investment may be diluted across too many small initiatives. To address this issue, Croatia could consider expanding the use of macro-regional co-operation instruments, such as the Slavonia, Baranja and Srijem development agreement. Signed by five counties in 2017, this agreement established a co-ordination council and has overseen the allocation of EUR 2.6 billion in EU and national development funds to regional projects (OECD, 2023[31]). Despite its success, many counties are not yet part of similar development agreements, as they have encountered challenges to identify sources to fund and finance macro-regional co-operation. Developing framework agreements with international financial institutions to ensure that macro-regional development councils can borrow from such institutions is one possible solution to this challenge.

A fourth and final area for improvement pertains to the need to review the financing model of RDAs, in order to shore up their operational sustainability. RDAs depend on two sources of revenue to carry out their mandate, namely i) supporting county-level strategic planning and ii) identifying funding calls and helping local governments develop project proposals. RDA base funding comes from their founding members (typically counties). This generally represents 25% to 30% of RDA revenue (OECD, 2023[18]). The remainder of RDA funding comes from EU Technical Assistance, which is channelled through the MRDEUF. Funding from EU Technical Assistance will end in December 2025, by which time Croatia aims to have strengthened the RDA funding model. In order to ensure that RDAs have the necessary financial resources to execute their tasks and responsibilities, Croatia can consider complementary actions. For instance, it could call on RDA founders (i.e. county governments) to increase their financial support to RDAs. Following the example of RDAs in different OECD Member countries (e.g. Belgium, Spain), the government could also consider allowing RDAs to once again generate a portion of their revenue through paid activities or services. Additionally, the government could provide direct funding for RDA activities through the national budget.

References

Croatian Bureau of Statistics (2023), "Mid-year Estimate of Population", *Population - Review by Counties*, https://podaci.dzs.hr/en/search?q=natural%20change%20population%20counties%20review (accessed on 4 January 2024). [15]

Croatian Bureau of Statistics (2023), *Popis stanovništva, kućanstava i stanova 2021. - Stanovništvo [Census of population, households and apartments 2021 - Population]*, https://dzs.gov.hr/u-fokusu/popis-2021/88 (accessed on 4 March 2024). [25]

Eurostat (2023), *At-Risk-of-Poverty Rate by NUTS 2 Regions*, https://ec.europa.eu/eurostat/databrowser/view/tgs00103/default/table?lang=en (accessed on 4 January 2024). [11]

Eurostat (2023), *At-Risk-of-Poverty Rate of Older People, by Age and Sex - EU-SILC and ECHP Surveys*, https://ec.europa.eu/eurostat/databrowser/view/ILC_PNS1/default/table?lang=en&category=livcon.ilc_ip.ilc_li (accessed on 3 January 2024). [5]

Eurostat (2023), *Causes of Death - Standardised Death Rate by NUTS 2 Region of Residence*, https://ec.europa.eu/eurostat/databrowser/view/HLTH_CD_ASDR2__custom_7230661/bookmark/table?lang=en&bookmarkId=92306057-8219-4299-9974-ebc5ead5c255 (accessed on 4 January 2024). [12]

Eurostat (2023), "Government revenue, expenditure and main aggregates", *Government finance statistics (EDP and ESA 2010)*, https://ec.europa.eu/eurostat/databrowser/view/GOV_10A_MAIN__custom_7657932/default/table?lang=en (accessed on 3 October 2023). [29]

Eurostat (2023), *Gross Domestic Product (GDP) at Current Market Prices by NUTS 3 Regions*, https://ec.europa.eu/eurostat/databrowser/view/NAMA_10R_3GDP/default/table?lang=en&category=na10.nama10.nama_10reg.nama_10r_gdp (accessed on 4 January 2024). [14]

Eurostat (2023), *Infant Mortality Rates by NUTS 2 Region*, https://ec.europa.eu/eurostat/databrowser/view/demo_r_minfind/default/table?lang=en (accessed on 4 January 2024). [10]

Eurostat (2023), *Life Expectancy at Birth by Sex and NUTS 2 Region*, https://ec.europa.eu/eurostat/databrowser/view/tgs00101/default/table?lang=en (accessed on 4 January 2024). [9]

Eurostat (2023), *Main GDP aggregates per capita*, https://ec.europa.eu/eurostat/databrowser/view/NAMA_10_PC/default/table?lang=en&category=na10.nama10.nama_10_aux (accessed on 2 January 2024). [2]

Eurostat (2023), *Nominal Labour productivity by NUTS 2 regions*, https://ec.europa.eu/eurostat/databrowser/view/nama_10r_2nlp/default/table?lang=en (accessed on 3 January 2024). [6]

Eurostat (2023), *Population by Educational Attainment Level, Sex, Age, Country of Birth and NUTS 2 Regions (%)*, https://ec.europa.eu/eurostat/databrowser/view/edat_lfs_9917__custom_8658906/default/table?lang=en (accessed on 4 January 2024). [13]

Eurostat (2023), *Population projections*, https://ec.europa.eu/eurostat/databrowser/view/TPS00002/default/table?lang=en (accessed on 18 September 2023). [4]

Eurostat (2023), *Regional Gross Domestic Product (PPS per Inhabitant) by NUTS 2 Regions*, https://ec.europa.eu/eurostat/databrowser/view/TGS00005/default/table?lang=en&category=na10.nama10.nama_10reg.nama_10r_gdp (accessed on 3 January 2024). [8]

Eurostat (2023), *Unemployment rate by NUTS 2 regions*, https://ec.europa.eu/eurostat/databrowser/view/tgs00010/default/table?lang=en (accessed on 3 January 2024). [7]

Government of Poland (n.d.), *Komisja Wspólna Rządu i Samorządu Terytorialnego [Joint Commission of the Government and Local Government]*, https://www.gov.pl/web/kwrist-mswia (accessed on 30 October 2023). [20]

Government of Poland (n.d.), *Unpublished documents.* [21]

Lublinska, M. (2017), *Decentralisation and multi-level governance in Poland: Ensuring coherence between national and subnational development strategies/policies*, https://www.oecd.org/regional/regional-policy/Decentralisation-and-multi-level-governance-in-Poland.pdf (accessed on 2 October 2023). [22]

Ministry of Finance (2023), *Subnational government accounts*, https://mfin.gov.hr/istaknute-teme/lokalna-samouprava/financijski-izvjestaji-jlp-r-s/pr-ras-i-ras-funkc-za-razdoblje-2014-2020/3173. [30]

MRDEUF (2023), *Upisnik regionalnih koordinatora i lokalnih razvojnih agencija [Register of regional coordinators and local development agencies]*, https://razvoj.gov.hr/upisnik-regionalnih-koordinatora-i-lokalnih-razvojnih-agencija/4007 (accessed on 2 December 2023). [17]

OECD (2023), *General Government Accounts - Government deficit/surplus, revenue, expenditure and main aggregates*, https://stats-3.oecd.org/index.aspx?DatasetCode=SNA_TABLE12. [27]

OECD (2023), *Interviews conducted as part of the "Enhanced Strategic Planning at the Regional and Local Levels in Croatia" project*. [18]

OECD (2023), *Interviews with local stakeholders conducted as part of the "Enhanced Strategic Planning at the Regional and Local Levels in Croatia" project*. [31]

OECD (2023), *OECD Economic Outlook, Volume 2023 Issue 1*, OECD Publishing, Paris, https://doi.org/10.1787/ce188438-en. [1]

OECD (2023), *OECD Public Governance Reviews: Czech Republic: Towards a More Modern and Effective Public Administration*, OECD Public Governance Reviews, OECD Publishing, Paris, https://doi.org/10.1787/41fd9e5c-en. [23]

OECD (2023), *Subnational governments in OECD countries: Key data (Brochure)*, OECD Publishing. [24]

OECD (2022), *OECD Project Questionnaire: Enhanced Strategic Planning at the Regional and Local Levels in Croatia - questionnaire addressed to Croatia's regional development agencies*. [26]

OECD (2022), *Response to the project questionnaire "Enhanced Strategic Planning at the Regional and Local Levels in Croatia" addressed to Croatia's regional development agencies*. [16]

OECD (2020), "The Future of Regional Development and Public Investment in Wales, United Kingdom", *OECD Multi-level Governance Studies*, https://doi.org/10.1787/e6f5201d-en (accessed on 2 October 2023). [19]

OECD/UCLG (2022), *Country profiles - Croatia*, https://www.sng-wofi.org/country-profiles/ (accessed on 7 April 2023). [28]

World Bank (2024), *GDP per capita, PPP (current international $)*, https://data.worldbank.org/indicator/NY.GDP.PCAP.PP.CD?end=2022&locations=OE&start=2013 (accessed on 2 January 2024). [3]

2 Setting the scene: Regional development trends in Croatia

This chapter provides an overview of regional development trends in Croatia at the national, regional and county levels. By analysing a wide range of demographic, economic and well-being indicators, this chapter provides the foundation for the policy assessment and recommendations that will appear in subsequent chapters. Main findings confirm trends such as a rapidly shrinking population, fast economic growth and modest improvements in citizen well-being at the national level but with large disparities across regions and counties. Regional inequalities remain large in Croatia, with residents in Zagreb and coastal counties earning higher incomes than in other parts of the country, for example.

Introduction

Since joining the EU in 2013, substantial improvement has been achieved throughout Croatia. Its economic performance, whether measured by GDP, the unemployment rate or the growth in trade, has been especially encouraging. However, geographic inequalities persist, for example in terms of the quality of life available to Croatian residents and the speed of demographic change. Residents of Zagreb City, and to a lesser extent coastal areas, live longer, and have higher incomes and greater educational attainment, on average, than those living further inland. In contrast, population loss is concentrated in the northeast, with emigration, low birth rates and limited employment opportunities all contributing to population shrinkage. These trends provide the backdrop against which Croatia has designed and implemented its regional development policies, such as the 2017-2020 National Strategy for Regional Development and the National Development Strategy 2030, which include a focus on balanced regional development. The data presented in this chapter can support evidence-informed decision making by the Croatian government as it continues to build institutional, financial and human resource capacity at all levels of government to design, implement, fund and track territorial development policies that seek to address territorial disparities.

This chapter provides a high-level analysis of Croatia's territorial development over the past decade, using data on a variety of governance, economic, demographic and well-being indicators. The analysis provides valuable insights into the development context for which Croatia has set up an elaborate regional development policy framework. The analysis includes evidence at the national, regional and county level, and demonstrates significant successes, areas of stagnation and well-entrenched disparities in outcomes for the residents of different geographic localities.

The first part of this chapter examines national trends, for which the available data are the most in-depth and international comparisons are most instructive. It includes indicators on governance, the economy, demography and well-being, and identifies numerous areas of success. Several indicators (e.g. inequality and democracy) have not changed significantly over the past decade, especially in comparison with neighbouring countries and EU economies comparable with Croatia in terms of their size and geographic location (Box 2.1). However, in absolute terms the general trend is both positive and sustained. The second section of this chapter focuses on Croatia's four TL2 (NUTS 2) areas (statistical regions) and reveals significant territorial disparities between Zagreb City and Adriatic Croatia, on the one hand, and the two inland regions of Pannonian Croatia and Northern Croatia, on the other, with the former demonstrating higher levels of GDP and well-being. The third part of this chapter analyses the relatively small number of indicators available at the county level. Many of these data have only been collected in previous censuses, which are conducted every ten years, the last one in 2021. However, the evidence of disparities at county level is clear, with stark differences in life expectancy, GDP and unemployment. It shows that despite widespread progress throughout Croatia in the past decade, there is still ample opportunity to further reduce territorial disparities.

Box 2.1. International benchmarks and data availability

The analysis of governance, economic, demographic and well-being indicators in Croatia includes comparisons, where available, with a consistent selection of benchmark countries. These include selected neighbouring countries (Hungary, Serbia, and Slovenia), other Eastern European countries (Bulgaria, Lithuania, and Slovak Republic) and a more developed economy (Italy) in close proximity to Croatia. The European Union and OECD averages are also included where possible. The chapter is based on data available in Q1 2023 and is therefore able to isolate the short-term impacts of the COVID-19 pandemic and the subsequent return to the historical trend in most cases. Some data used in this chapter are only available up until 2021, especially at the regional and county levels. In a few instances, 2020 is the last full year available.

National trends in Croatia since joining the EU

The data and analysis contained in this section covers the time period directly following Croatia's accession to the EU and aims to identify any significant changes within the Croatian system of governance, economy, demography and the well-being of its residents. Although these trends, and the absence of change on several indicators, cannot solely be attributed to EU membership, they provide insights into the positive impacts of membership and help identify areas where proactive domestic policies will be required to catch-up with neighbouring economies.

The governance dimension

Croatia is a relatively small country, with a territory of 56 594 km² (comparable to Latvia) (Croatian Bureau of Statistics, 2022[1]) and a population of 3.8 million inhabitants in 2021 (comparable to Lithuania and New Zealand), 58% of which live in urban areas as defined by the national classification[1].

The 1990 Croatian Constitution declared the country's independence from Yugoslavia and established the Republic of Croatia as a "unitary and indivisible democratic and social state". In 1992, Croatia was admitted as a member of the United Nations, became a member of the European Union in 2013 and joined the Eurozone and Schengen area in January 2023. In 2017, Croatia presented a formal application of accession to the OECD, and in January 2022, the OECD Council agreed to open accession discussions.

Since joining the EU in 2013, Croatia has undertaken several reforms to its governing institutions and territorial divisions. However, its constitution, political system, county structure and international borders remain largely unchanged, and the role of the state in the economy, as reflected in the tax-GDP ratio, has remained steady.

Croatia's territorial-administrative structure has remained stable

Since 1992, Croatia has had a unitary system of government with a directly elected president. In addition, Croatia has a Prime Minister who heads the executive branch of government and is accountable to parliament, which consists of one chamber. Croatia's territorial-administrative structure is composed of two levels of subnational government: regional and local self-governments (Table 2.1). At the regional level, Croatia is divided into 20 counties (or regional self-governments) and Zagreb City, which operates at the county level. Each county, with the exception of Zagreb City, is governed by a prefect and an assembly, both of which are elected by popular vote for four-year mandates. Zagreb City is governed by a mayor and a city assembly. At the local level, Croatia is comprised of 428 municipalities and 127 towns, each with their own mayor and local council, which are also directly elected for four-year terms. Croatia also has four non-administrative, statistical regions (TL2): Adriatic Croatia, Northern Croatia, Pannonian Croatia and Zagreb City.

Table 2.1. Croatia's territorial-administrative organisation, 2023

Tier/level of subnational government		Administrative unit	Number of units
Second tier	Regional (TL3)	Counties *(županije)*	20
		Zagreb City	1
Third tier	Municipal	428 municipalities *(općina)*	555
		127 towns *(grad)*	

Source: Author's elaboration, based on (Croatian Ministry of Regional Development and EU Funds, 2022[2]; SNG-WOFI, 2022[3]).

Progress in governance has been modest since EU accession

The strength of Croatian democracy has held firm, with smooth transfers of power occurring since 2013 and voter turnout for parliamentary and presidential elections averaging around 50%. According to the Economist Democracy Index (The Economist Intelligence Unit, 2022[4]), in 2022, Croatia ranked 59 out of 167 countries overall, scoring very high on its electoral process and pluralism, but moderately on the functioning of government, political participation and civil liberties.

Croatia's score on the World Bank's Worldwide Governance Indicators (Figure 2.1), which evaluate perceptions of governance quality across six categories in over 200 countries, also suggests moderate progress in a number of areas. Notably, Croatia's rankings in relation to political stability, regulatory quality, rule of law, and voice and accountability moderately improved in 2022 compared to 2013.

Figure 2.1. Worldwide governance indicators in Croatia, 2013 and 2022

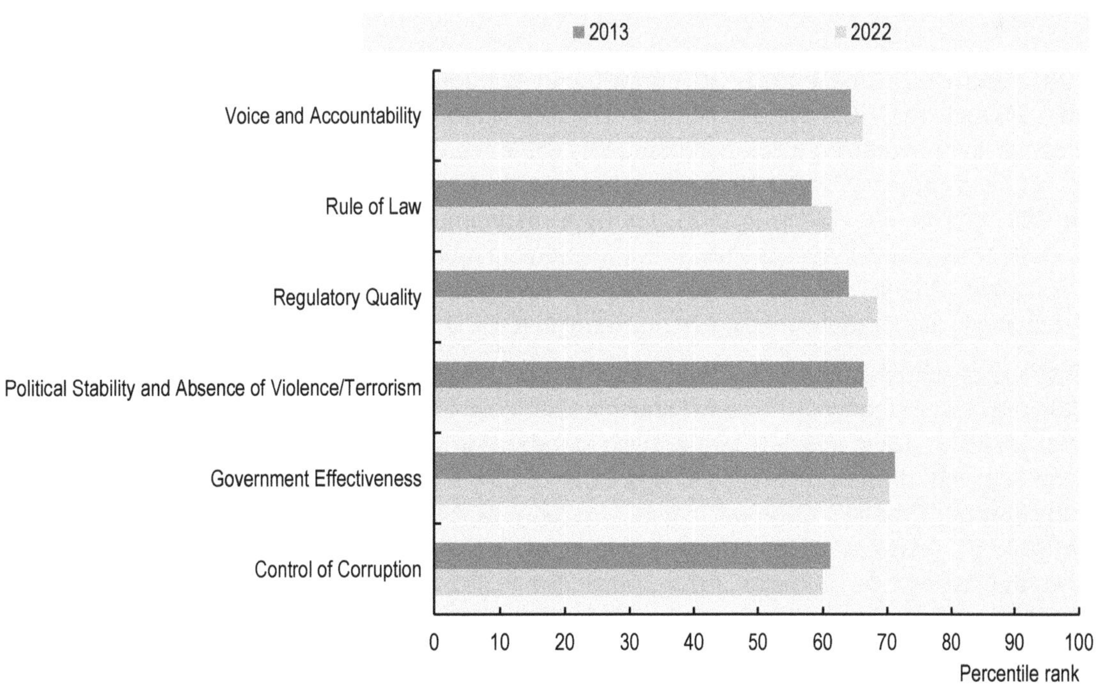

Note: The figure shows the rank of Croatia among all countries covered by each aggregate indicator, with 0 corresponding to the lowest rank, and 100 to the highest. The Worldwide Governance Indicators are composite governance indicators based on over 30 underlying data sources.
Source: Author's elaboration, based on (Kaufmann and Kraay, 2023[5]).

On 1 January 2023, Croatia adopted the euro as its official currency and formally joined the Schengen Area. These changes were part of the EU accession process and brought with them the expectation that they would reduce barriers to trade, tourism, skilled migration and investment, all of which would contribute to greater integration with the EU and support economic development. While EU accession in 2013 prompted a spike in emigration, particularly to countries such as Germany and Austria, and increased trade, investment and tourism, the impact of these two developments are yet to be seen. However, due to the kuna's pegging to the euro since 2003, and the high degree of access to EU labour markets already available to Croatian residents, the disruption caused by Schengen membership and the adoption of the euro are both anticipated to be small.

The economic dimension

Croatia's macroeconomic performance since 2013 has been strong, with substantial progress on several indicators. The most significant economic advances include:

- **Living standards:** GDP per capita (PPS)[2] increased from EUR 15 978 in 2013 to EUR 25 634 in 2022, averaging 5.4% growth annually, above the EU average of 3.4% and the OECD average of 3.9% (Eurostat, 2023[6]; World Bank, 2024[7]).
- **Unemployment:** Long-term unemployment fell from 11.0% in 2013 to 2.4% in 2022. Over the same time period, the average rate of long-term unemployment in the EU fell from 5.4% to 2.4% (Eurostat, 2023[8]).
- **Inflation:** Croatia successfully maintained price stability, with average inflation rarely exceeding 2% and only narrowly falling below 0% in 2015-16. Between 2013-22, the annual rate of inflation in Croatia averaged 1.9%, slightly below the EU average of 2.0% (Eurostat, 2023[9]).
- **Productivity:** Real labour productivity per person employed grew at an average annual rate of 1.4% between 2013-21, significantly higher than the EU average of 0.7% (Eurostat, 2023[10]).

Economic growth has exceeded the EU average

Between 2013 and 2022, Croatian real GDP grew by an average of 2.8%, which was faster than the EU average of 1.7% and the OECD average of 1.9%. The rate of real GDP growth was even more impressive at the per capita level, averaging 3.8%, compared to 1.6% in the EU and 1.3% in the OECD. The Croatian economy's rebound from the COVID-19 pandemic was particularly noteworthy. After shrinking by -8.5% in 2020, real GDP growth was 13.1% in 2021, led by a resurgence in tourism. Further, the latest *OECD Economic Outlook* forecasts that economic growth will remain robust over the near term, with the economy expected to grow 2.1% in 2023 and 2.5% in 2024. Rising wages and employment growth are also predicted, leading to higher real spending by households (OECD, 2023[11]).

In comparison to benchmark countries, Croatia's GDP growth has been less exceptional, with economies such as Bulgaria (4%), Hungary (3.7%) and Lithuania (3.8%) achieving comparable economic growth rates per capita since 2013. Yet in absolute terms, living standards in Croatia have clearly improved. GDP per capita, when adjusted for price differentials, was EUR 25 634 in 2022 compared to EUR 15 978 in 2013 (Figure 2.2). Further, Croatia's GDP per capita was only 27.2% lower than the EU average in 2022, compared to 38.6% lower in 2013, providing further evidence of broadly successful economic policy settings over the last decade (Eurostat, 2023[6]; World Bank, 2024[7]).

Figure 2.2. GDP per capita (PPS) in Croatia and benchmark countries, 2013 and 2022

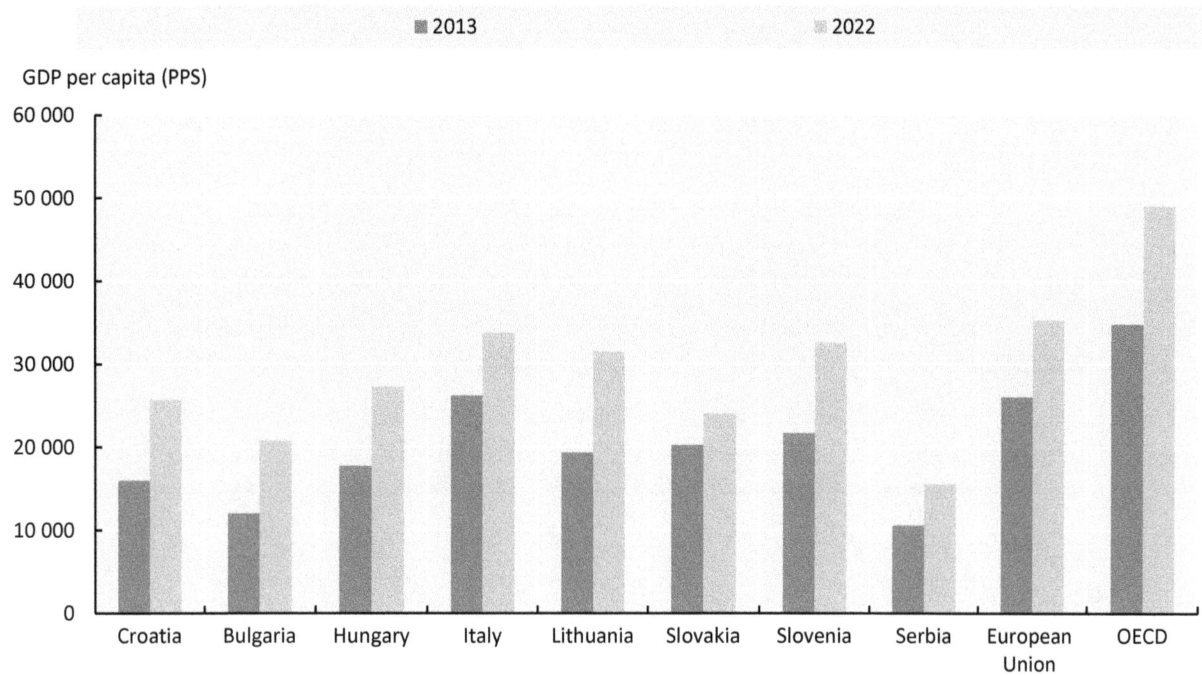

Note: Purchasing Power Standard. OECD estimate derived from Purchasing Power Parity.
Source: Author's elaboration with data from (Eurostat, 2023[6]; World Bank, 2024[7]).

One factor contributing to economic growth over the last decade is increased exports. Since Croatia joined the EU in 2013, the value of total goods that have been exported has grown at an average annual rate of 10.8%. This growth has been broadly consistent across Croatia's major export industries and suggests that EU accession did not disproportionately coincide with negative impacts caused by increased competition in industries such as food and live animals, which tend to be concentrated in rural areas (Figure 2.3). In 2022, the three largest export categories were machinery and transport equipment; mineral fuels and lubricants; and manufactured goods.

Figure 2.3. Croatian goods exports, 2013 and 2022

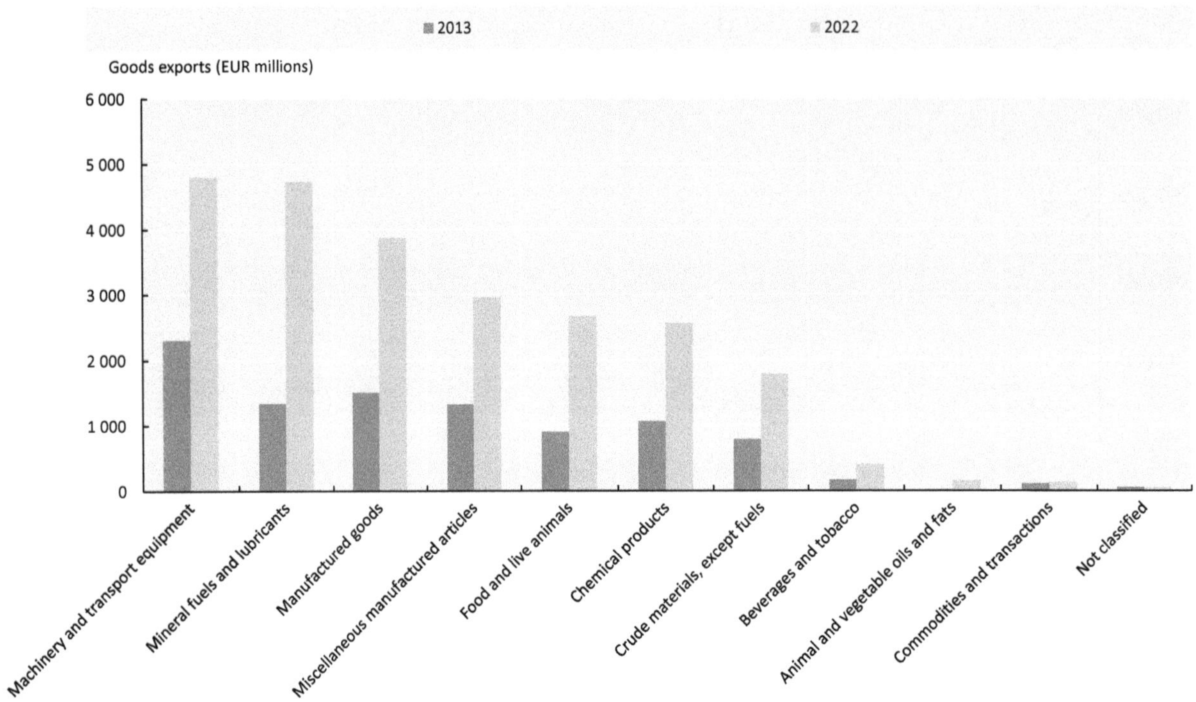

Source: Author's elaboration with data from (Croatian Bureau of Statistics, 2023[12]).

Despite the fast rate of economic growth, prices have remained stable in Croatia throughout the last decade, with an average inflation rate of only 0.9% from 2013-21 (Eurostat, 2023[9]). The OECD average throughout this period was 1.9% (OECD, n.d.[13]). In 2022, consumer prices in Croatia rose by 10.7%, in alignment with global developments and at a comparable speed to the EU average of 9.2% and OECD average of 9.6%.

Unemployment has fallen considerably since 2013

The most striking development in the Croatian economy since 2013 has been the rapid and sustained fall in long-term unemployment: from 11.0% to 2.4% between 2013 and 2022 (Eurostat, 2023[8]). Unlike total unemployment, which rises and falls in response to the business cycle, long-term unemployment (i.e. unemployment exceeding 12 months) reflects a structural imbalance in the labour market. This positive change has been driven by a combination of sustained economic growth and the ongoing development of labour-intensive sectors such as tourism. High rates of emigration to other EU economies, particularly Germany, have also contributed by providing new economic opportunities directly to the long-term unemployed.

The fall in long-term unemployment in Croatia, however, is broadly in line with a downward trend seen across the OECD, EU and benchmark countries (Figure 2.4). In the EU, long-term unemployment fell from 5.4% to 2.4% between 2013 and 2022. Long-term unemployment in Serbia, which was the highest of the benchmark countries in 2013, fell from 16.0% to 3.8% over the same period.

Figure 2.4. Long-term unemployment rate in Croatia and benchmark countries, 2013 and 2022

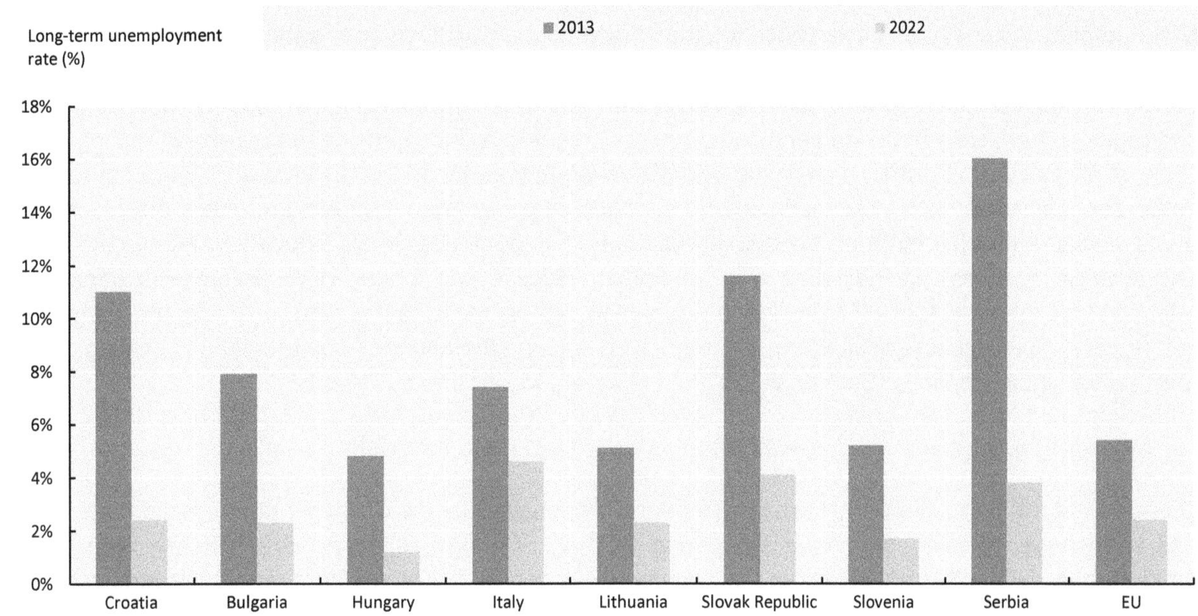

Note: 15-74 age group, percentage of the labour force.
Source: Author's elaboration with data from (Eurostat, 2023[8]).

The demographic dimension

Croatia has experienced significant demographic changes in the last decade. Like many countries in southern Europe, fertility rates are low and the average age of its residents continues to increase gradually each year. Although a reversal of this long-term trend is unlikely to be achievable, governments in Croatia will nonetheless be required to make significant reforms in a range of policy areas to adequately adapt to, and ameliorate, some of the negative impacts of demographic changes that are currently affecting the country.

Croatia's population is both shrinking and ageing

Croatia's population has become significantly smaller since 2013, and by 2022 had approximately 399 835 fewer residents (-9.4%). On average, this equates to Croatia losing 1.1% of its population annually during the last nine years. Population decline has been caused by low fertility rates and net outward migration. Over the last decade, the number of births has remained reasonably constant at around 40 000 per year but has been unable to offset the approximately 50 000 deaths recorded annually. This trend was exacerbated by the COVID-19 pandemic, which led to sharp increases in mortality in 2020 and 2021 (Eurostat, 2023[14]).

In addition to a reduced number of permanent residents, the population of Croatia has also aged significantly. In 2011, only 17.7% of the population were aged 64 or older, but by 2021 this had increased to 22.5%. Croatia's low fertility rate suggests that the proportion of elderly residents will continue to grow in the coming decade (Eurostat, 2023[14]).

Croatia's low birth rate, relative to mortality rates, is not exceptional for the region. In 2021, Croatia's fertility rate was approximately 1.6 births per woman. Most neighbouring countries and the EU as a whole are also averaging less than 2.1 births per woman, which is the standard threshold required to maintain positive population growth. In the long term, Croatia's population is forecast to decline from 3.86 million in 2022 to 3.31 million in 2050 (-13.3%) (Eurostat, 2023[14]).

Demographic decline can have wide-ranging effects on public finances, service delivery and socio-economic development, which need to be considered by policy makers. For example, with a diminishing population, the labour force also shrinks, which can lead to labour shortages across the economy. Such shortages, in turn, can affect firm behaviour, and may result in reduced business operations and job losses (Šerý et al., 2018[15]). Further, a declining population leads to reduced tax revenue and user charges from public services, which can strain national and subnational government budgets and affect the provision of public services that benefit from economies of scale (e.g. public transport, education, healthcare, water and sewage systems). In the same way, population decline can hinder local government capacity to maintain vital infrastructure. The decline in population can also lead to the closure of schools, community centres and other public facilities (e.g. libraries), thus eroding the sense of community and limiting access to essential public services (Šerý et al., 2018[15]; Beunen, Meijer and de Vries, 2020[16]).

Migration has contributed significantly to population decline

Croatia's natural population decreases have been compounded by the country's net migration rate, which has been negative every year over the period 2013-21. During this period over 96 000 more people emigrated from Croatia than settled in the country. However, in 2022 Croatia reversed this long-run trend and recorded positive net migration of 11 685 (Croatian Bureau of Statistics, 2023[17]).

Unlike the number of births and deaths, which have remained broadly consistent over the last ten years, migration patterns have fluctuated significantly in response to evolving international economic conditions and immigration policies. Following Croatia's accession to the EU in July 2013, 14 member countries became more easily accessible to Croatian workers, boosting emigration. However, the 13 remaining EU Member States maintained temporary restrictions. The removal of barriers to the German labour market in mid-2015 was particularly significant, opening up new employment opportunities. This contributed to a more than doubling of the number of annual emigrants in 2016 (Figure 2.5). The final EU member to lift labour market restrictions was Austria, in 2020.

Figure 2.5. Net migration in Croatia, 2013-22

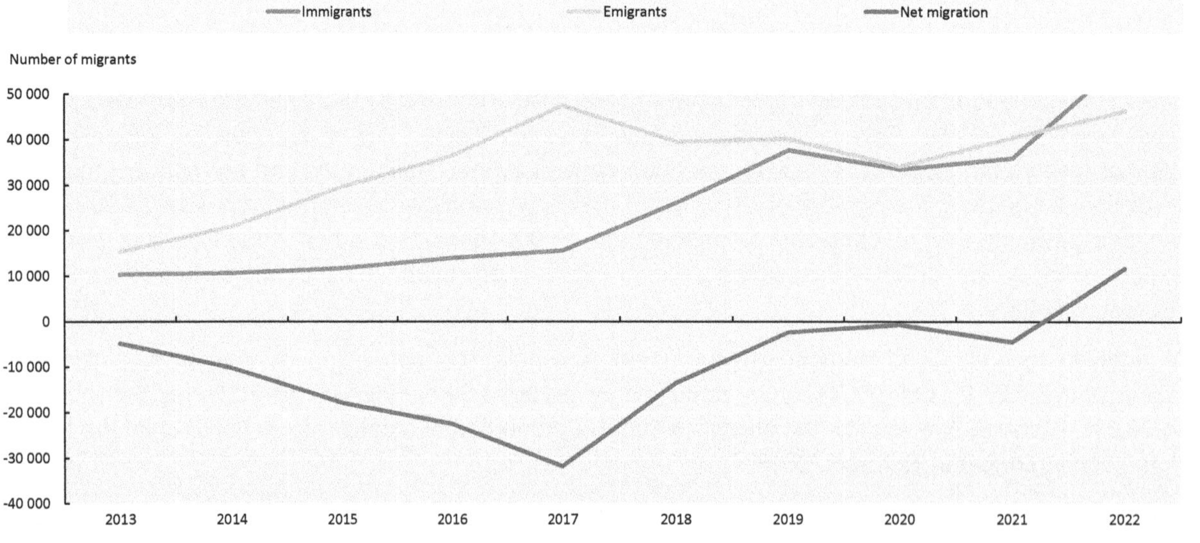

Source: Author's elaboration with data from (Croatian Bureau of Statistics, 2023[18]).

The vast majority of recorded emigration has been to other European economies, with Germany (44.1%), Bosnia and Herzegovina (12%) and Serbia (9.5%) being the most popular destinations. In recent years, Austria has also become a top emigration destination (Croatian Bureau of Statistics, 2022[19]). The largest sources of inward migration are also Bosnia and Herzegovina (32.4%), Germany (12.9%) and Serbia (10.8%), suggesting that some emigrants may be returning to Croatia after a period of living abroad (Croatian Bureau of Statistics, 2023[18]).

Another consequence of low fertility and the outward migration of working-age residents over the past decade are changes to the average age of the Croatian population. Elderly residents now make up 22.5% of the population (up from 15.7% in 2001), placing increasing pressure on government health services and annual pension costs (Table 2.2).

Table 2.2. Croatian population data, 2001, 2011 and 2021

Census	Population	0-14	15-64	65+
2001	4 437 460	17.1%	67.2%	15.7%
2011	4 284 889	15.2%	67.1%	17.7%
2021	3 871 833	14.3%	63.3%	22.5%

Source: Author's elaboration with data from (Croatian Bureau of Statistics, 2023[20]).

Croatia's ageing population is following a trajectory like in most European countries and poses a significant, but slow-moving, threat to the sustainability of the existing tax and transfer system (Čipin, 2017[21]). Research estimates that by 2050, the share of the state budget allocated to pensions and elderly healthcare could double (Nejašmić, 2011[22]). Government programmes and expenditure patterns in Croatia will therefore be required to adapt in the coming decade to accommodate the growing number of elderly residents and the steadily decreasing number of working-age, income-tax paying individuals.

Beyond government revenue and expenditure challenges, low fertility, and the decline in youth as a proportion of the total Croatian population, may have other long-term economic implications. For example, the current cohort of youth (between the ages of 0 and 14) in 2021, which will enter the labour market in the next twenty years, is significantly smaller than earlier generations (Figure 2.6), which could lead to future labour market shortages. Government policies to encourage the return of the Croatian diaspora, or to attract new working-age migrants from other countries, may therefore be required in periods of high employment. The relative decline in the working-age population could also limit future growth in GDP per capita, due to lower rates of participation (Croatian Bureau of Statistics, 2021[23]).

Figure 2.6. Population pyramid of Croatia, 2021

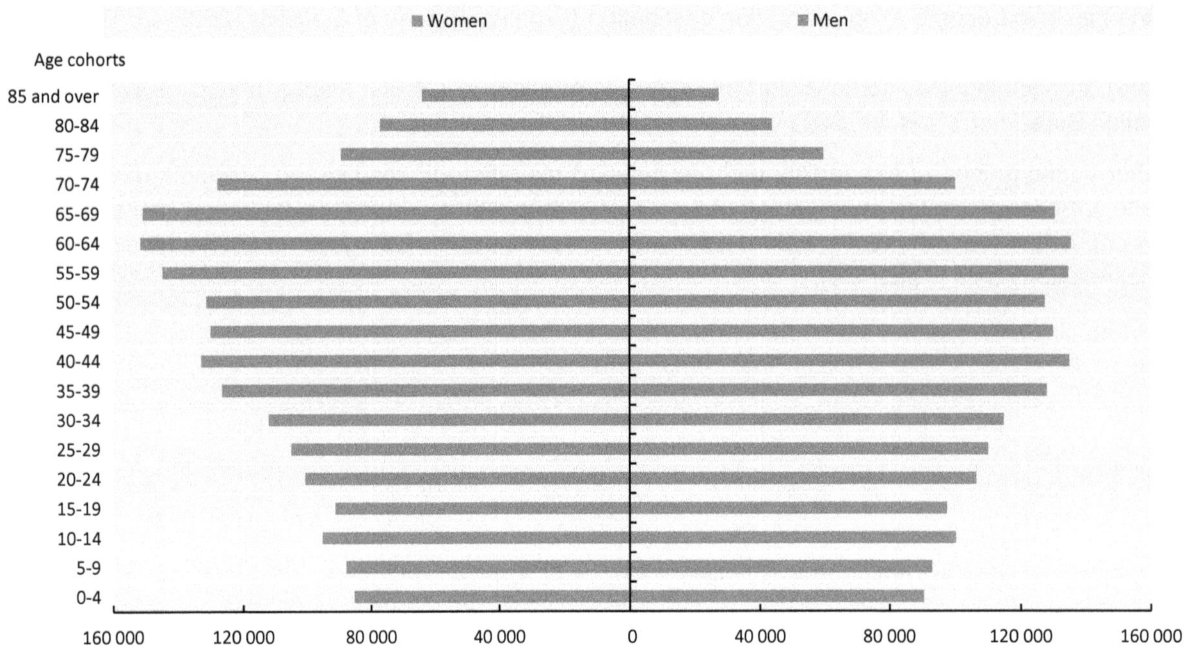

Source: Author's elaboration with data from (Croatian Bureau of Statistics, 2021[23]).

The well-being dimension

In comparison to economic indicators, progress on well-being has been more modest over the past decade. Since 2013, the rates of inequality and poverty in Croatia have improved marginally, and life expectancy remains largely unchanged and below the EU average.

Inequality, poverty and life expectancy has remained constant

Income inequality, as measured by the Gini coefficient, has not changed significantly over the last ten years. In 2021, Croatia scored 48.5, a slight improvement on the 49.3 recorded in 2013. On this measure, which is based on disposable income and includes pension payments, inequality in Croatia was slightly lower than the EU average (52.2). Of the benchmark countries, only Slovenia (42.8 in 2021) was notably more equal on this measure (Eurostat, 2024[24]).

The proportion of the population at risk of poverty within Croatia, however, has improved, falling from 18.8% in 2013 to 16.1% in 2022 (-2.7 percentage points) (Eurostat, 2023[25]). The risk of poverty in the EU and most benchmark countries has remained broadly stable, despite widespread improvements in per capita income, with only Hungary (-3.7 percentage points) among the benchmark countries to make more significant progress on this measure since 2013 (Figure 2.7). In direct comparison with benchmark countries, the 16.1% of the population at risk of poverty in Croatia in 2022 was higher than Slovenia (11.5%), roughly equal to the EU (16.2%) but significantly lower than Bulgaria (20.5%) and Italy (20.3%).

Figure 2.7. Share of the population considered at risk of poverty, 2013 and 2022

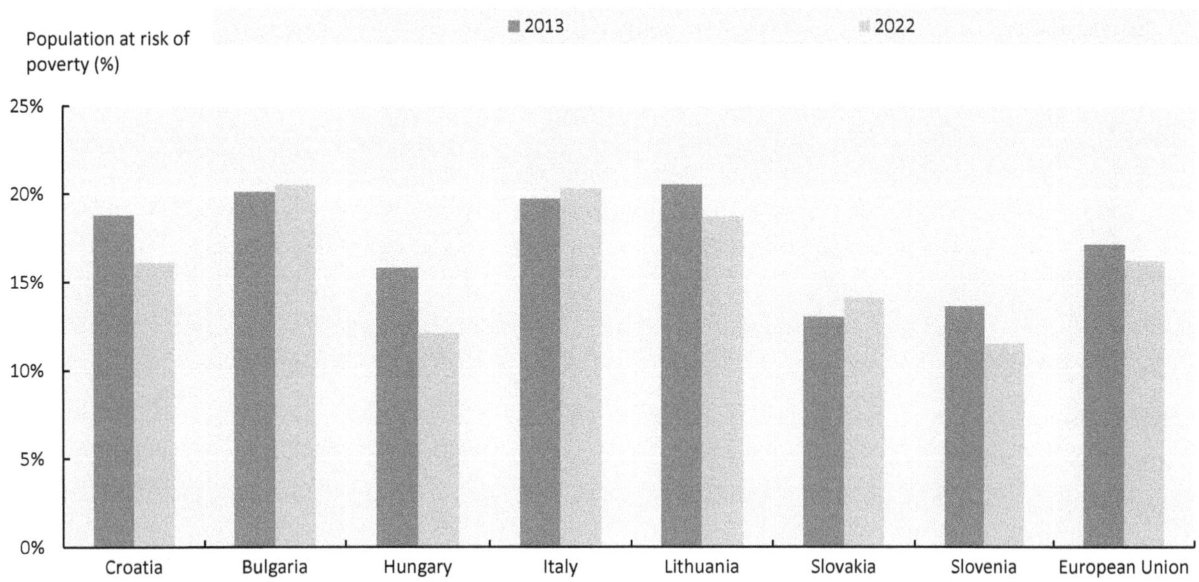

Note: Population under the age of 75.
Source: Author's elaboration with data from (Eurostat, 2023[25]).

Life expectancy at birth in Croatia has also failed to improve significantly. In 2022, the average Croatian could expect to live 77.7 years at birth, a slight decrease compared to the 77.8 estimated in 2013. Relative to benchmark countries, Croatia was near the median but remains significantly lower than the EU average of 80.4. For example, in 2022, life expectancy in Croatia remained lower than Italy (83.0) and Slovenia (81.3) but was higher than Bulgaria (74.3) and Hungary (76.2). Further investment in healthcare services and infrastructure, as well as education, will potentially be needed for life expectancy in Croatia to catch up with the EU average (Eurostat, 2023[25]).

Household internet access has increased rapidly throughout Croatia

Internet access is one area of substantial improvement, with the proportion of households reporting broadband connections growing by more than 20 percentage points since 2013 (Figure 2.8). Despite this growth, household access to broadband in Croatia remains at 86.1%, below the EU average of 92.3%. It also remains below most other benchmark countries, such as the Slovak Republic (90.0%) and Slovenia (93.0%) (Eurostat, 2023[26]; OECD, 2024[27]). Increasing household access to broadband is an important priority for Croatia for both social and economic reasons. Some of the benefits include reduced social isolation, additional flexibility in accessing government services, greater access to educational resources and an enhanced network of potential job opportunities.

Figure 2.8. Household broadband access, 2013 and 2022

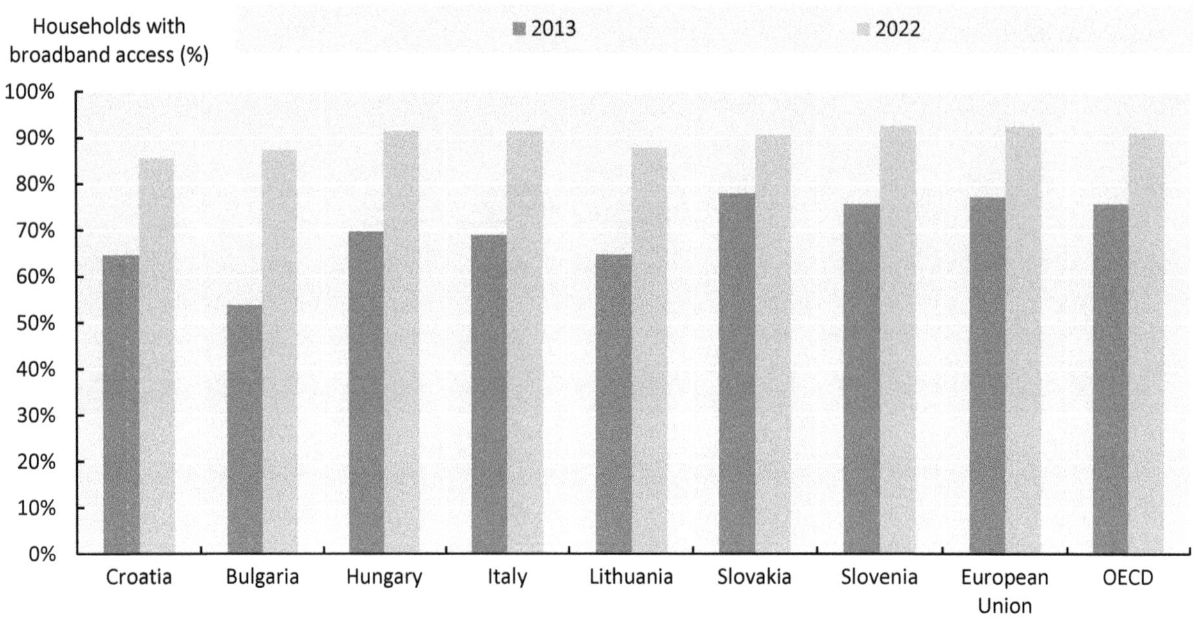

Source: Author's elaboration with data from (Eurostat, 2023[26]; OECD, 2024[27]).

Regional trends

Croatia's economic and demographic trends since 2013 have not been uniform, with large and sometimes growing disparities clearly identifiable among the country's four statistical (TL2) regions: Adriatic Croatia, Northern Croatia, Pannonian Croatia and Zagreb City (Figure 2.9). The available evidence suggests that Zagreb City and the Adriatic Croatia are more advanced economically and have higher levels of resident well-being, while population loss has been concentrated in Northern Croatia and Pannonian Croatia.

The four statistical regions of Croatia do not have independent political representation or policy-making capacity. They do, however, enable aggregation of the 20 counties and Zagreb City into distinct geographic zones that provide insights and additional depth to the analysis of national and subnational trends. This facilitates the design and implementation of various macro-regional development initiatives (e.g. smart specialisation and industrial transition policy) (see chapter 2).

Figure 2.9. Croatia's four TL2 regions

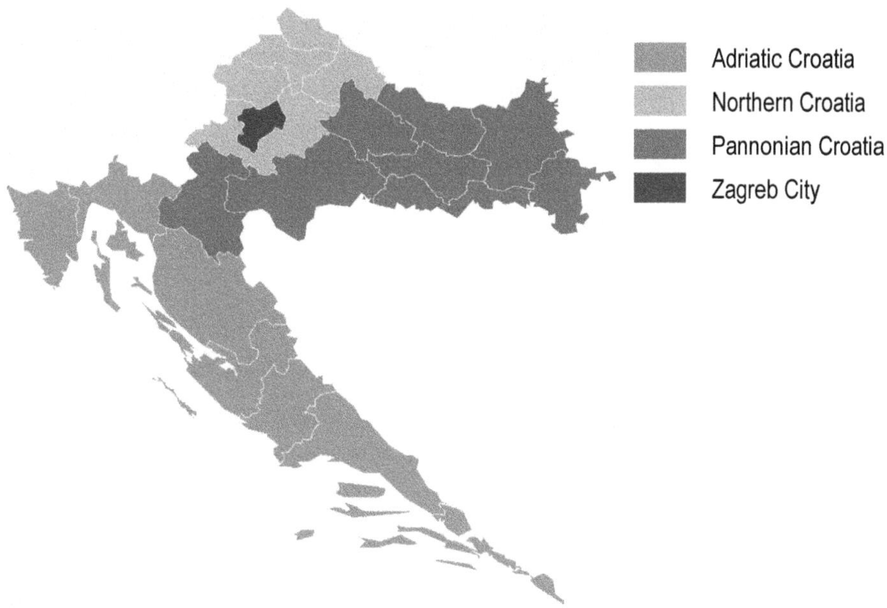

Source: Author's elaboration, based on (Croatian Bureau of Statistics, n.d.[28]).

From 2012-21, Croatian statistics were aggregated into only two regions – Adriatic Croatia and Pannonian Croatia – the former consisting of coastal counties and the latter of landlocked counties. The reconfiguration of 2021, which administratively divided Croatia into four separate TL2 regions (Adriatic Croatia, Northern Croatia, Pannonian Croatia and Zagreb City), has therefore created some limitations in the availability of data. For some indicators, which use the new configuration, data are only available from 2021 onwards and comparisons with the past decade are not possible. On others, data are available from 2013-21, but only include the two former TL2 classifications.

Further, several important indicators of governance, economic development and well-being available nationally are not collected or published at the regional level. It is therefore not possible to detect regional variations in the prevalence of inequality, corruption or Internet access. Nonetheless, the available data at the regional level provides valuable insights into how Croatia's territorial disparities have changed over the past decade.

The economic dimension

Significant economic disparities exist between Croatia's four TL2 regions, highlighted by the relatively strong performance of Zagreb City on a variety of economic indicators. For example, Zagreb City's productivity, employment and average income were twice as high as all other TL2 regions. Pannonian Croatia, in Croatia's northeast, was the lowest-performing region overall—although unemployment is just as high in Adriatic Croatia.

The regional disparities can be partially explained by several factors. First, Zagreb City is primarily a metropolitan area, while the other three consist of rural, regional and urban settlements. Second, as the seat of the central government, many public functions are concentrated in Zagreb. This adds to regional GDP, despite many of the government tasks being undertaken for the benefit of the entire country. Third, there may be a small measurement error caused by workers residing in Northern Croatia but working in Zagreb City. Such commuting patterns could affect regional per capita GDP estimates, which are calculated by dividing the total amount of regional output by the total number of permanent residents. This may slightly overstate the economic disparities between Northern Croatia and Zagreb City.

Zagreb City's economic dominance has grown, with other regions falling behind

Notwithstanding the above-mentioned considerations, Zagreb City is undeniably the most productive of the four TL2 regions and its residents enjoy a significantly higher standard of living than the national average. Further, the gap between Zagreb City and Pannonian Croatia, the least economically developed region, has widened. In 2013, GDP per capita in Pannonian Croatia was 63% lower than that of Zagreb City. This had increased to 66% by 2021 (Figure 2.10).

Figure 2.10. GDP per capita (PPS) in TL2 regions, 2013-21

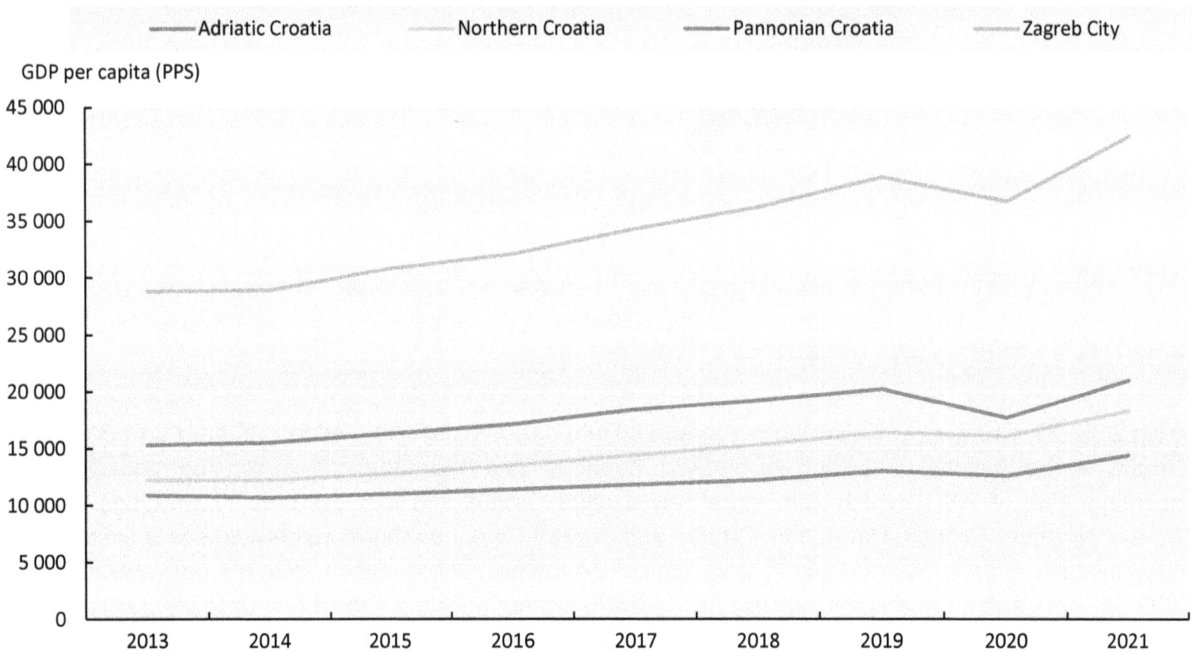

Note: Purchasing power standard.
Source: Author's elaboration with data from (Eurostat, 2023[29]).

Labour productivity in Croatia also varies significantly at the regional level. In Zagreb City, the average worker was able to produce EUR 20.60 of output, per hour, in 2020, which was significantly higher than in Adriatic Croatia (EUR 15.70), Northern Croatia (EUR 15.60) or Pannonian Croatia (EUR 13.00). Since 2013, labour productivity has increased in all regions except Adriatic Croatia, where it declined, albeit marginally (Figure 2.11).

Figure 2.11. Labour productivity in TL2 regions, 2013 and 2020

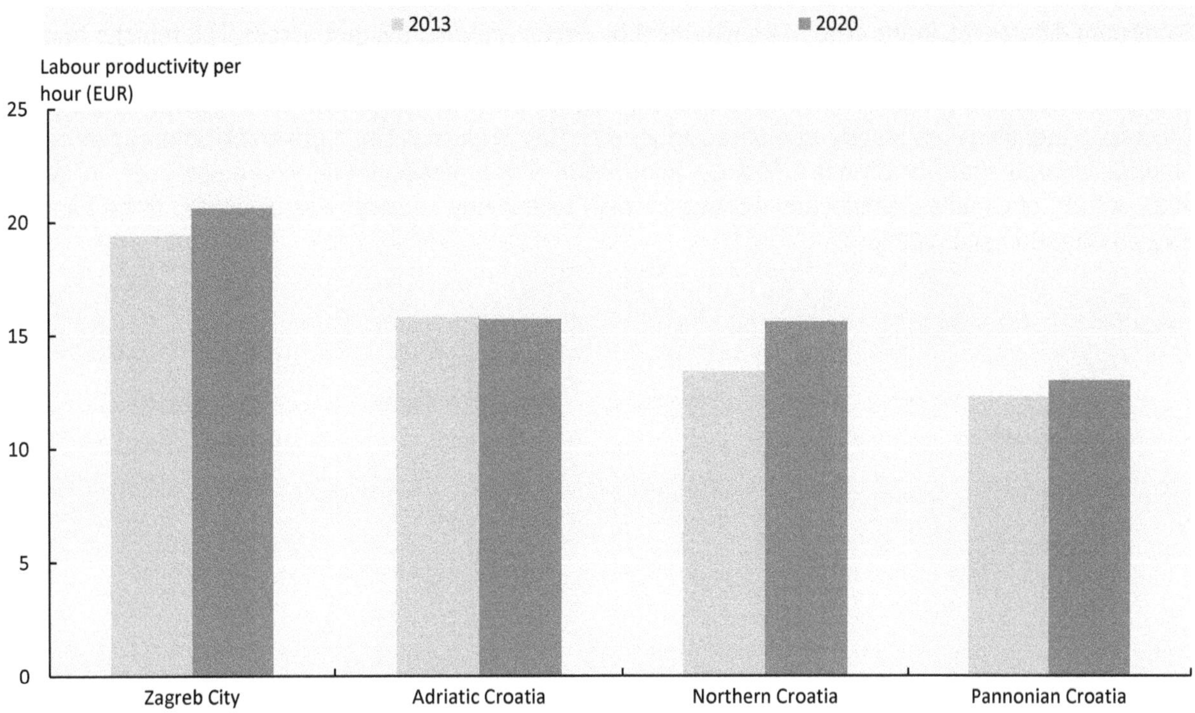

Source: Author's elaboration with data from (Eurostat, 2023[10]).

The distribution of employment and labour force participation across Croatia's four regions follows a similar pattern (Annex Table 2.A.1). While in Zagreb City only 5.2% of the labour force was unemployed in 2023, in Pannonian Croatia unemployment was the highest in the country at 12.4% (Table 2.3). Similarly, in Zagreb City, participation was very high, with 77.2% of the adult population economically active, while in Pannonian Croatia, only 64.8% of the same age cohort were economically active in 2023. Regional disparities in unemployment have remained broadly stable since 2016. Although the rate of unemployment has almost halved in Zagreb City, Adriatic Croatia and Northern Croatia since 2016, in Pannonian Croatia unemployment remains stubbornly high at 12.4%. These persistent disparities, however, do not detract from the rapid falls in unemployment that have been achieved in all of Croatia's TL2 regions in recent years.

Table 2.3. Unemployment in TL2 regions, 2016-23

	Unemployment 2023 (total)	Unemployment 2023 (men)	Unemployment 2023 (women)
Croatia	7.4% (-5.8 pp)	7.3% (-5.3 pp)	7.6% (-6.3 pp)
Adriatic Croatia	6.9% (-7.3 pp)	6.9% (-7.3 pp)	7.0% (-7.3 pp)
Northern Croatia	5.0% (-4.9 pp)	4.7% (-4.0 pp)	5.3% (-5.9 pp)
Pannonian Croatia	12.4% (-5.0 pp)	10.7% (-4.5 pp)	14.4% (-5.8 pp)
Zagreb City	5.2% (-4.5 pp)	6.6% (-4.2 pp)	3.9% (-4.7 pp)

Notes: Unemployed aged between 15-74. Data between parenthesis shows the percentage point [pp] change between 2016-23.
Source: Author's elaboration with data from (Eurostat, 2023[30]).

Participation rates have increased in all regions, since 2017, but the gap between the most and least economically active regions has increased only slightly. Zagreb City, where labour market participation is highest (77.2%), also experienced the largest increase (4.4 percentage points). The smallest increase was seen in Northern Croatia, with labour market participation increasing by 1.4 percentage points to 69.7% (Croatian Bureau of Statistics, 2023[31]).

Significant differences in the type of employment by sector are also evident across TL2 regions and can partially explain the large disparities in income and productivity. The landlocked TL2 regions of Pannonian Croatia and Northern Croatia have proportionally higher numbers of people employed in primary and secondary industries, especially compared to Zagreb City (Figure 2.12). Conversely, the capital region employs a large share of Croatia's finance, information and professional service employees. In fact, in 2022, 47.9% of Croatia's employees working in "high technology sectors" was estimated to be based in Zagreb City (Eurostat, 2023[32]).

Figure 2.12. Employment by activity type in TL2 regions, 2022

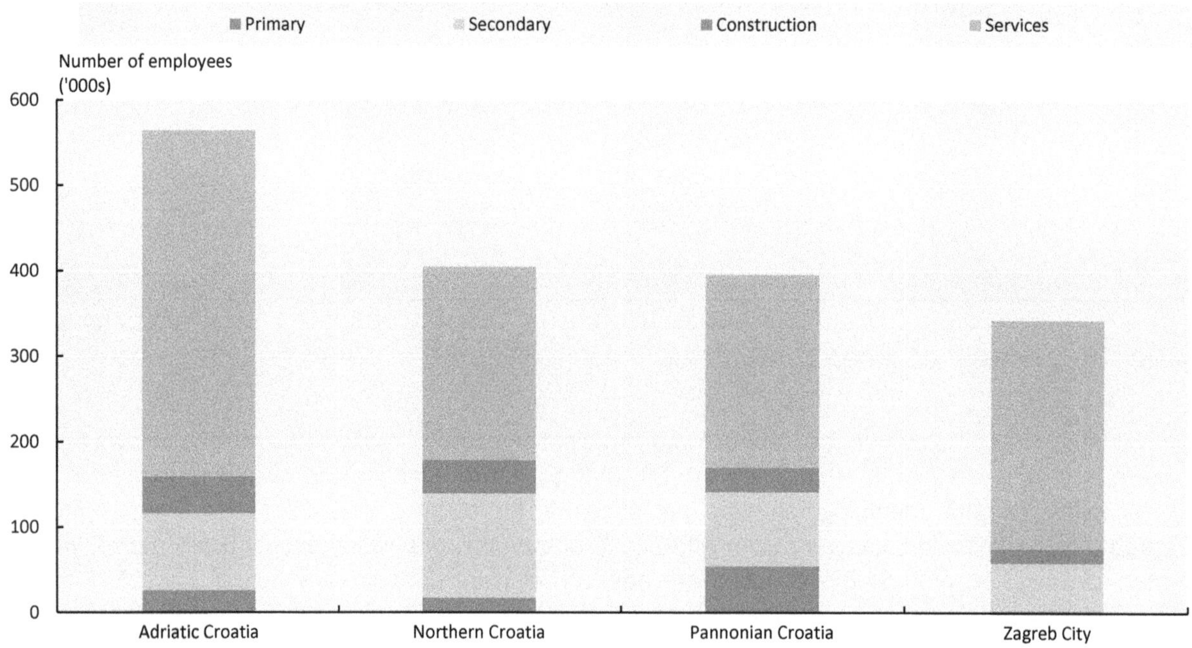

Note: All employees older than 15.
Source: Author's elaboration with data from (Eurostat, 2023[33]).

A further explanation of the economic disparities between TL2 regions relates to their innovation performance. In 2023, Adriatic Croatia, Northern Croatia and Pannonian Croatia were all classified as "emerging innovators +", the third-lowest ranking out of a possible 12 provided by the EU's Regional Innovation Scoreboard (Regional Innovation Scoreboard, 2023[34]). Scores on trademark applications, innovative SMEs collaborating, public-private co-publications and international scientific co-publications were below the Croatian average in all three of these regions. Zagreb City, by comparison, was considered a "strong innovator", the third-highest possible grouping, and scored above the EU average overall. Zagreb City scored particularly highly on the following criteria: lifelong learning; employment knowledge-intensive activities; R&D expenditures in the business sector, and international scientific co-publications.

The demographic dimension

The populations of all four of Croatia's TL2 regions are shrinking, ageing and affected by emigration. However, these demographic trends are worse in Pannonian Croatia. Between 2011 and 2022, Pannonian Croatia lost 17.4% of its population, which was an annual rate that was almost double that of the nation as a whole. In fact, Zagreb City only lost 2.9% of its population over the same period (Table 2.4).

Table 2.4. Population change in TL2 regions, 2011-22

	2011	2022	Total change	Average annual change
Croatia	4 275 984	3 854 000	-9.9%	-0.9%
Adriatic Croatia	1 411 935	1 296 210	-8.2%	-0.8%
Northern Croatia	855 837	785 699	-8.2%	-0.8%
Pannonian Croatia	1 227 100	1 013 572	-17.4%	-1.7%
Zagreb City	790 017	766 824	-2.9%	-0.3%

Source: Author's elaboration with data from (Croatian Bureau of Statistics, 2023[35]).

The high rate of population decline has been caused by the same factors evident at a national level. These include sustained low birth rates, accelerating mortality rates and international emigration. In Pannonian Croatia, between 2012-2021, an estimated 175 051 individuals permanently left the region. Around 68.7% of these emigrants left Croatia entirely, but nearly one third relocated to another region. Of the total number that emigrated to another region within Croatia between 2013-22, the largest share, approximately 30.7%, relocated to Zagreb City. Around 29.0% migrated to Adriatic Croatia, 21.5% to Northern Croatia and only 18.8% to Pannonian Croatia (Croatian Bureau of Statistics, 2023[35]).

The precipitous population decline in Adriatic Croatia, Northern Croatia and Pannonian Croatia has several important social and economic implications. Of particular concern is the loss of skilled and working-age residents, which could greatly limit the economic potential of these regions and lead to disruptions in essential services due to the low availability of qualified staff. New policies to boost regional attractiveness, such as additional investment in childcare facilities, affordable housing and targeted education programmes to match local residents with the employment needs of the region, have recently been introduced by the Croatian government to slow outward migration and attract new residents. These will require careful monitoring and evaluation to ensure they are appropriately targeted at the specific challenges present in each TL2 region.

The ageing in Croatia's four TL2 regions has occurred in a more consistent manner, with the growth of elderly residents and decline in working-age population broadly consistent with the national trend. However, within that broad demographic shift, the relative youth of Zagreb City is made clear by the nearly 4-year age difference between the average (median) resident compared to Pannonian Croatia (Table 2.5).

Table 2.5. Demographic profile of TL2 regions, 2022

	Median age	Youth	Working age	Elderly
Croatia	45.4	14%	63%	22%
Adriatic Croatia	46.3	14%	62%	24%
Northern Croatia	44.7	15%	64%	21%
Pannonian Croatia	46.9	14%	63%	23%
Zagreb City	43	15%	64%	21%

Note: Youth (0-14), working age (15-64) and elderly (>65)
Source: Author's elaboration with data from (Eurostat, 2023[36]; Eurostat, 2023[37]).

The well-being dimension

Regional disparities on well-being indicators echo the stark economic and demographic divergences across the four TL2 regions. In comparison with the national average, the residents of Zagreb City generally enjoy longer and healthier lives than residents in Northern Croatia and Pannonian Croatia, and are significantly less likely to endure poverty than residents in all other TL2 regions (Table 2.6).

Table 2.6. Well-being indicators in TL2 regions, 2021

	Life expectancy	Suicide rate (2020)	Infant mortality	Risk of poverty
Croatia	76.7	13.9	3.8	17.4%
Adriatic Croatia	77.9	12.7	4.2	18.1%
Northern Croatia	75.8	16.5	4.6	18.5%
Pannonian Croatia	75.2	16.3	3.9	27.0%
Zagreb City	77.8	9.5	2.2	11.6%

Note: Suicide rate per 100 000 residents; infant mortality rate per 1 000 births.
Source: Author's elaboration with data from (Eurostat, 2023[38]; Eurostat, 2023[39]; Eurostat, 2023[40]; Eurostat, 2023[41]).

The available evidence suggests that the well-being of residents in Pannonian Croatia, which is also the region with the lowest GDP per capita and the fastest rate of population decline, is considerably lower than other regions. Residents in Pannonian Croatia, on average, have lower life expectancy, are at significantly higher risk of poverty, and suffer rates of suicide and infant mortality above the national average (Eurostat, 2023[38]; Eurostat, 2023[39]; Eurostat, 2023[40]; Eurostat, 2023[41]). Taken together, and in recognition of the interrelationship between well-being and economic development, the case for direct, well-resourced, and region-specific policy intervention in the north-east of Croatia is compelling.

In Zagreb City, 42.7% of working-age adults had completed a tertiary qualification compared to only 17.6% in Pannonian Croatia in 2021 (Eurostat, 2023[42]). These statistics are based on the current population, so are likely to be a combination of both higher rates of study from existing residents and the long-term accumulation of migrating university graduates drawn to Zagreb City in pursuit of employment opportunities.

Conversely, working-age adults with very little education are concentrated in the landlocked TL2 regions (Table 2.7). An estimated 17.5% percent of adults in Pannonian Croatia and 15.6% of those in Northern Croatia have not progressed beyond lower secondary school, greatly limiting their employment prospects. Fortunately, these rates have declined in all regions since 2017, but relative inequities between regions have remained broadly similar. The concentration of highly-educated individuals in Zagreb City, and the relatively high rates of adults with limited education in Northern Croatia and Pannonian Croatia is a significant barrier to balanced regional development. Most critically, the professional skills and capacity of residents and employees in less educated regions are likely to be lower, which will in turn limit the effectiveness of local government, healthcare, education and other essential public services. Furthermore, future investment and entrepreneurial activity, which requires skilled labour, is likely to be drawn to regions with large numbers of educated workers and could therefore reinforce existing regional inequalities.

Table 2.7. Distribution of education attainment in TL2 regions, 2017-2022

	Tertiary Education (2022)	Completed only Lower Secondary or below (2022)
Croatia	25.4% (+1.7pp)	12.1% (-4.1pp)
Adriatic Croatia	24.9% (+1.2pp)	9.2% (-2.2pp)
Northern Croatia	20.3% (+2.3pp)	15.6% (-6.2pp)
Pannonian Croatia	17.2% (+2.1pp)	17.5% (-6.7pp)
Zagreb City	43.8% (+2.6pp)	5.3% (-2.4pp)

Note: 25-64 age group. Data between parenthesis shows the percentage point [pp] change between 2017-22.
Source: Author's elaboration with data from (Eurostat, 2023[42]).

County trends

Croatia's county structure has been in place since 1992, with few major changes to governance arrangements or territorial boundaries being made in the last decade (Table 2.8).

Table 2.8. Map of Croatia's TL3 regions

TL3 code	Counties and Zagreb City
HR021	Bjelovar-Bilogora
HR022	Virovitica-Podravina
HR023	Požega-Slavonia
HR024	Slavonski Brod-Posavina
HR025	Osijek-Baranja
HR026	Vukovar-Srijem
HR027	Karlovac
HR028	Sisak-Moslavina
HR031	Primorje-Gorski Kotar
HR032	Lika-Senj
HR033	Zadar
HR034	Šibenik-Knin
HR035	Split-Dalmatia
HR036	Istria
HR037	Dubrovnik-Neretva
HR050	Zagreb City
HR061	Međimurje
HR062	Varaždin
HR063	Koprivnica-Križevci
HR064	Krapina-Zagorje
HR065	Zagreb (county)

Source: Author's elaboration, based on (Croatian Bureau of Statistics, n.d.[28]).

Of the 20 counties and Zagreb City, several have exceptional characteristics that warrant particular attention. Zagreb City, with by far the largest population (767 131 inhabitants) and highest population density (1 197 per km²), is almost entirely urban. In contrast, Lika-Senj has a population of only 42 748 and is almost entirely rural. It is also the largest county, with an area of 5 353 km², over eight times larger than Zagreb City (just 641 km²) and more than seven times larger than Međimurje (729 km²). The remaining counties are broadly comparable to one another in terms of geographic area and population density, with a balance of both rural and urban areas within their borders (Table 2.9).

Table 2.9. Basic characteristics of Croatia's 20 counties and Zagreb City, 2021

County	Km²	Population	Pop/km²	Cities	Municipalities	Classification*
Bjelovar-Bilogora	2 640	101 879	39	5	18	Predominantly rural
Dubrovnik-Neretva	1 781	115 564	65	5	17	Intermediate
Istria	2 813	195 237	69	10	31	Predominantly rural
Karlovac	3 626	112 195	31	5	17	Predominantly rural
Koprivnica-Križevci	1 748	101 221	58	3	22	Predominantly rural
Krapina-Zagorje	1 229	120 702	98	7	25	Predominantly rural
Lika-Senj	5 353	42 748	8	4	8	Predominantly rural
Međimurje	729	105 250	144	3	22	Predominantly rural
Osijek-Baranja	4 155	258 026	62	7	35	Intermediate
Požega-Slavonia	1 823	64 084	35	5	5	Predominantly rural
Primorje-Gorski Kotar	3 588	265 419	74	14	22	Intermediate
Šibenik-Knin	2 984	96 381	32	5	15	Intermediate
Sisak-Moslavina	4 468	139 603	31	7	12	Predominantly rural
Slavonski Brod-Posavina	2 030	130 267	64	2	26	Intermediate
Split-Dalmatia	4 540	423 407	93	16	39	Intermediate
Varaždin	1 262	159 487	126	6	22	Intermediate
Virovitica-Podravina	2 024	70 368	35	3	13	Predominantly rural
Vukovar-Srijem	2 454	143 113	58	5	16	Predominantly rural
Zadar	3 646	159 766	44	6	28	Predominantly rural
Zagreb (county)	3 060	299 985	98	9	25	Predominantly rural
Zagreb City	641	767 131	1 197	1	0	Predominantly urban

Note: *Classification applied by the Croatian Bureau of Statistics based upon population density and continuity and in adherence with TL3 urban-rural typology.
Source: Author's elaboration, based on (Croatian Bureau of Statistics, 2024[43]; Eurostat, 2018[44]).

Economic changes at county level

As alluded to in the previous section on Croatia's TL2 regions, the country's economy is highly dependent on a single TL3 region, namely Zagreb City. Its economic output in 2021 was more than four times greater than Split-Dalmatia, the second-largest county economy (Eurostat, 2023[45]). Compared to Lika-Senj, which has the smallest economy at the county level, the GDP of Zagreb City is over 100 times larger (Figure 2.13). The share of national GDP concentrated in Zagreb City has also grown over the past decade. In 2013, its share of national GDP was 33.7%, but in 2021 this had risen to 34.8%.

The concentration of economic activity within Zagreb City is further demonstrated by the wide range of financial, cultural, industrial and educational institutions that are based there, not to mention the vast majority of Croatian ministries, government agencies and civil servants. Despite being only one of 21 TL3 regions in Croatia, approximately one-third (31.8%) of the country's entire workforce in 2022 was employed in Zagreb City (Croatian Bureau of Statistics, 2023[46]).

Figure 2.13. Total GDP by county, 2013 and 2021

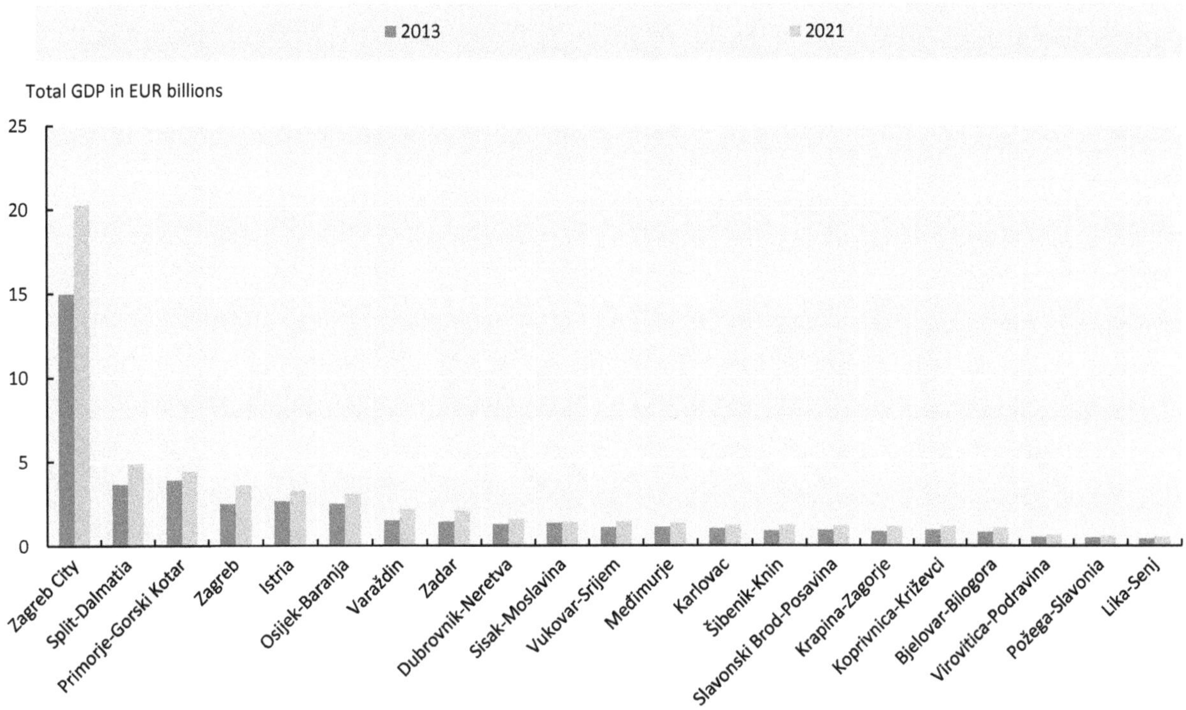

Source: Author's elaboration with data from (Eurostat, 2023[47]).

On a per capita basis, the GDP of Zagreb City remains by far the highest in Croatia (Figure 2.14). In 2020, GDP per capita was EUR 23 500 in Zagreb City, significantly higher than the Croatian average of EUR 12 500, but still well below the EU average of EUR 30 000 (Eurostat, 2023[48]). Based on this measure, an average resident in Zagreb City is able to obtain living standards up to three times greater than those residing in the bottom five (by GDP per capita) counties: Sisak-Moslavina, Vukovar-Srijem, Slavonski Brod-Posavina, Požega-Slavonia and Virovitica-Podravina. Notably, these five low-income counties are all landlocked, and are all located within Pannonian Croatia, in the country's north-east. Virovitica-Podravina, with GDP per capita of EUR 6 800, has the lowest standard of living among all 20 Croatian counties and Zagreb City. The average incomes of its residents, based on this metric, were equal to only approximately 54.4% of the Croatian average and only 22.7% of the EU average in 2020.

Figure 2.14. GDP per capita by county, 2013 and 2020

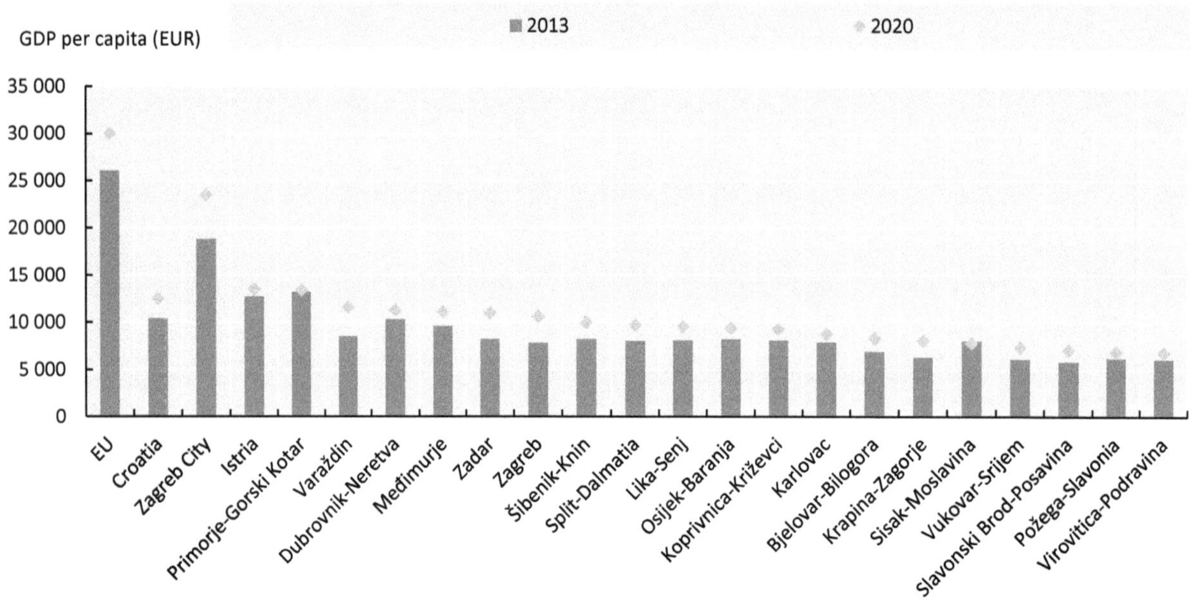

Source: Author's elaboration with data from (Eurostat, 2023[48]).

Since 2013, there has been limited evidence of economic convergence among the Croatian counties. The relative positions of Primorje-Gorski Kotar and Sisak-Moslavina, for example, have declined slightly since 2013. The counties of Varaždin and Krapina-Zagorje, in contrast, improved their position in the same period. Yet the overall distribution of GDP per capita remains largely unchanged, with very high levels in Zagreb City, above or around the Croatian average in coastal areas and below the national average for inland regions.

GVA is concentrated around Zagreb and coastal counties

The total value of output produced in Zagreb City, as measured by gross value added (GVA), is just as lopsided as GDP. Alongside Zagreb City, the counties of Split-Dalmatia, Primorjie-Gorski Kotor and Zagreb (county) produced approximately 57% of national GVA in 2021. The industrial composition of each county, as measured by GVA, provides some insights into the underlying disparities across counties (Figure 2.15). The best-performing counties, on both GDP and GVA, exhibit higher shares of tertiary industries compared to primary industries, such as agriculture and forestry. In Zagreb City, for example, approximately 83% of GVA can be attributed to tertiary sectors, compared to only 43% in Međimurje (Croatian Bureau of Statistics, 2023[49]).

Figure 2.15. Sectoral composition of GVA by county, 2020

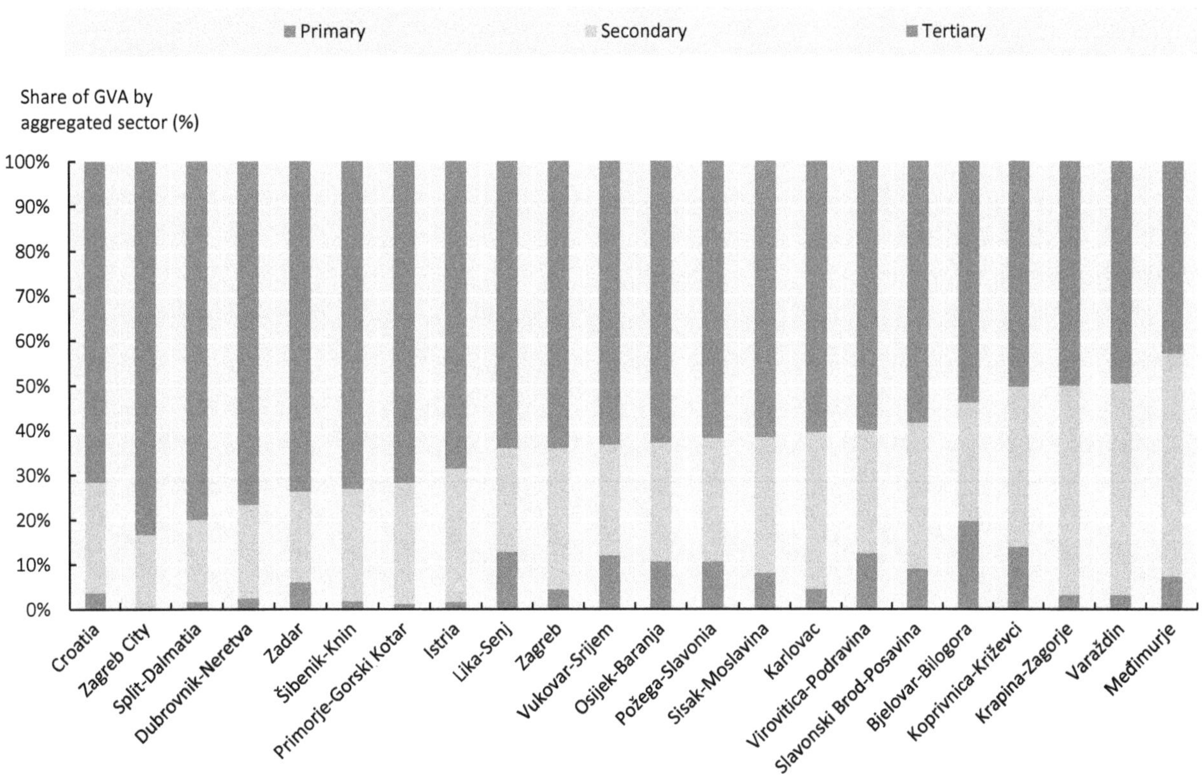

Note: Aggregates of primary (A), secondary (B-F) and tertiary (G-U) are estimated using the National Classification of Activities 2007.
Source: Author's elaboration with data from (Croatian Bureau of Statistics, 2023[49]).

The distribution of employment also varies significantly at the TL3 level (Eurostat, 2023[50]). In counties with high per capita GDP, such as Zagreb City and Istria, employment is concentrated in service industries (e.g. wholesale trade, retail, accommodation, hospitality, transportation and information technology). In low-income counties, such as Virovitica-Podravina and Požega-Slavonia, employment is much more evenly spread, with primary industries such as agriculture and forestry making up a relatively high share of total employment.

Tourism is booming but only in coastal areas

One of the most significant factors driving these sectoral differences is the concentration of tourism, one of Croatia's most important industries, within coastal localities. From the more than 82 million overnight stays from foreign visitors in 2022, of the landlocked counties only Zagreb City was able to attract more than one million (Figure 2.16). The concentration of tourists in coastal areas has both social and economic implications. Despite the employment, investment and tax revenue that the tourism sector has generated in recent years, some coastal localities have begun implementing strategies to help reduce the number of visitors to their areas, aiming to ease the congestion, environmental degradation and social disruption sometimes associated with mass tourism. For landlocked counties, which have generally achieved growth in tourist visits since 2013 (although tourists volumes were very low at that time), capitalising on Croatia's growing popularity as a holiday destination is a high priority and forms a key goal of the Strategy for Sustainable Tourism Development 2030 (Ministry of Tourism and Sport, 2024[51]).

Figure 2.16. Annual foreign visitor nights by county, 2013 and 2022

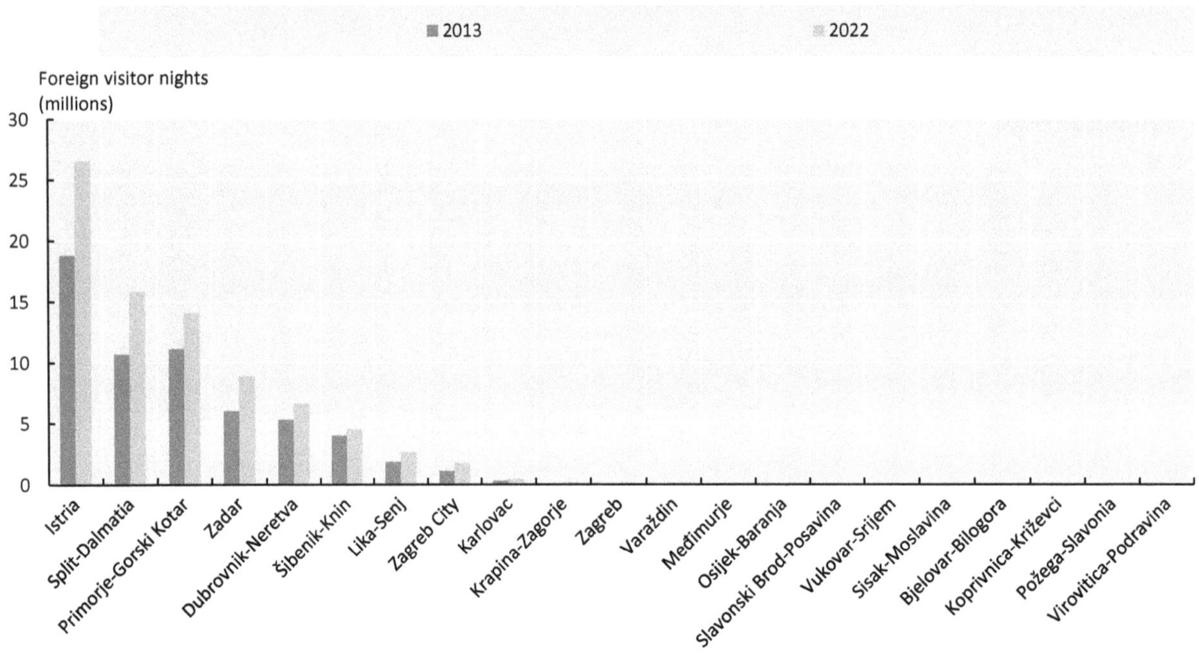

Note: In commercial establishments only.
Source: Author's elaboration with data from (Croatian Bureau of Statistics, 2022[52]).

Long-term unemployment has fallen rapidly in all counties and Zagreb City

The rapid decline in Croatia's long-term unemployment rate from 11% to 2.4% has been achieved through consistent improvement across all counties, both coastal and landlocked. On average, the absolute number of long-term unemployed in each county fell by 66.1% over the past decade (Croatian Bureau of Statistics, 2023[53]). This reduction, which represents a significant improvement in personal circumstances for some of the most disadvantaged individuals in each county, as well as reduced government costs for unemployment support, has been driven by a combination of factors. These factors include consistent economic growth, an ageing population and the ongoing expansion of the tourism industry that has increased demand for labour since 2013 and provided new employment opportunities.

Unemployment rates have fallen at a slower rate than long-term unemployment and are, in 2022, more varied at the county level. Eastern counties, and coastal counties with large urban centres, generally have unemployment rates above the national average of 7% and in many cases in excess of 10% (Figure 2.17). Zagreb City and the counties of the northwest were generally the best performers, with unemployment around only 4% in 2022. Despite these disparities, Croatia's rising economic tide has lifted all boats: unemployment rates have fallen dramatically in all counties since 2013. Nevertheless, it does indicate that the labour markets in some counties are less dynamic than others, and more targeted interventions will be required to address the geographic imbalance in unemployment.

Figure 2.17. Unemployment rate by county, 2013 and 2022

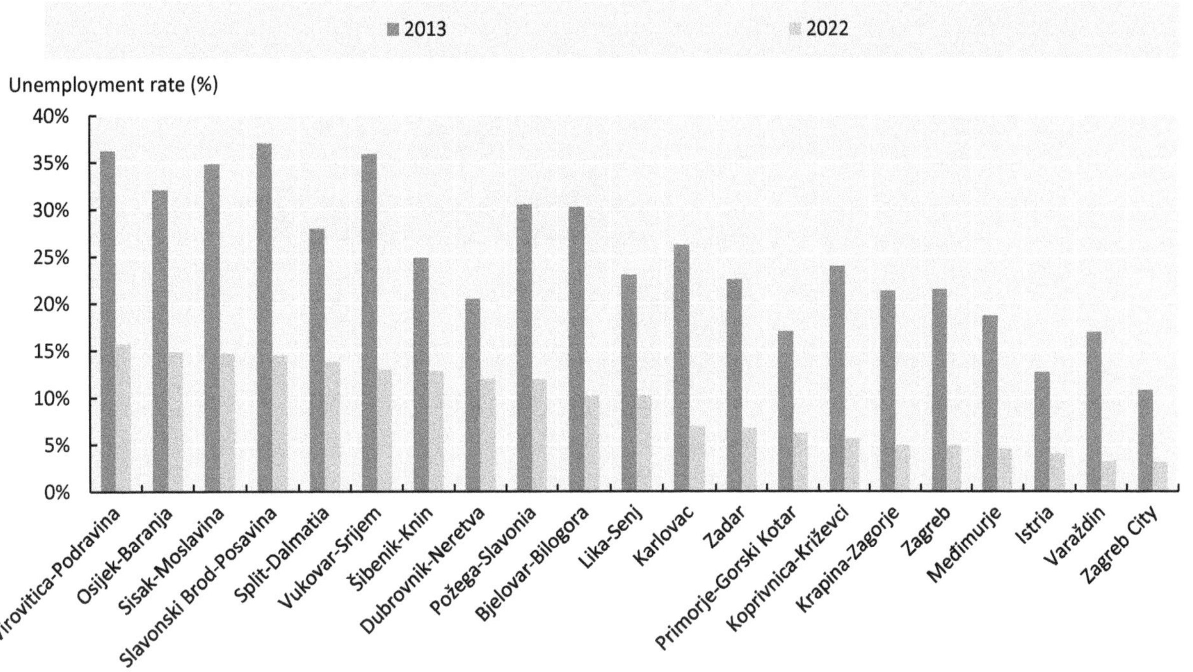

Note: Registered unemployment on 31 March.
Source: Author's elaboration with data from (Croatian Bureau of Statistics, 2023[53]).

Demographic changes at the county level

The rapid population decline in Croatia over the last decade has been unevenly distributed, with landlocked counties shrinking at a much faster rate than those on the coast. However, population decline has still occurred in all TL3 regions (Figure 2.18). Zagreb City, which reported the smallest decline, lost approximately 2.9% of its population between 2011-2021. In contrast, Vukovar-Srijem lost 20.3% of its population over the same period (Croatian Bureau of Statistics, 2023[20]).

Figure 2.18. Cumulative population decline by county, 2011-2021

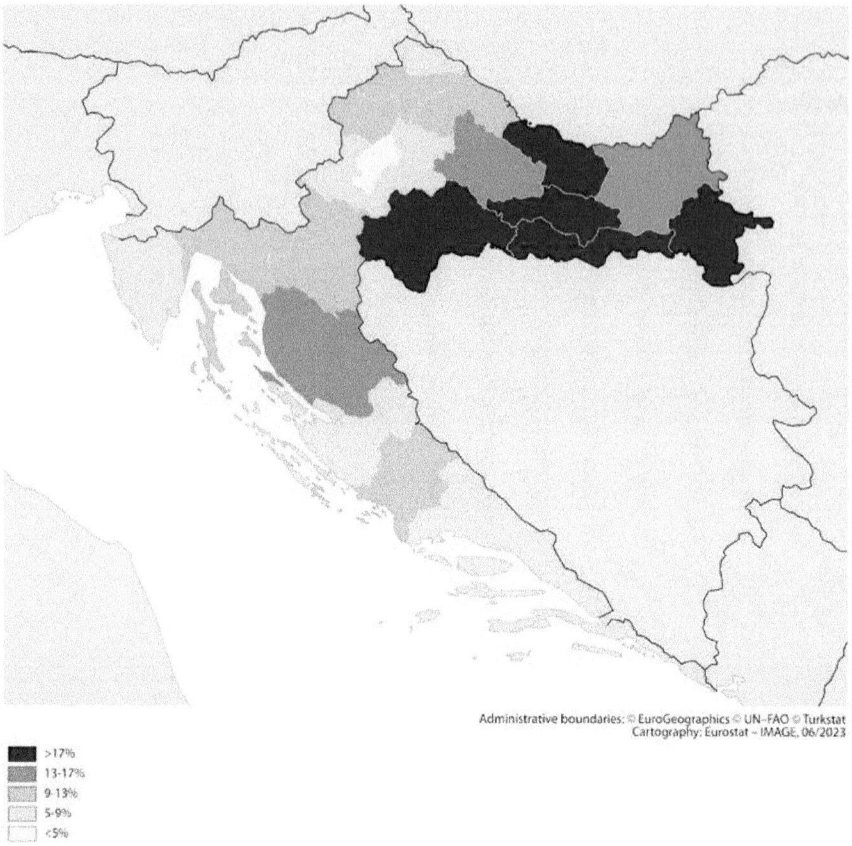

Source: (Croatian Bureau of Statistics, 2023[20]).

The uneven distribution of decline in population across Croatian counties and Zagreb City has been caused by two major factors—large variations in natural population decline and inconsistent migration patterns. Although natural population decline and emigration have affected all Croatian counties and Zagreb City to some degree, these national trends have occurred at vastly different rates. For example, between 2011 and 2021, the natural decrease of population, as a proportion of its 2011 population, was -10.9% in Lika-Senj. In Međimurje, the county with the smallest natural decline over the same period, the change was only -0.8% of the 2011 population (Croatian Bureau of Statistics, 2023[54]).

The range of net migration outcomes across counties between 2011 and 2021 is of a similar magnitude to the wide differences in natural population growth. In 15 out of Croatia's 21 counties, the total number of emigrants, including both international and inter-county, exceeded the total number of immigrants (Figure 2.19). Yet in Zagreb City, and in Dubrovnik-Neretva, Istria, Zadar and Zagreb counties, the total number of immigrants exceeded the number of emigrants. While the absolute numbers of net international migrants are small in some counties, as a proportion of 2011 populations, their impact can be significant. Ranging from a 3.8% increase in Zagreb City, to a 4.0% decrease in Vukovar-Srijem, net migration patterns have significantly accelerated population decline in some regions while slowing overall population decline in others (Croatian Bureau of Statistics, 2023[54]).

Figure 2.19. Aggregate international and inter-county migration, 2011-21

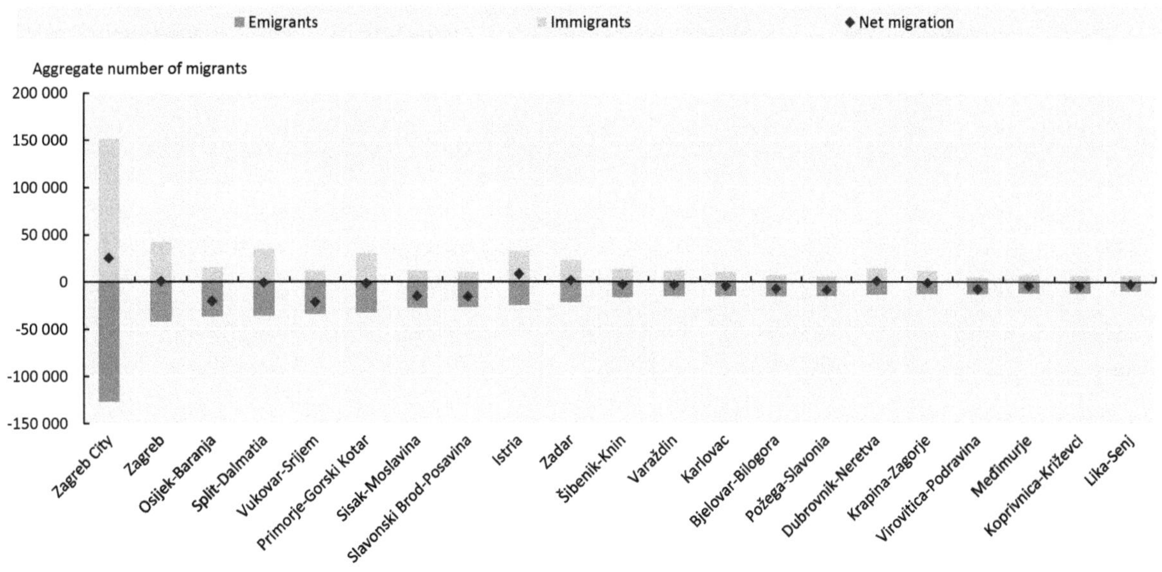

Note: Aggregate is the total number of emigrants and immigrants recorded in each county between 2011 and 2021.
Source: Author's elaboration with data from (Croatian Bureau of Statistics, 2023[54]).

In the five most rapidly shrinking counties, international migration has had a larger impact than inter-county migration, but both contributed significantly to population decreases between 2011-2021 (Figure 2.20). The average for all 20 counties and Zagreb City over the same period is more balanced, with migration flows—both inward and outward—following a similar trajectory for both county and international migration. This trend suggests that national and regional policy makers should tailor their demographic change and regional attractiveness strategies to the unique migration patterns of their counties. In counties experiencing rapid shrinkage, policies might focus on attracting and retaining residents, including through a combination of economic incentives, investment in affordable housing and connectivity (digital and by car, bus and train).

Figure 2.20. Aggregate net migration, fastest-shrinking counties, 2011-21

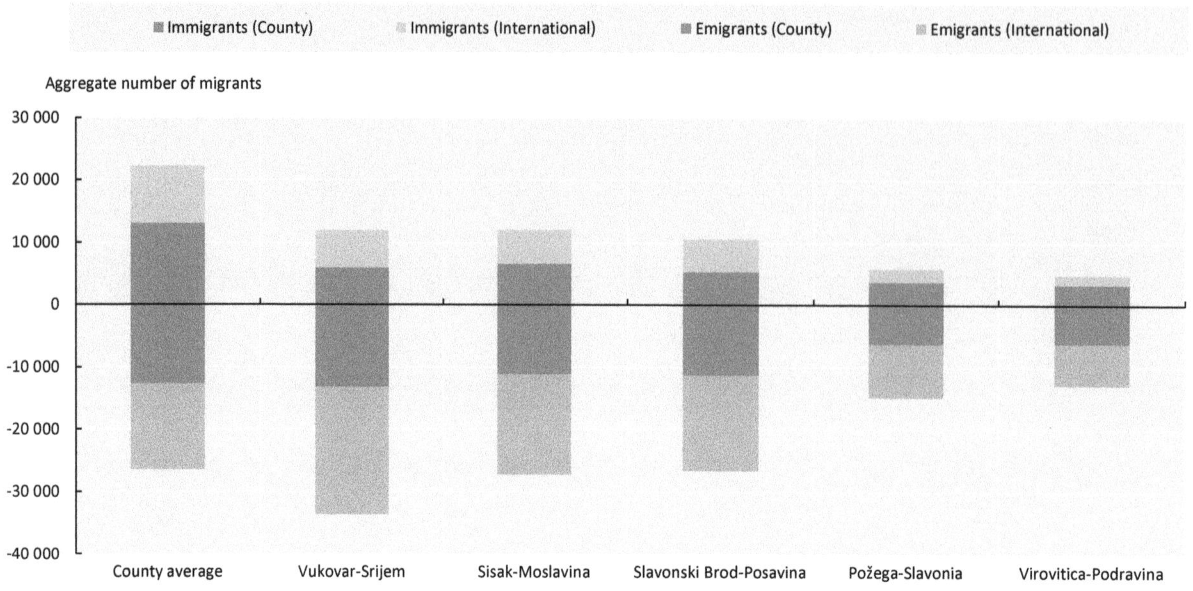

Source: Author's elaboration with data from (Croatian Bureau of Statistics, 2023[54]).

Well-being changes at the county level

The quality of life in Croatia has improved in the past decade, but large geographic disparities remain in several important indicators. For life expectancy at birth, the residents of coastal counties can generally expect to live 4-5 years longer, on average, than those in the landlocked locations (Figure 2.21). For the total population, Dubrovnik-Neretva recorded the highest life expectancy at birth in 2020, with 80.9 years. In contrast, Osijek-Baranja, the lowest-scoring county, recorded only 75.5 years. In every TL3 region, women are expected to live significantly longer than men. This gap is largest in Krapina-Zagorje, at 8.5 years, and smallest in Slavonski Brod-Posavina, at 4.5 years (Croatian Bureau of Statistics, 2022[55]). But the consistent divergence in health outcomes between men and women across all counties and Zagreb City suggests that further targeted programmes are needed to help improve the health outcomes of men throughout Croatia.

Figure 2.21. Life expectancy at birth by county, 2020

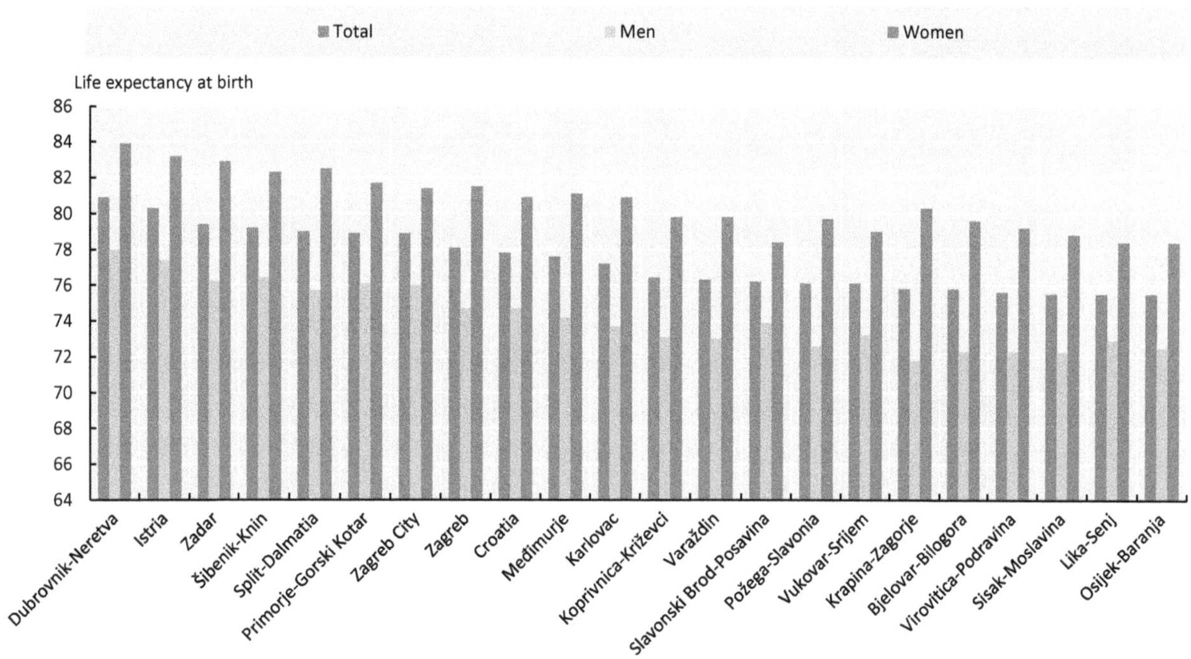

Source: Author's elaboration with data from (Croatian Bureau of Statistics, 2022[55]).

Health outcomes are highly uneven across counties and Zagreb City

The prevalence of disability, as defined by the Croatian Bureau of Statistics is unevenly distributed across counties, with Zagreb, Zagreb City and some coastal regions reporting significantly lower rates than landlocked counties in 2021 (Figure 2.22). The county with the lowest rate of disability was Istria, with only 10.8%, compared to 20.8% in Šibenik-Knin, the county with the highest rate of disability (Croatian Institute of Public Health, 2022[56]). Because the demographic profiles of Croatian counties are broadly comparable, with a similar proportion of elderly and working-age residents, these results are unlikely to be the direct result of variations in population characteristics. Lower population density, and a higher concentration of employment in primary industries, both of which could lead to a higher rate of accidents, and less developed health infrastructure, may partially explain the wide divergence. Lower average incomes, lower rates of education, higher rates of unemployment and other social factors may also be contributing to the regional disparities in terms of the disability rate. International and inter-county migration is also likely to have exacerbated these disparities, as individuals with a disability, for both health and economic reasons, are less likely to relocate to another country or county.

Figure 2.22. Percentage of the population with a disability by county, 2021

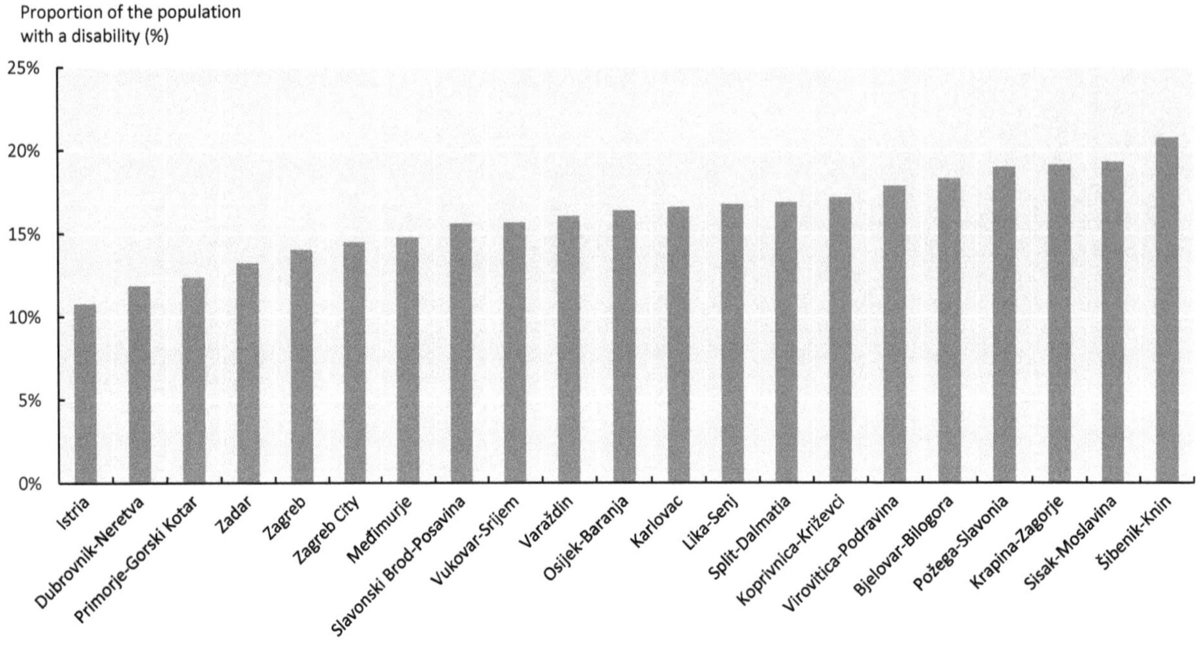

Source: Author's elaboration with data from (Croatian Institute of Public Health, 2022[56]).

Infant mortality rates across counties are also disparate, but do not align neatly with the high-income or coastal area narrative (Figure 2.23). Counties encompassing coastal areas, including Split-Dalmatia and Dubrovnik-Neretva, score relatively poorly, while Požega-Slavonia, in the north-east, has one of the lowest infant mortality rates in the country. Overall, Istria achieved the lowest infant mortality rate in 2021, with only 1.2 deaths per 1 000 births. Lika-Senj, the largest and most sparsely populated county, had the highest rate, at 10.1. Notably, infant mortality rates in the five worst-performing counties on this measure have increased since 2013, suggesting additional investment in medical services and infrastructure may be required in those localities (Croatian Bureau of Statistics, 2022[55]).

Figure 2.23. Infant mortality by county, 2013 and 2021

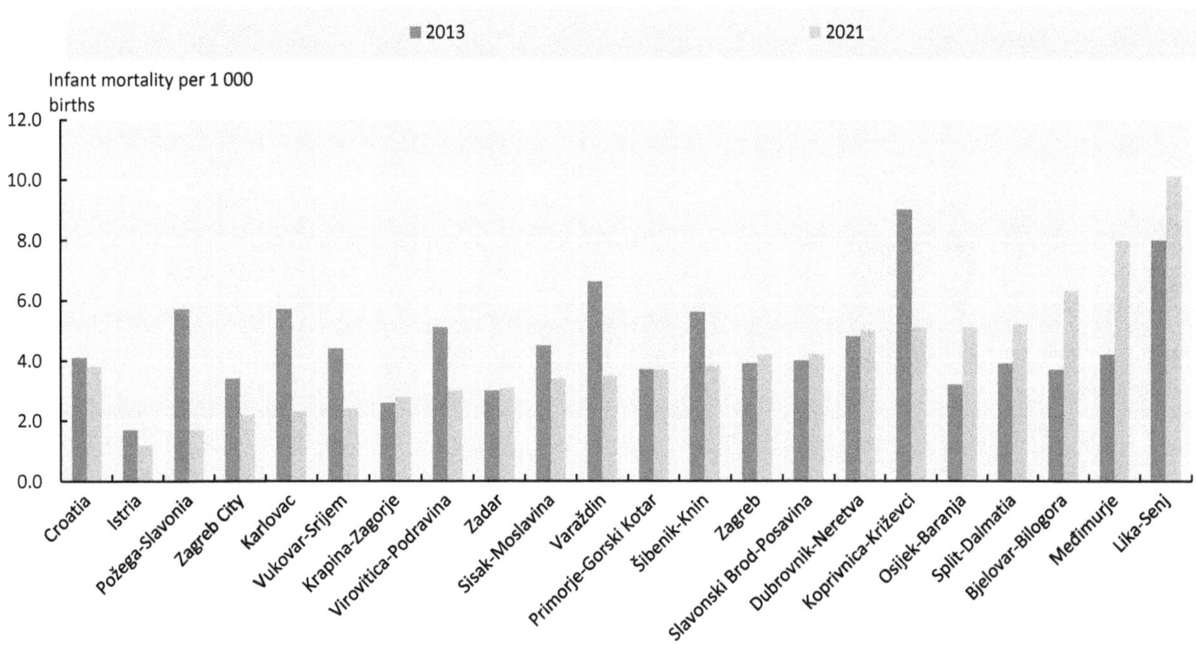

Note: Per 1 000 births.
Source: Author's elaboration with data from (Croatian Bureau of Statistics, 2022[55]).

One available indicator of medical facilities at the county level is the number of hospital beds per 10 000 residents. On this measure, there is significant variation on the distribution across counties, suggesting some unevenness in the provision of medical infrastructure (Figure 2.24). This variation, however, does not appear to correlate strongly with other health outcome indicators. Nonetheless, it highlights the potential challenges of accessing health services for some residents and the need for medical infrastructure to expand and evolve in line with demographic changes to ensure equity.

Figure 2.24. Hospital beds per 10 000 residents by county, 2021

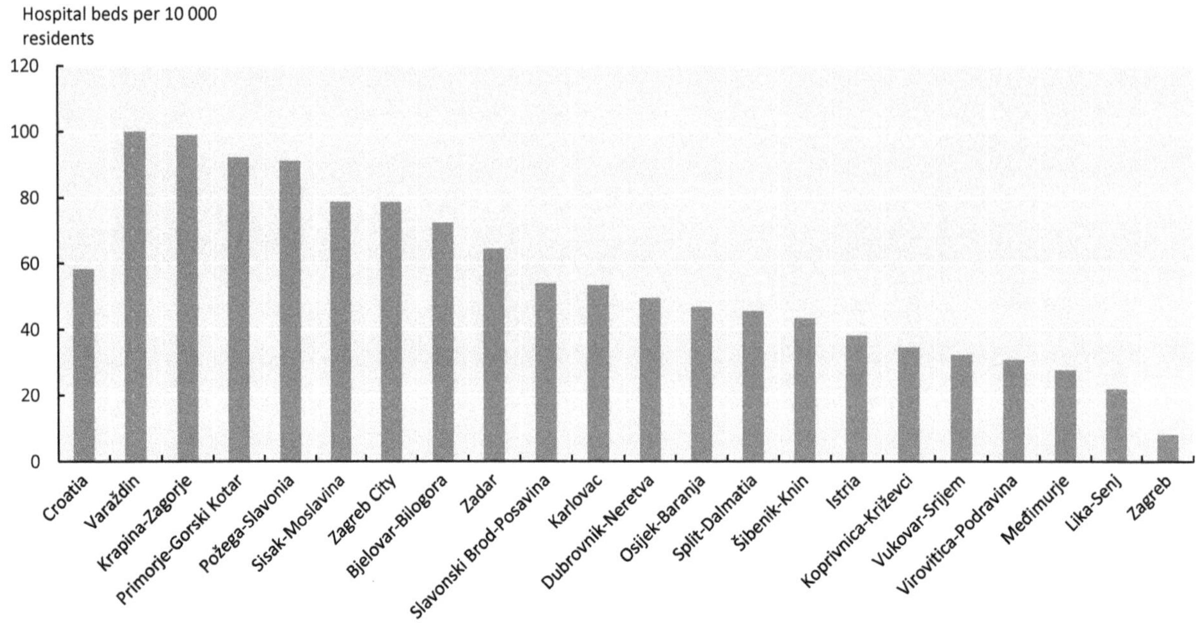

Note: Includes general hospitals, clinics, infirmaries and special hospitals.
Source: Author's elaboration with data from (Croatian Institute of Public Health, 2023[57]).

Crime rates vary across counties, but with no clear geographic pattern

Crime and traffic accidents, another indicator of well-being, also vary across Croatia, with residents in more remote and sparsely populated counties generally experiencing higher rates than others. When measured on a per capita basis, crime and traffic accidents are positively correlated, with Lika-Senj reporting the highest rates on both metrics (Figure 2.25). Interestingly, several high-income counties including Zadar and Istria have recorded relatively high rates of crime and traffic accidents. However, these statistics include crimes and accidents affecting non-permanent residents and tourists, so the actual impact on the average permanent resident may be smaller than these indicators suggest in coastal areas (Ministry of the Interior, 2022[58]; Ministry of the Interior, 2023[59]).

Figure 2.25. Reported crime and traffic accidents per capita by county, 2022

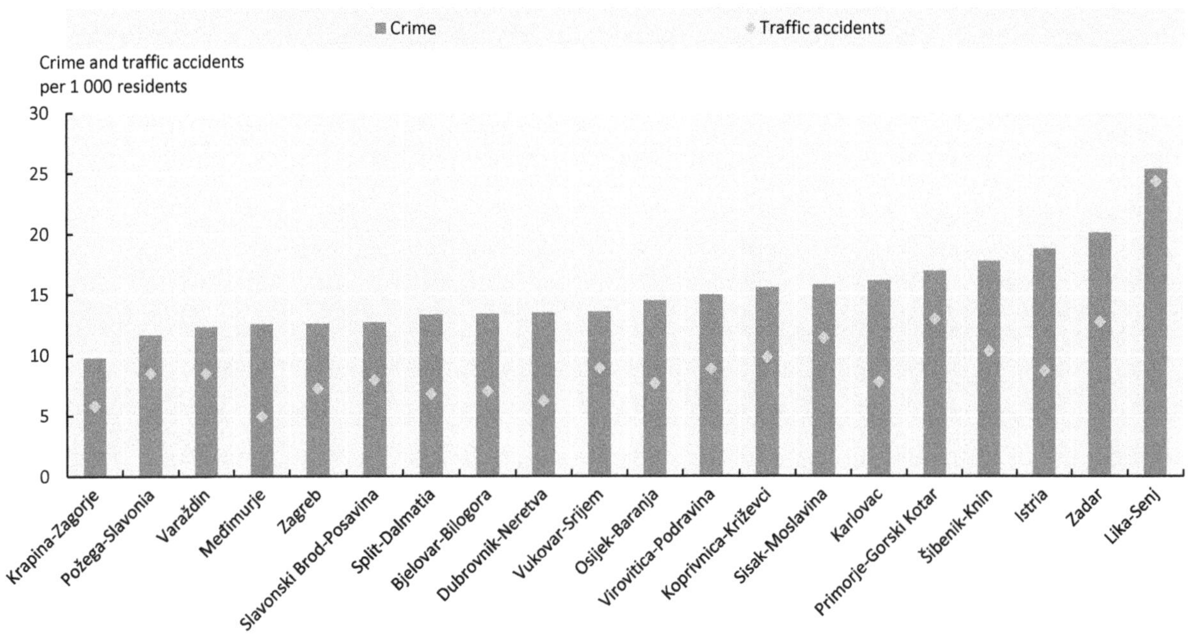

Note: Crime and traffic accident statistics for Zagreb City are included in Zagreb. Per capita estimates include the population of both.
Source: Author's elaboration with data from (Ministry of the Interior, 2022[58]; Ministry of the Interior, 2023[59]).

Internet speeds vary significantly across counties

Internet access is another indicator of well-being that is highly uneven across counties and Zagreb City. Although data for broadband access in the home is not available at the county level, the national rate of connection is 85.5%, suggesting widespread availability. Nonetheless, average download and upload speeds vary significantly, greatly limiting the practical use of an Internet connection in some localities. The average download speed available in Zagreb City in 2022, for example, was 124.8 megabytes per second (mbps), almost five times faster than the 25.3 available in Krapinsko-Zagorska (Ookla, n.d.[60]). These disparities can affect economic productivity, as areas with faster connectivity are more likely to attract and retain businesses. Furthermore, communities with limited Internet capabilities may face challenges in accessing government services and educational resources online. Further, low-speed Internet access could also hamper the overall attractiveness of a county, thus negatively affecting investment and tourism, among other impacts.

University graduation rates are broadly consistent across counties

Education levels across Croatian counties are difficult to measure due to insufficient data on the average number of years of schooling, or the total number of individuals holding different levels of qualification. The Croatian Bureau of Statistics does record the number of new university graduates each year, based on the county of permanent residence (Figure 2.26). These statistics may be slightly misleading, because recent graduates are highly mobile and may relocate shortly after completing university and entering the workforce. Therefore, the skills and educational attainment of the adult population actually residing within each county might be more unequal. But from an equity and upward mobility perspective, there is clear evidence that young people across all of Croatia are accessing, and graduating, from university at comparable rates (Croatian Bureau of Statistics, 2023[54]).

Figure 2.26. Number of university graduates per 10 000 residents in 20 counties and Zagreb City, 2013 and 2021

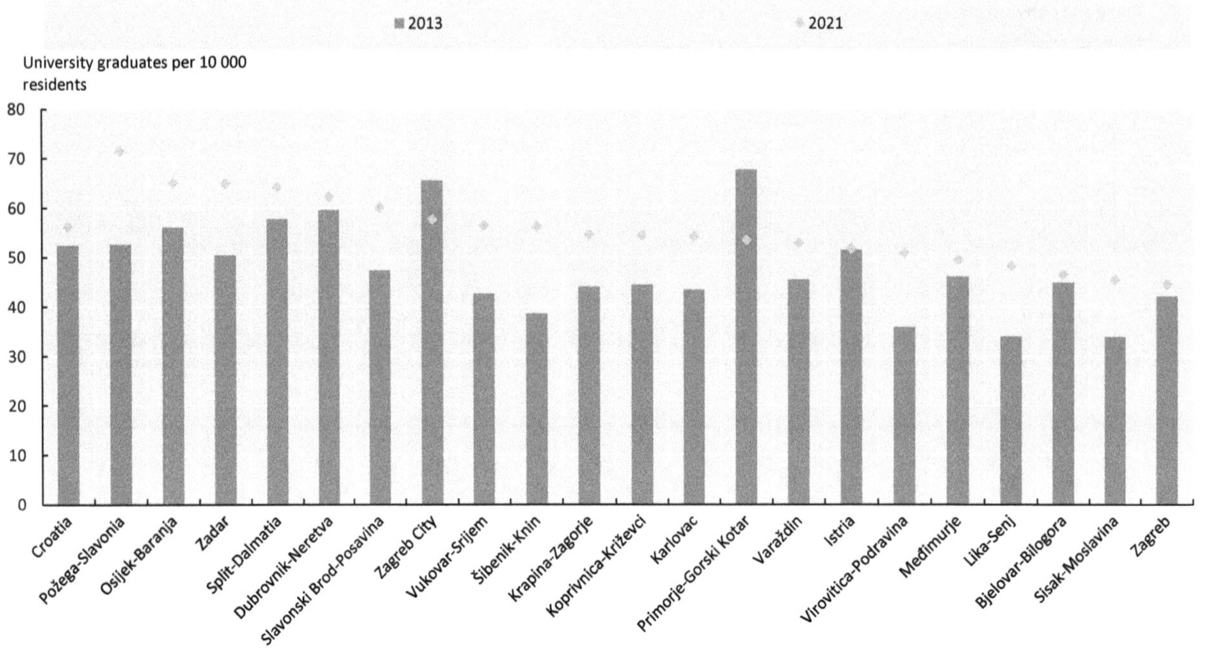

Source: Author's elaboration with data from (Croatian Bureau of Statistics, 2023[54]).

Conclusion

Croatia's performance overall since 2013 has been positive, with significant progress clearly evident on a number of indicators (e.g. reduced unemployment and higher GDP per capita) and modest improvements on several others (e.g. reduced risk of poverty and increased life expectancy). Long-term population decline remains an ongoing challenge, but Croatia's demographic profile is on par with many of its neighbours and does not pose an immediate threat to economic growth, well-being or the provision of government services. Regional inequalities remain large in Croatia, with residents in Zagreb and coastal counties earning higher incomes and experiencing a higher quality of life than landlocked areas. However, the fundamental conditions of all regions and counties are improving, and the additional level of investment and prioritisation required by the national and subnational governments to accelerate regional development and reduce inequality is unmistakably achievable.

In addition to well-targeted policies to address these inequalities, broader data collection and their more regular publication is also needed to help identify geographical disparities and measure progress to reduce them. Limited data, particularly at the county level, undermines efforts to identify such issues, set appropriate targets for improvement, develop suitable policy responses and measure the effectiveness of government programmes and interventions. Significant delays in the publication of data is also a concern in Croatia. Releasing data on key indicators on a more regular basis would enable policy makers to monitor the effectiveness of their strategies and plans more rapidly and allocate resources more effectively. It would also strengthen accountability, both at the county and national levels of government, while helping to support the case for renewed focus and investment in regional development.

References

Beunen, R., M. Meijer and J. de Vries (2020), “Planning strategies for dealing with population decline: Experiences from the Netherlands”, *Land Use Policy*, Vol. 93, https://doi.org/10.1016/J.LANDUSEPOL.2019.104107. [16]

Čipin, I. (2017), “Recent Demographic Trends and Policy Initiatives in Croatia”, in Čipin, I. and N. Ilieva (eds.), *Coping with Demographic Decline in Croatia and Bulgaria*, Friedrich Ebert Stiftung - Zagreb, https://library.fes.de/pdf-files/bueros/kroatien/13814.pdf (accessed on 8 September 2023). [21]

Croatian Bureau of Statistics (2024), *Urban-Rural Typology*, https://dzs.gov.hr/highlighted-themes/prostorne-klasifikacije-i-subnacionalne-statistike-2-694/urban-rural-typology/705 (accessed on 4 January 2024). [43]

Croatian Bureau of Statistics (2023), *Employment and Wages - Review by County*, https://podaci.dzs.hr/en/statistics-in-line/. [46]

Croatian Bureau of Statistics (2023), “Foreign Trade in Goods”, *Statistics in Sequence*, https://podaci.dzs.hr/hr/statistika-u-nizu/ (accessed on 2 January 2024). [12]

Croatian Bureau of Statistics (2023), *Gross Domestic Product (GDP) for Republic of Croatia, HR_NUTS 2021. – HR NUTS 2 and Counties, 2020*, https://podaci.dzs.hr/2023/en/58252 (accessed on 4 January 2024). [49]

Croatian Bureau of Statistics (2023), “International Migration”, *Migration of Population of Republic of Croatia, 2022*, https://podaci.dzs.hr/2023/en/58062 (accessed on 2 January 2024). [18]

Croatian Bureau of Statistics (2023), *Labour Force In The Republic of Croatia*, https://podaci.dzs.hr/2023/en/58050. [31]

Croatian Bureau of Statistics (2023), “Mid-year Estimate of Population”, *Population - Review by Counties*, https://podaci.dzs.hr/en/search?q=natural%20change%20population%20counties%20review (accessed on 4 January 2024). [35]

Croatian Bureau of Statistics (2023), *Migration of the Population of the Republic of Croatia, 2022*, https://podaci.dzs.hr/2023/en/58062#:~:text=The%20Republic%20of%20Croatia%20had,29.3%25%20of%20aliens%20emigrated%20abroad. [17]

Croatian Bureau of Statistics (2023), *Persons in Paid Employment, by Activities and Counties, Situation as on 31 March 2022.* [62]

Croatian Bureau of Statistics (2023), *Population Estimate, by age groups and sex, by Counties, 30 June*, https://web.dzs.hr/PXWeb/Table.aspx?layout=tableViewLayout1&px_tableid=SP21_1.px&px_path=Stanovni%c5%a1tvo__Procjene%20stanovni%c5%a1tva&px_language=en&px_db=Stanovni%c5%a1tvo&rxid=f67ec132-0425-40d2-b92b-d5bf6b61a5cc (accessed on 3 January 2024). [20]

Croatian Bureau of Statistics (2023), "Registered Unemployment Rate, Situation as on 31 March", *Employment and Wages - Review by Counties*, https://podaci.dzs.hr/media/1j5ahx5g/rad-2022-2-6_4-persons-in-paid-employment-by-sex-and-by-counties-2022.pdf (accessed on 4 January 2024). [53]

Croatian Bureau of Statistics (2023), *Towns in Statistics*, https://podaci.dzs.hr/en/statistics/population/. [54]

Croatian Bureau of Statistics (2022), *Croatia in Figures*, https://podaci.dzs.hr/media/l2wkiv1a/croinfig_2022.pdf. [1]

Croatian Bureau of Statistics (2022), *Migration of population of Republic of Croatia, 2021*, https://podaci.dzs.hr/2022/en/29029 (accessed on 2 April 2024). [19]

Croatian Bureau of Statistics (2022), *Statistical Information*. [55]

Croatian Bureau of Statistics (2022), "Tourist Arrivals and Overnights in Commercial Accomodation Establishments - Annual Data", *Tourism - Review by Counties*, https://podaci.dzs.hr/en/statistics/tourism/ (accessed on 4 January 2024). [52]

Croatian Bureau of Statistics (2021), *Population Census*, https://podaci.dzs.hr/2022/en/29031. [23]

Croatian Bureau of Statistics (2014), *Persons in Paid Employment, by Activities and Counties*. [61]

Croatian Bureau of Statistics (n.d.), *The NUTS classification in Croatia*, https://dzs.gov.hr/highlighted-themes/prostorne-klasifikacije-i-subnacionalne-statistike-2-694/the-nuts-classification-in-croatia/699 (accessed on 4 January 2024). [28]

Croatian Institute of Public Health (2023), *Croatian Health and Statistical Calendar for 2021 - Tabular Data*. [57]

Croatian Institute of Public Health (2022), *Report on Persons with Disabilities in the Republic of Croatia*. [56]

Croatian Ministry of Regional Development and EU Funds (2022), *Responses to the OECD national-level questionnaire for the "Enhanced Strategic Planning at the Regional and Local Levels in Croatia" project*. [2]

Eurostat (2024), *Gini coefficient of equivalised disposable income - EU-SILC survey*, https://ec.europa.eu/eurostat/databrowser/view/ILC_DI12/default/table?lang=en (accessed on 15 January 2024). [24]

Eurostat (2023), *At-Risk-of-Poverty Rate by NUTS 2 Regions*, https://ec.europa.eu/eurostat/databrowser/view/tgs00103/default/table?lang=en (accessed on 4 January 2024). [40]

Eurostat (2023), *At-Risk-of-Poverty Rate of Older People, by Age and Sex - EU-SILC and ECHP Surveys*, https://ec.europa.eu/eurostat/databrowser/view/ILC_PNS1/default/table?lang=en&category=livcon.ilc.ilc_ip.ilc_li (accessed on 3 January 2024). [25]

Eurostat (2023), *Causes of Death - Standardised Death Rate by NUTS 2 Region of Residence*, https://ec.europa.eu/eurostat/databrowser/view/HLTH_CD_ASDR2__custom_7230661/bookmark/table?lang=en&bookmarkId=92306057-8219-4299-9974-ebc5ead5c255 (accessed on 4 January 2024). [41]

Eurostat (2023), *Employment (thousand persons) by NUTS 3 regions*. [50]

Eurostat (2023), *Employment by Sex, Age, Economic Activity and NUTS 2 Regions*, https://ec.europa.eu/eurostat/databrowser/view/lfst_r_lfe2en2__custom_8297463/default/table?lang=en (accessed on 3 January 2024). [33]

Eurostat (2023), *Employment in High-tech Sectors by NUTS 2 Regions*, https://ec.europa.eu/eurostat/databrowser/view/tgs00039/default/table?lang=en&category=t_reg.t_reg_sct (accessed on 5 January 2024). [32]

Eurostat (2023), *Gross domestic product (GDP) at current market prices by NUTS 3 regions*. [45]

Eurostat (2023), *Gross Domestic Product (GDP) at Current Market Prices by NUTS 3 Regions*, https://ec.europa.eu/eurostat/databrowser/view/NAMA_10R_3GDP/default/table?lang=en&category=na10.nama10.nama_10reg.nama_10r_gdp (accessed on 4 January 2024). [47]

Eurostat (2023), *Gross Domestic Product (GDP) at Current Market Prices by NUTS 3 Regions*, https://ec.europa.eu/eurostat/databrowser/view/NAMA_10R_3GDP/default/table?lang=en&category=na10.nama10.nama_10reg.nama_10r_gdp (accessed on 4 January 2024). [48]

Eurostat (2023), *HICP - annual data (average index and rate of change)*, https://ec.europa.eu/eurostat/databrowser/view/PRC_HICP_AIND__custom_7002518/default/table?lang=en (accessed on 23 November 2023). [9]

Eurostat (2023), *Households - Level of Internet Access*, https://ec.europa.eu/eurostat/databrowser/view/ISOC_CI_IN_H/default/table?lang=en (accessed on 3 January 2024). [26]

Eurostat (2023), *Infant Mortality Rates by NUTS 2 Region*, https://ec.europa.eu/eurostat/databrowser/view/demo_r_minfind/default/table?lang=en (accessed on 4 January 2024). [39]

Eurostat (2023), *Life Expectancy at Birth by Sex and NUTS 2 Region*, https://ec.europa.eu/eurostat/databrowser/view/tgs00101/default/table?lang=en (accessed on 4 January 2024). [38]

Eurostat (2023), *Long-term Unemployment by Sex - Annual Data*, https://ec.europa.eu/eurostat/databrowser/view/UNE_LTU_A/default/table?lang=en&category=labour.employ.lfsi.une (accessed on 2 January 2024). [8]

Eurostat (2023), *Main GDP aggregates per capita*, https://ec.europa.eu/eurostat/databrowser/view/NAMA_10_PC/default/table?lang=en&category=na10.nama10.nama_10_aux (accessed on 2 January 2024). [6]

Eurostat (2023), *Nominal Labour productivity by NUTS 2 regions*, https://ec.europa.eu/eurostat/databrowser/view/nama_10r_2nlp/default/table?lang=en (accessed on 3 January 2024). [10]

Eurostat (2023), *Population by Educational Attainment Level, Sex, Age, Country of Birth and NUTS 2 Regions (%)*, https://ec.europa.eu/eurostat/databrowser/view/edat_lfs_9917__custom_8658906/default/table?lang=en (accessed on 4 January 2024). [42]

Eurostat (2023), *Population on 1 January by Broad Age Group, Sex and NUTS 3 Region*, https://ec.europa.eu/eurostat/databrowser/view/demo_r_pjanaggr3__custom_8297895/default/table?lang=en (accessed on 4 January 2024). [36]

Eurostat (2023), *Population projections*, https://ec.europa.eu/eurostat/databrowser/view/TPS00002/default/table?lang=en (accessed on 18 September 2023). [14]

Eurostat (2023), *Population structure indicators by NUTS 3 region*, https://ec.europa.eu/eurostat/databrowser/view/demo_r_pjanind3/default/table?lang=en (accessed on 4 January 2024). [37]

Eurostat (2023), *Regional Gross Domestic Product (PPS per Inhabitant) by NUTS 2 Regions*, https://ec.europa.eu/eurostat/databrowser/view/TGS00005/default/table?lang=en&category=na10.nama10.nama_10reg.nama_10r_gdp (accessed on 3 January 2024). [29]

Eurostat (2023), *Unemployment rate by NUTS 2 regions*, https://ec.europa.eu/eurostat/databrowser/view/tgs00010/default/table?lang=en (accessed on 3 January 2024). [30]

Eurostat (2018), "Glossary: Urban-Rural Typology", *Eurostat Statistics Explained*, https://ec.europa.eu/eurostat/statistics-explained/index.php?title=Glossary:Urban-rural_typology (accessed on 9 January 2024). [44]

Kaufmann, D. and A. Kraay (2023), *Worldwide Governance Indicators, 2023 Update (www.govindicators.org), Accessed on 11/1/2023.*, https://www.govindicators.org/ (accessed on 1 November 2023). [5]

Ministry of the Interior (2023), *Overview of the Basic Indicators for Public Safety in the Republic of Croatia for 2013-2022.* [59]

Ministry of the Interior (2022), *Survey of Basic Indicators.* [58]

Ministry of Tourism and Sport (2024), *Sustainable tourism development strategy until 2030*, https://mint.gov.hr/strategija-razvoja-odrzivog-turizma-do-2030-godine/11411 (accessed on 13 February 2024). [51]

Nejašmić, I. (2011), "Consequences of future demographic changes in Croatia", *Acta Geographica Croatica*, Vol. 38./1., pp. 1-14. [22]

OECD (2024), *ICT Access and Usage by Households and Individuals*, https://stats.oecd.org/index.aspx?r=656108# (accessed on 3 January 2024). [27]

OECD (2023), *OECD Economic Outlook, Volume 2023 Issue 1*, OECD Publishing, Paris, https://doi.org/10.1787/ce188438-en. [11]

OECD (n.d.), *Consumer Prises - Annual Inflation*, https://stats.oecd.org/index.aspx?r=656108# (accessed on 18 December 2023). [13]

Ookla (n.d.), *Internet speed*, https://github.com/EDJNet/internet_speed/tree/main/data (accessed on 23 November 2023). [60]

Regional Innovation Scoreboard (2023), *Regional Profiles Croatia*, https://ec.europa.eu/assets/rtd/ris/2023/ec_rtd_ris-regional-profiles-croatia.pdf. [34]

Šerý, O. et al. (2018), "Shrinking of cities in the Czech Republic and its reflection on society: Case study of Karviná City", *Geographica Pannonica*, Vol. 22/1, pp. 68-80, https://doi.org/10.5937/22-16622. [15]

SNG-WOFI (2022), "Country and Territory Profiles", *Croatia*, https://www.sng-wofi.org/country-profiles/croatia.html (accessed on 2 January 2024). [3]

The Economist Intelligence Unit (2022), *Democracy Index 2022*. [4]

World Bank (2024), *GDP per capita, PPP (current international $)*, https://data.worldbank.org/indicator/NY.GDP.PCAP.PP.CD?end=2022&locations=OE&start=2013 (accessed on 2 January 2024). [7]

Annex 2.A. Employment by sector and county

Annex Table 2.A.1. Employment by sector and county, 2013-22

Largest employment sector per NUTS 3 region as a share of total regional employment

NUTS 3 region	2013		2022	
	Largest employment sector	Share of total employment	Largest employment sector	Share of total employment
Bjelovar-Bilogora	Manufacturing	27.4%	Manufacturing	24.1%
Dubrovnik-Neretva	Wholesale and retail trade	13.6%	Accommodation and food service activities	15.3%
Istria	Manufacturing	20.1%	Accommodation and food service activities	15.0%
Karlovac	Manufacturing	25.4%	Manufacturing	27.3%
Koprivnica-Križevci	Manufacturing	32.9%	Manufacturing	33.4%
Krapina-Zagorje	Manufacturing	32.6%	Manufacturing	33.3%
Lika-Senj	Public administration and defence	19.2%	Public administration and defence	16.0%
Međimurje	Manufacturing	41.6%	Manufacturing	43.2%
Osijek-Baranja	Manufacturing	17.7%	Manufacturing	16.4%
Požega-Slavonia	Manufacturing	26.6%	Manufacturing	22.4%
Primorje-Gorski Kotar	Wholesale and retail trade	15.8%	Wholesale and retail trade	15.5%
Šibenik-Knin	Manufacturing	14.8%	Wholesale and retail trade	13.7%
Sisak-Moslavina	Manufacturing	26.3%	Manufacturing	22.0%
Slavonski Brod-Posavina	Manufacturing	27.1%	Manufacturing	28.6%
Split-Dalmatia	Wholesale and retail trade	18.6%	Wholesale and retail trade	17.7%
Varaždin	Manufacturing	40.5%	Manufacturing	38.4%
Virovitica-Podravina	Manufacturing	24.2%	Manufacturing	27.5%
Vukovar-Srijem	Manufacturing	15.2%	Manufacturing	17.4%
Zadar	Wholesale and retail trade	16.6%	Wholesale and retail trade	16.6%
Zagreb (County)	Manufacturing	23.7%	Manufacturing	22.8%
Zagreb City	Wholesale and retail trade	18.5%	Wholesale and retail trade	17.3%

Note: Paid employment in legal entities as of 31 March 2022.

Source: Author's elaboration with data provided by (Croatian Bureau of Statistics, 2014[61]; Croatian Bureau of Statistics, 2023[62])

Notes

[1] Predominantly urban regions are those where more than 80% of the population lives in 'urban clusters' or contains a city of more than 500 000 inhabitants representing at least 25% of the region's total population. The classification is estimated at the NUTS 3 level.

[2] Purchasing power standard is an artificial currency unit developed by Eurostat to enable comparisons of national accounts aggregates. It is calculated by multiplying aggregate production, in the local currency, by purchasing power parities, which are indicators of price level differences across countries.

3 Croatia's regional development governance framework

This chapter examines recent advances in Croatia's regional development policy and how it could be strengthened. First, it looks at how the country has reformed its legislative and regulatory framework for regional development since 2014. Second, the chapter explores the tasks and responsibilities of the main public actors involved in designing and implementing the country's regional and local development planning documents. In particular, it focuses on the mandate of Croatia's 21 regional development agencies and their position in the country's multi-level governance framework. Finally, the chapter assesses the effectiveness of existing co-ordination mechanisms for regional development in ensuring vertical and horizontal policy coherence.

Introduction

Since joining the European Union (EU) in 2013, Croatia has taken significant steps to establish an extensive legislative and policy framework for regional and local development. Key legislative achievements include the adoption of the 2014 Law on Regional Development, which created a legal basis for place-based regional development policy making. These efforts were further supported by the passing of laws for the development of specific territories, including hilly and mountainous areas, and islands. Croatia also enacted the 2017 Law on the System of Strategic Planning and Development Management, which created a comprehensive and hierarchical framework for strategic planning across and among levels of government, while reducing the overall number of territorial development planning documents.

Together, these reforms established a clear range of long-, medium- and short-term national, county and local-level planning documents. These include the National Development Strategy 2030 (NDS), which identifies balanced regional development among its main strategic objectives. Medium-term county development plans that seek to guide regional and local development efforts have also been introduced.

Furthermore, the legislative and policy changes provided more clarity regarding the responsibilities of actors involved in the design, implementation, monitoring and evaluation of regional development plans and programmes. For example, Croatia's 21 regional development agencies (RDAs), which, prior to 2017, had existed as limited liability companies that predominantly focused on providing paid consulting services, were reconstituted as public regional co-ordinators responsible for regional development planning. Moreover, different horizontal and vertical co-ordination mechanisms were established to support regional development policy design and implementation. These include the national-level network of strategic co-ordinators and the county-level network of RDAs.

To capitalise on the results of the above-mentioned reforms and to support the effectiveness of its regional development governance framework, there are various areas that Croatia could further strengthen. First, there are opportunities to further streamline Croatia's regional development planning framework, for example by updating the Law on Regional Development so that it no longer mentions obsolete planning responsibilities. Second, RDAs have reported skills gaps in areas such as procurement, the digital and green transitions, and monitoring and evaluation that need to be addressed. Strengthening these skills would make it easier for the agencies to support subnational governments to design competitive project proposals and report on the implementation of their development plans. Third, the complex relationship that RDAs have to county administrations and the national government presents a series of challenges (e.g. in terms of accountability) that can hamper the agencies' ability to guide medium-term regional development efforts. Fourth, while there are specific benefits to Croatia's RDAs operating at the TL3 (NUTS 3) instead of TL2 (NUTS 2) level (e.g. to identify local development needs), it also affects their ability to address macro-regional development challenges, support the mobilisation of regional development financing, and pool expertise. Fifth, while Croatia has set up several co-ordination bodies for regional development, there is scope to improve the quality of exchange across and among levels of government.

This chapter focuses on the legislative and policy framework for regional development, as well as the multi-level governance structures that support place-based development in Croatia. It begins by analysing Croatia's progress towards establishing a more robust legal and regulatory framework for regional development. The chapter then assesses the roles and responsibilities of the main actors involved in the development and implementation of the country's regional development planning documents. In particular, it focuses on the role of the RDAs in supporting regional development planning. The chapter concludes with a discussion of the country's horizontal and vertical co-ordination mechanisms that support the design, implementation, monitoring and evaluation of territorial development plans and programmes.

Box 3.1. Key recommendations to further strengthen Croatia's regional development governance framework

To strengthen the current legislative and policy framework for regional development, Croatia is advised to:

- Review and update the Law on Regional Development to ensure it is more closely aligned with the Law on the System of Strategic Planning and Development Management, in particular in terms of the planning requirements for national and subnational government bodies.
- Carry out periodic assessments of the planning responsibilities of national and subnational governments, and of their capacity to design, implement, monitor and evaluate such documents. On the basis of these assessments, the government could determine whether certain planning requirements may be excessive or too complex, and if so, streamline as appropriate.

To enhance the capacity of subnational actors to support the implementation of regional development policy, Croatia could:

- Conduct an annual training needs assessment for RDAs, in order to identify gaps in their knowledge and skills. On the basis of this assessment, the Ministry of Regional Development and EU Funds (MRDEUF) can develop an RDA capacity building plan that identifies training priorities and proposes concrete learning opportunities (e.g. MRDEUF seminars, workshops delivered by the State School for Public Administration).
- Clarify the complex relationship that RDAs have to county administrations and the MRDEUF, in order to address tensions over which strategic and operational tasks the RDAs should prioritise—those coming from the counties or from the Ministry.
- Implement an outreach campaign, led by the MRDEUF, to ensure increased understanding among county leaderships regarding the laws governing regional development and strategic planning, and how those apply to the counties and their RDAs.
- Conduct a formal assessment of the benefits, costs, legal and political obstacles to establishing the RDAs at the TL2 (NUTS 2) level. The purpose of the assessment would be to understand whether adjusting the territorial scale at which the RDAs operate could help address the financial, human resource and co-ordination challenges associated with RDAs operating at the TL3 level. Such an assessment should also consider intermediate alternatives that might achieve the benefits of scale without the full reconfiguration of RDAs (e.g. piloting the creation of one RDA at the NUTS 2 level).

To strengthen the effectiveness of vertical and horizontal co-ordination and co-operation mechanisms for regional development, Croatia is recommended to:

- Strengthen the impact of the Prime Minister-led regional development co-ordination body, which has been operational since 2016 by:
    - Ensuring that the body's meetings include the systematic participation of all national government bodies with portfolios that support regional development policy (e.g. Croatian Bureau of Statistics);
    - Reorganising the body into two chambers: one to support inter-ministerial co-ordination of regional development policy and the other to support the policy's vertical co-ordination among different levels of government.

- Incorporating the Prime Minister-led co-ordination body in the Law on Regional Development, replacing the Council for Regional Development, which has not been operationalised.
- Improve peer-to-peer learning and exchange opportunities among RDAs, for example by establishing a new forum or organisational unit within the Croatian Association of Counties that is dedicated to RDAs, or setting up a separate national RDA association.

Croatia's legislative framework for regional development

Over the past decade, Croatia has taken important steps in setting up a comprehensive framework for regional and local development, enabling governments at all levels to play a role in designing and implementing regional and local development initiatives. Progress in this area has been closely linked to the adoption of the 2014 Law on Regional Development, which laid the groundwork for regional development policy in Croatia. Even more important, however, were a series of legislative changes between 2017 and 2018, including the adoption of the 2017 Law on the System of Strategic Planning and Development Management, which sought to streamline the country's multi-level strategic development system and clarify the roles and responsibilities of public bodies at all levels of government to support place-based development.

One challenge to the reform process, however, has been the fact that the Law on Regional Development identifies several planning documents (e.g. urban development strategies) that subnational governments are no longer expected to develop and/or have been replaced by separate planning documents (e.g. Integrated Territorial Investment strategies). This risks creating uncertainty regarding the planning responsibilities of respective stakeholders and undermining policy coherence (MRDEUF, 2024[1]). Going forward, moreover, to support good-quality planning, policy makers should ensure that the administrative burdens being imposed on national- and subnational-level stakeholders responsible for developing plans and programmes (i.e. strategic planning co-ordinators and RDAs) are not overly burdensome.

Regional development policies and strategies across the OECD

Regional development refers to a general effort to reduce regional disparities and foster balanced and inclusive growth in a country, an individual region, or a metropolitan, urban or rural area (OECD, 2022[2]). Over time, the main objective of regional development has evolved from top-down interventions designed to reduce regional disparities by compensating less developed areas, into a much broader approach aimed at improving regional competitiveness, often by adopting a strategy that builds on a region's unique development strengths and challenges. This perspective emphasises co-operation across and among levels of government, as well as leveraging the contribution of non-governmental actors.

OECD Member countries conceptualise regional development policy as a medium- to long-term, cross-sectoral, multi-level policy—composed of laws, regulations, as well as planning and budgeting instruments—that aims to improve the contribution of all regions to national performance and reduce inequalities between places and between people. It can do so by promoting long-term sustainable development in all regions through strategic and targeted public policy, investment and service provision measures that are tailored to the specific needs and opportunities of regions and their inhabitants (OECD, 2023[3]). The 2023 *OECD Recommendation of the Council on Regional Development Policy* identifies ten complementary pillars that support regional development policy making and implementation (Box 3.2).

Box 3.2. OECD Recommendation of the Council on Regional Development Policy

The OECD Recommendation of the Council on Regional Development Policy, adopted by OECD Member countries in 2023, identifies ten complementary pillars to support regional development policy making and implementation. They include the following:

1. **Designing and implementing an integrated and balanced regional development strategy** tailored to different places.
2. **Targeting the appropriate territorial scale(s) for policy action** to account for all types of interdependencies across and within regions.
3. **Engaging actively with regional and local communities and stakeholders** throughout the policy-making cycle to gather and co-produce the knowledge needed to identify regions' needs and leverage their specific assets.
4. **Leveraging regional development policy to address the asymmetric impact of global megatrends and shocks**, and deliver on a sustainable and just green transition.
5. **Promoting the availability and quality of internationally comparable data and indicators** at different territorial scales to inform regional development policy and produce evidence for decision-making.
6. **Establishing sound multi-level governance arrangements** to foster coherent regional development policy.
7. **Strengthening administrative, strategic, and technical capacities** for regional development policy design and implementation at national and subnational levels of government.
8. **Mobilising diversified, balanced, and sustainable financial resources** to adequately fund regional development policy at the national and subnational levels.
9. **Promoting integrity, transparency, and accountability** in regional development policy to ensure the effective use of public resources and strengthen trust in national and subnational governments.
10. **Fostering robust performance management mechanisms** that promote evidence-based regional development policy.

Source: Author's elaboration, based on (OECD, 2023[3]).

A regional development strategy, by contrast, is a long-term planning instrument to achieve specified territorial objectives. It can bring together the strategies of diverse policy sectors to support their coherent implementation and contribution to a territory's productivity and attractiveness, not to mention the well-being of its citizens (OECD, 2020[4]). The effective implementation of a regional development strategy depends on several elements, such as sectoral policies. It also depends on the contributions of subnational governments with whom policy responsibilities may be shared, and non-governmental actors, including civil society organisations, the private sector, social economy organisations, civil society organisations, and citizens (OECD, 2022[2]).

Many OECD member countries (e.g. Brazil, Chile, Germany, Greece, Ireland, Mexico, the Netherlands, Portugal, Switzerland, the Republic of Türkiye and the United Kingdom) have a document outlining a strategic vision for their country. However, these often have a relatively short-time horizon (e.g. one to six years). Nevertheless, countries increasingly aim to develop strategies that span one to two decades or even longer (e.g. Costa Rica, Czechia, Finland, Hungary, Israel, Lithuania, Norway, and Slovenia) (OECD,

2020[4]). In countries where changes in government generally imply a marked shift in priorities, the development of a long-term strategic plan can contribute to policy continuity and improved outcomes.

Implications of top-down versus bottom-up regional development planning

A country's approach to regional development can be top-down, bottom-up or a combination of the two. In the case of the former, the national government sets the development vision and takes a command-and-control approach to policy design and implementation. Conversely, a bottom-up approach implies that subnational governments or other subnational actors identify local needs, and establish and implement plans to meet them (OECD, 2022[2]). On their own, neither approach will likely be effective or sustainable. While top-down approaches tend to meet strong implementation resistance from local stakeholders, adopting an approach that focuses primarily on bottom-up development may limit policy coherence, lead to disconnected investments across territories, and face funding and financing constraints.

A key question policy makers need to answer is how to strike an appropriate balance between the two approaches (OECD, 2020[4]). There is evidence that strategies combining a bottom-up and top-down approach are among the most effective (Crescenzi and Giua, 2016[5]). The development and implementation of a national-level, long-term regional development strategy that is the result of extensive stakeholder consultation processes can promote policy coherence among sectors and levels of government, and enhancing the efficient use of resources. It can provide the framework for action that enables different actors to take responsibility for implementing the initiatives necessary to achieve a society's long-term development vision, and builds their understanding of the need for collaboration (Rojas, Cuadrado-Roura and Fernández Güell, 2008[6]).

In order to help achieve long-term regional development objectives, in many OECD Member countries national-level strategic documents are complemented by regional and local development strategies, plans and projects designed by subnational actors (OECD, 2016[7]; OECD, 2019[8]). This is also the case in Croatia.

Croatia's legislative framework for regional development

The foundations of Croatia's current legislative framework for regional development (Table 3.1) were laid in 2014, when the government passed the Law on Regional Development. The law regulates the goals and principles of regional development in Croatia. In particular, it stipulates that the overarching aim of regional development policy is to create conditions in which all territories can strengthen their competitiveness and fulfil their development potential with a view to supporting the country's sustainable socio-economic development (Official Gazette of Croatia No 147 et al., 2018[9]). In pursuit of this goal, the Law states that policy makers should focus particularly on:

- Linking regional and local development needs with national-level priorities and EU Cohesion Policy objectives;
- Helping to address development challenges in economically lagging areas;
- Adopting specific measures to support the development of territories in border areas; and
- Promoting territorial co-operation and an efficient use of EU funds to support regional development.

A key component of the Law on Regional Development is its regulation of the national and subnational plans and bodies involved in supporting regional development policy. For instance, the Law tasked the MRDEUF with developing a national-level regional development strategy. Simultaneously, county administrations were made responsible for designing and adopting county development plans. City and municipal administrations were granted the option of designing and adopting their own local development plans. The Law also tasked the country's 21 RDAs, which are integrated into each of the county governments, with supporting the design, implementation, monitoring and evaluation of regional development policy (Official Gazette of Croatia No 147 et al., 2018[9]).

2017-2018 adjustments of the legislative framework for strategic planning

In 2017 and 2018, the government took legislative action to improve the coherence with which strategic planning is conducted among levels of government. First, the government recognised the need for a long-term development strategy for the country as a whole. Second, it identified an excess of planning documents. For example, there were 110 overlapping strategies and plans at the national level (OECD, 2023[10]), which created uncertainty regarding the country's sectoral and multi-sectoral development aims. This could have led to fragmented implementation processes and a sub-optimal use of public resources, while complicating monitoring and evaluation efforts. Third, the process for designing the different national and subnational planning documents was not co-ordinated or streamlined, resulting in parallel planning processes for different purposes. Finally, there was limited clarity regarding which actors were responsible for implementation and whether the results set in the different planning documents could, in fact, be achieved (OECD, 2023[11]; OECD, 2023[10]).

To help address the multiple challenges related to Croatia's development planning and implementation mechanisms and processes, the 2014 Law on Regional Development was amended in 2017. First, the amendments established RDAs as public institutions (whereas previously many of them had been established as private companies) and made them responsible for supporting the co-ordination of Croatia's strategic planning system among levels of government (Official Gazette of Croatia No 147 et al., 2018[9]).

Second, and for the first time ever, the government adopted a new Law on the System of Strategic Planning and Development Management in the same year (Official Gazette of Croatia No 123/2017, 2017[12]). The Law regulates strategic planning across and among levels of government. In particular, it establishes a clear hierarchy between the different long- (10+ years), medium- (5-10 years) and short-term (1-4 years) planning documents that need to be developed at national and subnational government levels in order to ensure greater policy coherence. Furthermore, the Law stipulates that the strategic planning documents must be linked to relevant budgets. Lastly, the Law outlines the actors responsible for the design, implementation, monitoring and evaluation of plans (Official Gazette of Croatia No 123/2017, 2017[12]). Table 3.1 provides an overview of the main laws governing regional development in Croatia.

Table 3.1. Main laws governing regional development in Croatia

Legislation	Description
2014 Law on Regional Development (amended in 2017 and 2018)	• Regulates the goals and principles of regional development in Croatia. • Stipulates that the aim of regional development policy is to create conditions in which all territories can strengthen their competitiveness and realise their development potential in order to support the country's sustainable socio-economic development. • Introduced the Regional Development Index, a composite indicator system used to monitor and evaluate the level of development of local governments. • Identified functional areas in need of special attention and support (e.g. 'assisted areas').
2017 Law on the System of Strategic Planning and Development Management (amended in 2022)	• Regulates strategic planning at all levels of government. • Establishes the hierarchy between the different long-, medium- and short-term strategic planning documents and defines their link to public budgets. • Defines the actors responsible for the design, implementation, monitoring and evaluation of plans, as well as the period for their design and implementation.

2018 Law on Assisted Areas	• Regulates the management of development in assisted areas. • Mandates the design and implementation of short-term programmes at national level that guide projects for 'assisted areas' at the regional and local levels. • Requires all counties, cities and municipalities to ensure the necessary preconditions for strengthening the competitiveness of the assisted areas and realising their development potential. • Stipulates that RDAs must assist in strengthening the capacity of counties, cities and municipalities located in assisted areas.
2018 Law on Hilly and Mountainous Areas	• Regulates the management of development in hilly and mountainous areas. • Defines hilly and mountainous areas. • Mandates the design and implementation of 1) short-term programmes at the national level that guide measures and 2) projects for hilly and mountainous areas. • Tasks all counties, cities and municipalities with providing the necessary preconditions for strengthening competitiveness of hilly and mountainous areas and realising their development potential
2018 Law on Islands (amended in 2020 and 2021)	• Regulates the management of development for Croatian islands and islets, including the manner in which their assets can be sustainably used and developed. • Sets out a classification of islands according to geographical criteria and territorial jurisdiction. • Establishes island development indicators used to evaluate development in these areas. • Stipulates the establishment of an Island Council, an advisory body to be consulted during the creation and implementation of programmes. • Introduces the National Island Development Plan and a further Island Development Plan at regional level.
2001 Law on Local and Regional Self-government (amended 13 times since its adoption)	• Regulates counties, cities and municipalities, their scope and organisation, the way their bodies work, the supervision of their acts and works, and other matters of significance for their work. • Allocates responsibilities in a wide range of domains to counties, cities and municipalities. • Outlines the conditions necessary and the bodies in charge of co-operation agreements between Croatian local governments, and those between Croatian local governments and those of other countries. • Outlines the main sources of revenue and the financial responsibilities of counties, cities and municipalities.

Source: Authors elaboration, based on (Official Gazette of Croatia No 118/18, 2018[13]; Official Gazette of Croatia No 118/2018, 2018[14]; Official Gazette of Croatia No 123/2017, 2017[15]; Official Gazette of Croatia No 123/2017, 2017[12]; Official Gazette of Croatia No 144/2020, 2017[16]; Official Gazette of Croatia No 147 et al., 2018[9]; Official Gazette of Croatia No 151/22, 2022[17]).

Strength of Croatia's current legislative framework for regional development

Croatia's current legislative arrangements supporting regional development provide policy makers at the national and subnational levels with a clear framework that guides the design, implementation, monitoring and evaluation of place-based planning documents. This is evident in several key areas. First, the Law on Regional Development forms a legal basis for regional development policy, and for a place-based approach to policy making that aims to address territories' specific development challenges. The Law also identifies regional development as a cross-cutting government priority, with the MRDEUF tasked with ensuring its co-ordination across and among levels of government. It also stipulates that RDAs should drive county and local development.

Second, the government's place-based approach to regional development has been reinforced by supplementary legislation, such as the 2018 laws on Islands, Hilly and Mountainous Areas and Assisted Areas, which establish strategic objectives for both types of territories. For example, the former law calls for the stable economic development of islands, a fair distribution of social opportunities for all island communities and an increase in their resilience to climate change.

Third, the Law on the System of Strategic Planning and Development Management created a comprehensive and hierarchical framework for strategic planning across and among levels of government. This has limited the significant overlap that previously existed among national and subnational government planning documents.

Fourth, the Law on the System of Strategic Planning and Development Management has introduced a legal basis for cross-government monitoring, evaluation and reporting of the strategic planning system (Official Gazette of Croatia No 123/2017, 2017[12]). Under the provisions of the law, the MRDEUF has developed a standardised Library of Indicators. The Library is a registry that is regularly maintained and updated with new indicators, which must be used by all public authorities in order to ensure standardised performance measurement across government (OECD, 2023[18]; OECD, 2023[10]).

Main strategic planning documents supporting Croatia's regional development framework

As stated, the Law on the System of Strategic Planning and Development Management provides a clear overview of key long-, medium- and short-term planning documents to be developed and implemented at the national and subnational levels (Figure 3.1). The Law on Regional Development established a number of additional planning documents to be developed, including a national-level regional development strategy, medium-term programmes for different development territories (e.g. assisted areas, hilly and mountainous areas), and urban development strategies for the country's major cities. However, it has not been updated to reflect the planning requirements that were set out in the 2017 Law on the System of Strategic Planning and Development Management. As a result, certain planning expectations set out in the former Law are out of date (MRDEUF, 2024[1]).

Figure 3.1. Croatia's system of strategic planning documents

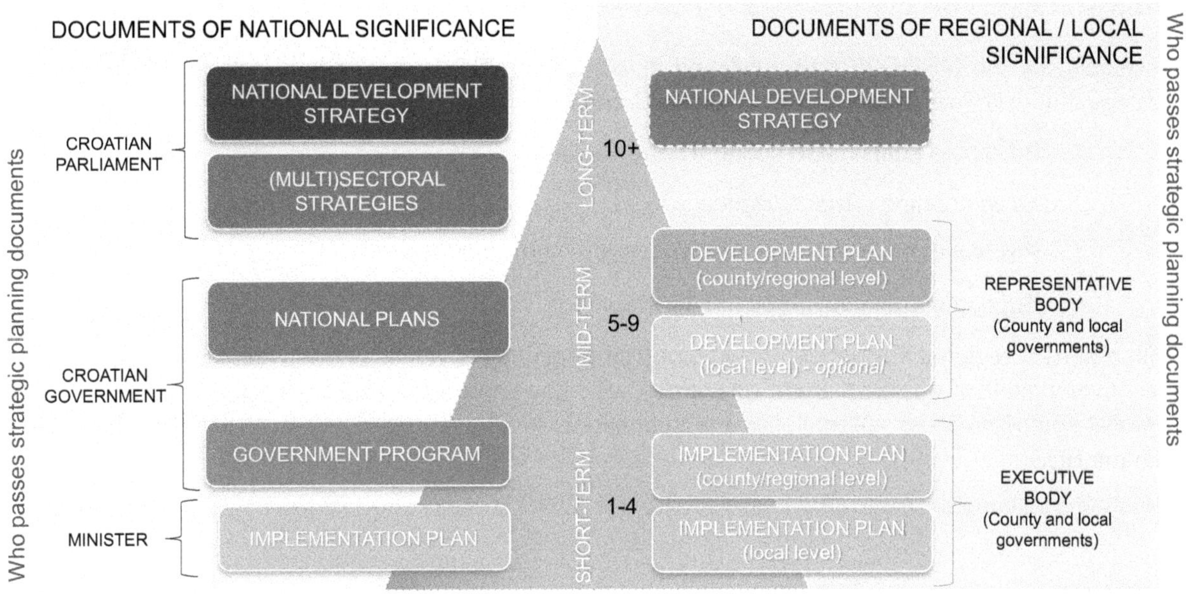

Source: Author's elaboration based on (MRDEUF, 2023[19]).

Croatia's national-level planning documents supporting regional development

The highest-level national strategic planning document supporting Croatia's regional development framework is the National Development Strategy (NDS) 2030 (Box 3.3). It identifies balanced regional development as one of its four strategic axes. To support the implementation of the NDS, national government bodies are responsible for adopting a set of medium- and short-term planning documents. For example, the Government Programme 2020-2024 is a whole-of-government planning document that covers the duration of the current administration and reflects its political priorities. One of its core aims is to support balanced regional development and decentralisation (Government of Croatia, 2020[20]). In particular, this priority area focuses on supporting greater fiscal decentralisation, and more extensive inter-regional and inter-municipal co-operation, as well as investing in broadband and transport infrastructure (e.g. railways).

Box 3.3. Croatia's National Development Strategy 2030

Developed by the MRDEUF and published in 2021, the NDS is a long-term, whole-of-government strategy that delineates four strategic axes for Croatia:

1. Building a sustainable economy and society;
2. Strengthening crisis resilience;
3. Promoting the green and digital transition; and
4. Supporting balanced regional development.

With regard to regional development, two broad strategic objectives have been identified: i) supporting the development of assisted areas and areas with development specificities; and ii) strengthening regional competitiveness. All national and subnational level planning documents have to be aligned with the NDS.

Source: Author's elaboration, based on (Official Gazette of Croatia No 13/2021, 2021[21]).

In addition to the NDS 2030 and the Government Programme, are a series of medium- and short-term strategies, plans and programmes that have a distinct territorial focus. For example, to support the smart specialisation goals outlined in the NDS, the Croatian Ministry of Science and Education is developing a Smart Specialisation Strategy (S3) 2029. The S3, which includes plans for specific TL2 regions, aims to improve the competitiveness and industrial transformation of Croatia's territories by building innovation capacity (Croatian Ministry of Science and Education, 2022[22]).

Croatia has also adopted different planning documents for territories that require specific attention. This includes the National Island Development Plan 2021-2027, which was developed by the MRDEUF and sets out the goals of the NDS in relation to island development (MRDEUF, 2021[23]). In 2022, Croatia also published separate short-term programmes for assisted areas and for hilly and mountainous areas, both of which were developed by the MRDEUF for the 2022-2025 period (MRDEUF, 2022[24]).

The implementation of the NDS, including its objective of balanced regional development is further supported by different national plans that are directly linked to EU funding mechanisms. These include:

- **The Competitiveness and Cohesion Programme 2021-2027** was developed to enable Croatia to secure EU Cohesion Policy funds. The Programme identifies a number of priorities for supporting the development of assisted, and hilly and mountainous areas (MRDEUF, n.d.[25]).
- **The Integrated Territorial Programme 2021-2027** was developed to secure funding through the European Regional Development Fund and the Just Transition Fund. The Programme has four main objectives that support territorial development, including supporting the industrial transition of Croatian regions, as well as the development of urban and island areas (MRDEUF, n.d.[25]).
- **The National Recovery and Resilience Plan 2021-2026** was developed to receive and allocate EU funding to support recovery in the wake of the COVID-19 pandemic (European Commission, 2023[26]). One of the objectives of the plan is to improve the institutional capacity of county and local governments, including on topics such as strategic planning (Government of Croatia, 2021[27]).

Croatia's county and local-level planning documents supporting territorial development

At the subnational level, the main strategic planning documents are (medium-term) county development plans, which must be adopted by county administrations. However, in light of the limited human resource capacity of many city and municipal governments, local administrations have the option of designing and adopting local development plans. All subnational governments (including city and municipal administrations) must, however, develop a short-term implementation programme that identifies policy measures that can help to meet their objectives (as well as the objectives of higher-level strategic plans) (Official Gazette of Croatia No 151/22, 2022[17]). In the case of cities and municipalities that do not have their own medium-term development plans, the local implementation programmes need to be vertically aligned with the county development plan. Legislation also prompts certain local governments to develop an urban development strategy. These include: i) urban agglomerations (Zagreb, Split, Rijeka and Osijek); ii) large urban areas (i.e. other cities with more than 35 000 inhabitants); iii) small urban areas (cities that have between 10 000 and 35 000 inhabitants or are the seats of the county government) (Official Gazette of Croatia No 123/2017, 2017[12]). In practice, this planning responsibility has been supplanted by Integrated Territorial Investment strategies, which have been developed for Croatia's major urban areas (see chapter 5) (MRDEUF, 2024[1]).

In addition, as part of Croatia's strategic framework for improving regional competitiveness (and under the auspices of Croatia's NDS and the S3), counties are required to co-operate with the MRDEUF to develop macro-regional Plans of Industrial Transition. Such plans aim to increase the competitiveness of TL2 regions—which lag behind the EU average—by strengthening regional value chains, boosting innovation through strategic partnerships, and supporting new upskilling, reskilling and training initiatives. In particular, the objective of the Plans of Industrial Transition is to equip workers with skills that are expected to be valuable and in-demand in the future. Three Plans of Industrial Transition have been developed, covering Pannonian Croatia, Northern Croatia and Adriatic Croatia respectively (OECD, 2023[10]). The plans were designed by the MRDEUF with support from the RDAs, based on a participatory process involving representatives from public bodies, and the private sector, academia, civil society and government, following the quadruple helix model. Co-ordinating councils comprised of the prefects of each TL2 region supervised the development of the plans and approved them (MRDEUF, 2024[1]).

Opportunities to further streamline Croatia's multi-level planning framework for regional development

There are, however, a number of areas that Croatia could explore to strengthen its multi-level planning framework for regional development. For instance, despite having streamlined planning requirements through the 2017 Law on the System of Strategic Planning and Development Management, the Law on Regional Development has not been adjusted to reflect these changes (e.g. it still mandates the development of urban development strategies). This creates a measure of uncertainty regarding the planning responsibilities of various actors, although in practice, national and subnational actors typically derive their responsibilities from the Law on the System of Strategic Planning and Development Management, in recognition of the fact that the Law on Regional Development is out of date (MRDEUF, 2024[1]).

Nevertheless, the government has acknowledged this issue, and is planning a review and update of the Law on Regional Development (MRDEUF, 2024[1]). As part of this exercise, the government should conduct a mapping of existing planning responsibilities at the national and subnational levels, in order to evaluate whether there are any possibilities to further streamline existing planning requirements. In so doing, it should also consult with representatives from respective levels of government regarding their capacity to support the design, delivery, monitoring and evaluation of existing planning obligations.

National and subnational actors supporting regional development

The governance setup supporting regional development policy matters. A clear assignment of responsibilities across and among levels of government in areas such as strategic planning, economic development, and education is particularly crucial. This clarity ensures that all levels of government know their role, responsibilities, and the expectations placed upon them, for example in terms of guiding policy design, funding or ensuring the implementation of specific projects.

Moreover, it is essential for tasks and responsibilities to be allocated at the appropriate level of government, in order to maximise their impact. However, identifying the level of government at which tasks should be allocated requires policy makers to navigate a series of trade-offs. For instance, while assigning tasks to a lower level of government may enable policy makers to more effectively leverage local knowledge and networks when identifying development needs, assigning tasks to a higher level of government may help to deliver other benefits (e.g. economies of scale in public investment and service delivery).

Another important element that supports an effective governance setup is ensuring that the public bodies charged with advancing regional development policy have the necessary funding and skilled personnel to carry out their mandates. Without sufficient resources, even the most well-designed regional development plans can fail to achieve their intended outcomes.

The legislative changes Croatia undertook in 2014 and 2017-2018 have sought to improve the governance setup for regional development. In particular, they have helped to provide significant clarity regarding which bodies should lead or contribute to regional and local development planning and implementation. Despite these advances, however, several challenges have strained the effectiveness of Croatia's governance arrangements supporting regional development. These include the complex relationship of the RDAs with their respective county administration and with the MRDEUF, which largely guides and oversees RDA work. Other challenges include the relatively local territorial level at which the RDAs operate and the high degree of municipal fragmentation, which limits their financial and human capacities to support development planning and implementation.

National-level actors involved in supporting Croatia's regional development governance framework

A wide array of public actors is involved in Croatia's regional development governance framework (Table 3.2). These include the Croatian Parliament, which adopts key long-term strategic planning documents (e.g. NDS and the national-level regional development strategy). They also include central executive bodies, including a variety of line ministries (e.g. the MRDEUF and ministries of Economy and Sustainable Development, Agriculture and Science and Education). These executive bodies are typically responsible for adopting national mid- and short-term planning documents that identify sectoral priorities and lines of action to achieve them, as well as contribute to the fulfilment of higher-level, long-term strategic objectives (e.g. those outlined in the NDS). To support coherent strategic planning at the national level, including for regional development, each line ministry has a strategic planning co-ordinator, which assists ministerial units with the design, implementation, monitoring and evaluation of planning documents.

Table 3.2. Main national-level government bodies involved in regional development planning

Actor	Responsibilities
Croatian Parliament	The Croatian Parliament adopts the NDS and other long-term (10+ years) strategic planning documents, such as sectoral and multi-sectoral strategies. It also approves monitoring reports on the implementation of the NDS. The Parliament is also charged with adopting a national-level regional development strategy.
Government of Croatia (general)	The Government of Croatia adopts medium-term (5-9 years) planning documents such as National Plans, and short-term strategic planning documents such as the Government Programme.
Line ministries	Line ministries adopt and implement short-term (1-4 years) planning documents, such as implementation programmes, which contribute to the fulfilment of higher-level strategic objectives (e.g. those outlined in the National Plans or the Government Programme).
The Ministry of Regional Development and EU Funds (MRDEUF)	The MRDEUF is responsible for co-ordinating the overall system of strategic planning in Croatia, including managing the design, implementation, monitoring and evaluation of the NDS. Other responsibilities include: • Submitting an annual report to the government on the implementation of the NDS; • Developing a legal framework, guidelines and methodology for the drafting, implementation, monitoring and evaluation of strategic planning documents across government; and • Determining the compliance of national-level strategic documents (e.g. sectoral and multi-sectoral strategies, national plans and implementation programmes of central government bodies) with the NDS. The MRDEUF also chairs the network of strategic planning co-ordinators and provides feedback on the alignment of strategic sectoral planning documents with the NDS. Finally, the MRDEUF is in charge of and manages the allocation of EU funds.
Strategic planning co-ordinators	Strategic planning co-ordinators are organisational units within line ministries that are responsible for overseeing strategic planning activities, and assisting other ministerial units with the design, implementation, monitoring and evaluation of strategic planning documents, including those related to regional development. They are also tasked with reporting to the MRDEUF on the implementation of strategic planning documents within their own government departments (through the network of strategic planning co-ordinators). Strategic planning co-ordinators could, in principle, help to ensure a regional lens is applied to sectoral planning documents and their implementation.

Source: Author's elaboration, based on (Official Gazette of Croatia No 147 et al., 2018[9]; Official Gazette of Croatia No 151/22, 2022[17]).

The MRDEUF, however, is the key body responsible for the country's regional development policy and for co-ordinating the overall system of strategic planning in Croatia. Its set of responsibilities include leading the design, implementation, monitoring and evaluation of the NDS (Official Gazette of Croatia No 147 et al., 2018[9]; Official Gazette of Croatia No 151/22, 2022[17]). Specific responsibilities include preparing regulations and other support material to guide the design, monitoring and evaluation of county and local development plans and implementation programmes. Also included are reviewing and commenting on draft county development plans that provide technical advice and channel financial support to the RDAs.

Subnational actors supporting regional development

At the regional level of government, county administrations are in charge of developing and leading the implementation of the county development plans in co-operation with local governments (Official Gazette of Croatia No 144/2020, 2017[16]; Official Gazette of Croatia No 151/22, 2022[17]). Counties are responsible for several tasks of regional importance, including maintaining county roads, supporting the development of regional public transport networks, and managing secondary education, and secondary healthcare (e.g. hospitals) (Official Gazette of Croatia No 144/2020, 2017[16]). To fund these responsibilities, counties receive a share of personal income tax, and depend heavily on earmarked intergovernmental transfers (e.g. for education, healthcare). As such, they have limited financial flexibility to orient service delivery to meet specific, territorially-differentiated needs (see chapter 5) (OECD, 2023[18]).

At the local level, Croatia's territorial-administrative structure includes two units of local government—cities and municipalities—both of which are responsible for supporting local development efforts. Croatia's territory includes 127 cities (excluding Zagreb City) and 428 municipalities[1]. According to the law, cities and municipalities are responsible for carrying out tasks of local importance, including maintaining local roads and managing primary education, as well as primary healthcare (Table 3 3). However, legislation also allows for an asymmetric assignment of responsibilities at the local level. In particular, a city or municipal administration can decide to transfer certain tasks and responsibilities to the county level. For instance, despite primary education formally being a local competence, this task is managed by county administrations in all but 35 cities (OECD, 2022[28]). Unlike counties, cities and municipalities can generate own-source revenue by leveraging different taxes (e.g. on real estate transactions, consumption, vacation homes and public area use) (OECD/UCLG, 2022[29]). This provides them with additional leeway to direct local funding to meet specific local needs.

Table 3 3. Division of selected tasks and responsibilities at the subnational level in Croatia

Sectors and sub-sectors	Regional level	Local level
Administrative services	Regional administrative services; issuance of construction and renting permits (except for large cities)	Local administrative services; issuance of construction and renting permits (only for large cities)
Public order and safety	Civil protection	Firefighting (only for large cities); civil protection
Economic affairs	Economic development	Not applicable
Roads and public transport	Maintenance of county and local roads (except for large cities); transport and traffic infrastructure	Maintenance of local roads (only for large cities)
Healthcare	Secondary healthcare (e.g. hospitals); preventative healthcare; primary healthcare*	Primary healthcare (e.g. general practitioners)
Education	Secondary education; primary education*	Primary education

Note: An * indicates that the county delivers the task when the local government considers that it lacks the administrative or financial capacity to do so.
Source: Author's elaboration, based on sources including: (Official Gazette of Croatia No 144/2020, 2017[16]; OECD/UCLG, 2022[29]; OECD, 2022[28]; Official Gazette of Croatia No 20/2021, 2021[30]).

The distribution of sectoral tasks and responsibilities indicates that both counties and local governments can influence policy areas relevant for regional and local development (e.g. economic development, education), and support the implementation of the county development plans. However, as counties are more dependent on earmarked intergovernmental transfers than cities and municipalities, they have less flexibility to orient spending to specific regional needs. This risks placing the onus for ensuring place-based implementation of territorial development initiatives on cities and municipalities.

Moreover, while in certain sectors (e.g. utilities), there is no overlap in competence between counties, and cities and municipalities, in others their mandates are very much aligned and may even overlap (e.g. roads and public transport). This reality requires counties and local governments to have a very clear understanding of what their specific responsibilities are and where they overlap. It also requires good co-ordination mechanisms to prevent a duplication of efforts.

RDAs are critical to subnational development planning

County administrations have various planning obligations that are linked to regional development. In particular, they are responsible for adopting and implementing county development plans (medium-term) and county implementation programmes (short-term). All plans are subject to ex ante approval by the county assembly (MRDEUF, 2023[31]; Official Gazette of Croatia No 151/22, 2022[17]). To help them carry out these tasks, county administrations rely on their RDAs.

In 2017, the RDAs became regional co-ordinators after previously having operated as Limited Liability Companies (OECD, 2022[28]). The RDA reconfiguration served two purposes. First, it sought to shift the focus of the RDAs from providing paid services to boost local economic development, to guiding strategic planning for regional development. The change was meant to strengthen the ability of counties to support the subnational implementation of national policies, as well as the 2017 National Strategy for Regional Development. Second, by curtailing their ability to provide paid services, the government sought to address concerns that RDAs had an unfair competitive advantage over private sector consultants. As public entities, RDAs could potentially access resources (e.g. financial support from county governments) and information (e.g. on upcoming calls for projects) that were not as readily available to private firms. Per the 2017 amendment, all county administrations were mandated to establish an RDA and ensure sufficient funding for their activities.

Key RDA responsibilities in the field of strategic planning include (Official Gazette of Croatia No 147 et al., 2018[9]; OECD, 2023[18]):

- Drafting county development plans and other strategic documents on their county's behalf and supporting implementation, while contributing to the design of national-level planning documents related to regional development (e.g. S3);
- Verifying the compliance of county planning documents with higher-level strategic planning documents (e.g. the NDS);
- Monitoring and reporting on the implementation of county planning documents, as well as regional and local development projects, to the county administration and the MRDEUF.

In addition, RDAs are responsible for helping counties, cities, municipalities and non-governmental actors to identify relevant EU and national funding calls and providing them with support to develop project proposals (Official Gazette of Croatia No 147 et al., 2018[9]). The combination of tasks and responsibilities of Croatian RDAs, which emphasises their leading role in supporting strategic planning, sets them apart from many of their peers in OECD Member countries, where RDAs focus primarily on business development and job creation, and have a less active role in territorial development planning (Box 3.4).

Box 3.4. Regional Development Agencies across the OECD

Regional development agencies (RDAs) operate in many OECD Member countries. They are generally charged with increasing economic development and regional attractiveness. However, there is much variation in the way RDAs are constituted (e.g. whether they are created by the national government or by a group of regional and local public and non-governmental actors), the levels at which they operate (e.g. TL2 or TL3 regions), and how they are funded (e.g. through membership fees, grants and/or project-based funding). Furthermore, RDA tasks and responsibilities also vary significantly – from supporting strategic planning for regional development and managing EU Cohesion Policy Funds, to promoting business internationalisation and managing public service delivery. The RDAs that operate in Belgium, the Netherlands, Romania and Spain illustrate this diversity.

Wallonia, Belgium

The Wallonia region in Belgium has eight territorial development agencies (*Agences de développement territorial*) that generally operate at the TL3 level. These RDAs are consortiums of regional and local public actors that seek to promote regional attractiveness and encourage investment in the regional economy. They offer a wide range of services (e.g. coaching, organising business events and providing financial support) to help businesses settle and grow in Wallonia's different regions. Several RDAs support municipalities in their urban and rural development planning. For example, subnational public bodies can contract the Regional Development Agency of Picardy Wallonia (IDETA) to carry out project application, appraisal, implementation, and monitoring and evaluation processes. This includes identifying project funding opportunities, conducting impact assessments and report writing. In addition, several RDAs manage specific public services, or own business parks and industrial land, which they can sell or rent out. For instance, the Regional Development Agency Charleroi and South Hainaut (IGRETEC) operates regional wastewater treatment plants, and functions as an energy purchasing centre for public bodies located in the region (e.g. cities and towns).

The Netherlands

The Netherlands has eight RDAs, which generally operate at the TL2 level, that function as territorial development corporations with public shareholders. The aim of the RDAs is to strengthen regional economies and increase employment, for example by encouraging innovation, investment and internationalisation activities. They do so by helping local and international businesses identify funding opportunities and employees, and by building their business networks. The RDAs can receive funding from the national government, provinces, municipalities, as well as non-governmental organisations such as research institutions. Most revenue is spent on investing in innovative businesses, and the (re)development of industrial estates and business parks.

Romania

In 1999, Romania established eight development regions that align with the country's TL2 territories. It also formed a regional development council and agency in each region, along with a framework to elaborate, implement and assess regional development strategies. The RDAs, which operate as non-governmental organisations, are responsible for encouraging territorial development and boosting regional attractiveness. They are charged with drafting and implementing territorial development strategies, plans and programmes (including smart specialisation strategies). They also support the implementation of regional development projects financed by the EU. In addition, the RDAs contribute to attracting foreign investment, offer business support services and promote innovation. The oversight of each RDA falls under a regional development council, composed of elected county and local government officials, and can include representatives of non-governmental organisations. The councils are responsible for reviewing and approving their RDA's regional development planning documents.

Since 2021, the RDAs also act as regional Managing Authorities for EU Cohesion Policy funds, which means they are entrusted with the design and implementation of the EU-funded Regional Operational Programme 2021-2017. This shift in responsibility renders the agencies responsible for managing EU funds exceeding EUR 1 billion per development region.

Spain

Spain has 19 RDAs that operate at the level of Spain's autonomous regions (TL2 level). While there is some variation across Spanish RDAs in terms of their mandate, their objective is to support regional economic development and citizen well-being. Their main fields of activity include: providing technical advice to businesses, including on internationalisation; managing investment funds, subsidies and loans; developing and managing industrial parks; and facilitating networking and exchange among public bodies, the private sector and research institutes. For instance, the regional development agency Andalucía TRADE has established a Project Accelerator Unit to fast-track investment attraction for strategic projects by providing preferential administrative procedures and technical support throughout the investment process.

In terms of planning, the RDAs are generally responsible for the design and implementation of the regional S3. The governments of Spain's autonomous regions, of which the RDAs are part, are responsible for overall strategic regional development planning, as well as the design and management of regional Operational Programmes for the EU 2021-2027 programming period. The main sources of RDA revenue to operate and support project implementation are funds from Spain's regional governments, as well as EU funds.

Source: Author's elaboration. Belgium: (IDETA, 2023[32]; IGRETEC, n.d.[33]; Wallonie Developpement, n.d.[34]); the Netherlands: (Netherlands Chamber of Commerce, n.d.[35]); Romania: (ROREG, 2022[36]; EURADA, n.d.[37]; OECD, 2023[38]); and Spain: (Andalucía TRADE, n.d.[39]; Foro ARD, n.d.[40]).

While RDA human resource capacity has increased sharply, skills gaps remain

There is a significant variation in the financial and human resource capacity of RDAs to carry out their responsibilities (Figure 3.2). As of 2023, for example, while some RDAs had more than 50 employees (e.g. Zadar County RDA), others had as few as 11 (e.g. Bjelovar-Bilogora County RDA and Istria County RDA). The variation in staffing numbers can affect their ability to ensure similar levels of support to county, city and municipal administrations (MRDEUF, 2023[41]).

County-based comparisons can help to highlight this disparity. For instance, while Primorje-Gorski Kotar and Zadar counties include a similar number of cities and municipalities (36 and 34 in total, respectively), their RDA staff numbers are quite different. In 2023, Zadar County RDA had 56 employees, compared to only 20 in Primorje-Gorski Kotar County RDA. This suggests that, at least on paper, the capacity of Zadar RDA to provide tailored support to cities and municipalities, such as helping them identify EU funding opportunities and prepare competitive project proposals is significantly greater than that of other RDAs.

Figure 3.2. Staffing of RDAs, 2018 and 2023

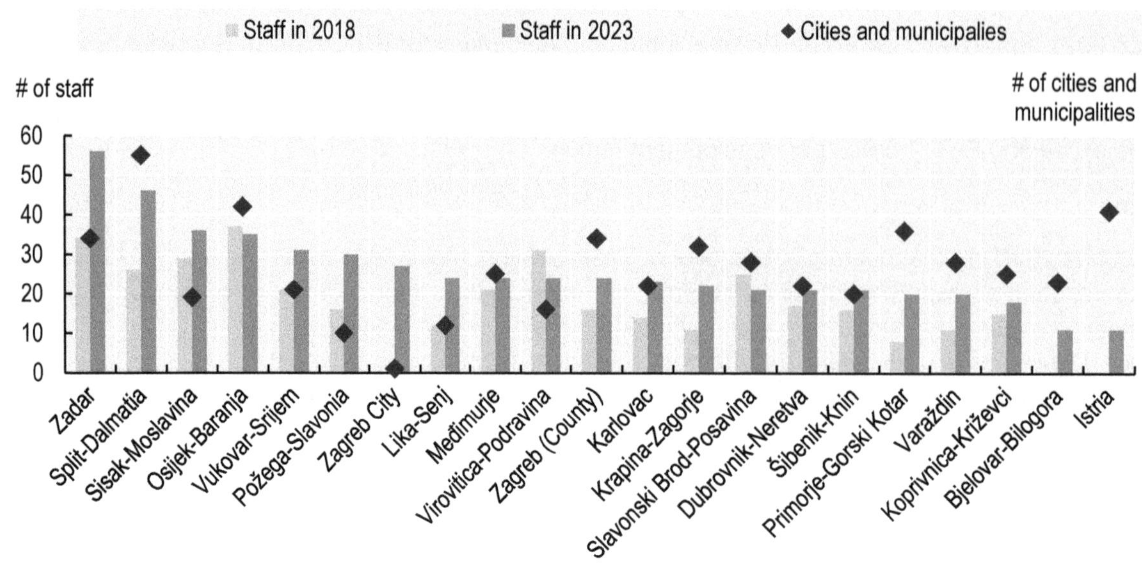

Source: Author's elaboration, based on (OECD, 2022[42]; MRDEUF, 2023[43]).

Notwithstanding the above-mentioned disparity, it is important to note that the payrolls of RDAs surged following the 2017-2018 legislative changes to Croatia's regional development and strategic planning frameworks. Figure 3.2 suggests that the total number of RDA employees across Croatia increased from 360 to 545 between 2018 and 2023, with staffing levels in several RDAs rising by more than 75% (e.g. Požega-Slavonia RDA, Lika-Senj County RDA and Krapina-Zagorje County RDA). This change reflects the funding from EU Technical Assistance available to RDAs during this period, which many RDAs used to attract staff (see chapter 5) (OECD, 2023[18]).

The increase in RDA staffing levels has helped strengthen their capacity to carry out their mandate—to support the design of county development plans, to identify funding opportunities for counties, cities, and municipalities, and to facilitate the implementation of strategic regional initiatives. In response to an OECD questionnaire completed by all 21 RDAs, 76% of RDAs considered that they had sufficient staff to execute their responsibilities, and 91% of RDAs indicated that their staff had the necessary expertise to carry out their mandate (Figure 3.3). However, there are also concerns among national government representatives that the RDAs may in fact be overstaffed, raising questions about the sustainability and cost-effectiveness of their operations, especially in the context of future funding uncertainty (OECD, 2023[10]).

Figure 3.3. Self-reported resource capacity of Croatia RDAs

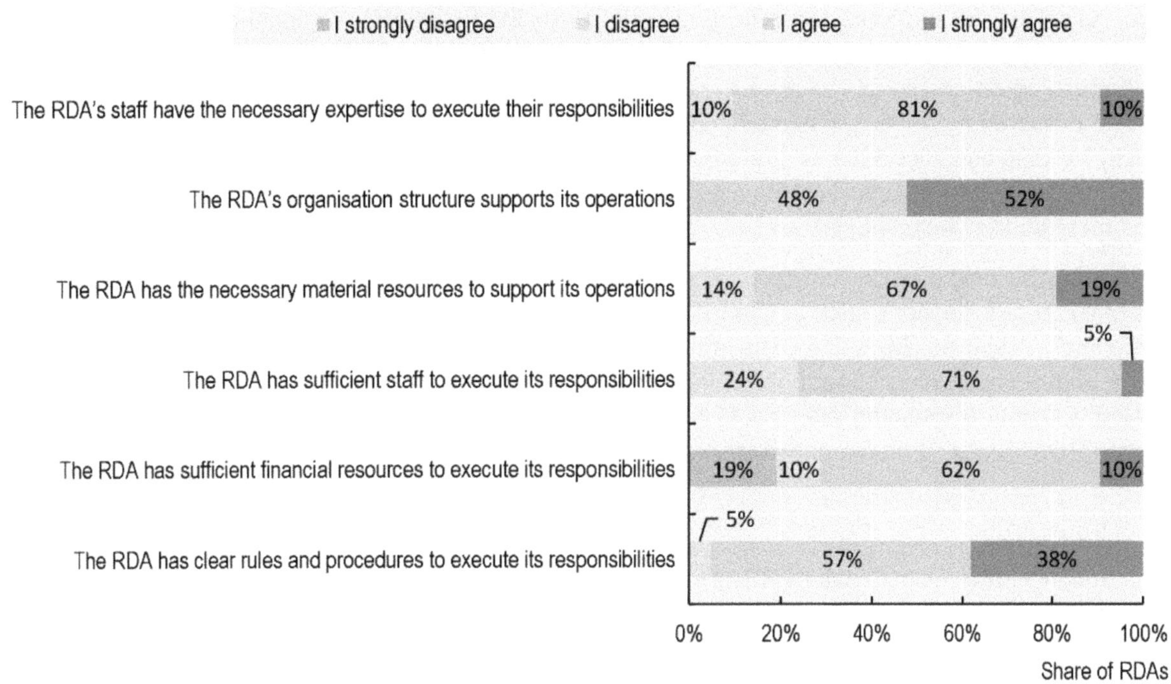

Note: Questionnaire question: To what extent do you agree with the following statements? Full statements: The RDA has clear internal rules, procedures and mechanisms in place to carry out its various tasks; The RDA has sufficient financial resources to execute its responsibilities; The RDA has sufficient staff to execute its responsibilities; The RDA has the necessary material resources (e.g. office space, computers) to support its operations; The RDA's organisation structure supports its operations (e.g. having dedicated units for various tasks); The RDA's staff have the necessary expertise to execute their responsibilities; Does your RDA have the necessary human resources (including expertise) to effectively carry out the following tasks related to the regional development planning process? N=21.
Source: Author's elaboration, based on (OECD, 2022[28]).

While these data portray a very positive image of RDA resource capacity, they reflect a particular point in time. In 2022, RDAs were still receiving significant funding through EU Technical Assistance. Moreover, in 2021-2022, many RDAs were primarily focused on the design of county development plans, an activity that demands particular skills (e.g. strategic planning, stakeholder consultation). Now that all county development plans have been adopted, the workload of the RDAs has shifted more towards issues such as monitoring and reporting, and helping county, city and municipal administrations to identify and apply to EU and national funding calls. Such activities require a different skill set.

Despite the increase in staffing levels since 2018, interviews with RDAs revealed skills gaps in areas such as public procurement, monitoring and evaluation, and advancing the green and digital transitions (OECD, 2023[18]). Enhancing skills in these areas is crucial for effectively implementing, monitoring and evaluating county development plans. Moreover, EU funding and financing opportunities at the regional and local levels are increasingly focused on projects linked to renewable energy, energy efficiency, and digital innovation. Improving RDA knowledge and skills vis-à-vis green and digital initiatives is vital, given an expertise gap within city and municipal governments that limits their ability to develop strong project proposals, and access relevant funding and financing opportunities. Furthermore, while RDAs receive ample requests from cities and municipalities to support their strategic planning processes (e.g. to prepare implementation programmes), they also signalled having limited expertise in financial and strategic planning at the local government level (OECD, 2023[18]).

To overcome these challenges, the MRDEUF and RDAs should consider conducting a periodic, potentially annual, training needs assessment. On the basis of the assessment, an RDA capacity building plan could be designed to identify training priorities for the upcoming period and propose concrete training opportunities. For example, the MRDEUF could expand its current training offer to RDAs, including on official guidelines for progress reporting and changes to EU funding for regional development projects (OECD, 2023[18]). The MRDEUF should also identify which other national bodies would be best placed to provide training on additional topics (e.g. public procurement). For example, capacity building initiatives could be delivered by training institutes such as the State School for Public Administration, which offers capacity building on topics such as strategic planning and management of EU funds (OECD, 2023[10]). For example, the State School could create a series of training opportunities specifically targeted to subnational government bodies, including RDAs.

The capacity building plan could, however, also feature training offered by national and international non-governmental organisations such as the Institute of Economics, Zagreb and the European Association of Development Agencies (EURADA). The latter represents regional and local development agencies across Europe and offers training opportunities, including through international peer-to-peer exchange (OECD, 2024[44]). Finally, the training plan could also identify opportunities for peer-to-peer exchange across Croatian RDAs, building on the particular expertise that some agencies may have developed.

Oversight of RDAs is shared between county administrations and the MRDEUF

The oversight structures of Croatia's RDAs are complex, with the latter having legal, functional and financial ties to both the county administrations and the national government. Their dependence on both types of public bodies, which represent different interests, presents a series of accountability challenges.

Croatia's RDAs are formally part of the county administrations, which are generally their sole founder. As such, the *de jure* accountability of Croatian RDAs is typically to county governments, and not to the national government, cities or municipalities. The formal ties between the county and RDA are underscored by the fact that their directors are appointed by the county prefect to a four-year term and that core RDA funding comes from the county budget (see chapter 5). These arrangements make the RDAs accountable to the county administrations.

There is, however, a concern among RDAs that the county administrations do not fully understand: i) the purpose of strategic planning for regional development; ii) the counties' responsibilities under the Law on Regional Development; and iii) RDA mandates. This lack of understanding could lead to a number of negative outcomes, such as county leadership teams not placing sufficient importance on strategic planning for regional development or failing to provide the RDAs with the tools or information to carry out their mandate. For example, RDAs indicated that county departments have not always provided timely information that the agencies need to draft monitoring reports (OECD, 2023[10]).

There are also reports of county executives insisting that their RDAs draft project proposals for specific local governments to help them apply to EU funding, despite RDAs knowing that such proposals would not be successful (e.g. because it was not sufficiently connected to the topic of the call). Such examples illustrate the way in which RDAs' lack of an arms-length relationship with county administrations can undermine their effectiveness in guiding regional development (OECD, 2023[10]).

At the same time, RDAs are also accountable to the MRDEUF, for example for the EU Technical Assistance funds that the Ministry channels to the RDAs. Moreover, the MRDEUF needs to formally accredit the RDAs before they can act as regional co-ordinators. In practical terms, this means that the RDAs must comply with a set of national-level requirements relating to, for example, their human resource management, as well as accounting and transparency procedures (Official Gazette of Croatia No 147 et al., 2018[9]).

The complex relationship that RDAs have to county administrations and the MRDEUF creates tension over which strategic and operational tasks the RDAs should prioritise – those coming from the county leadership or from the Ministry. This can be particularly challenging when the parties in power at the county and national levels are different.

To resolve the complex positioning of the RDAs vis-à-vis the county administrations and the MRDEUF, a number of measures could be taken. For instance, the government could reassess the division of roles and responsibilities among the RDAs, county administrations, and the MRDEUF. This would involve adapting the Law on Regional Development and relevant regulations to provide additional detail on the strategic and operational tasks for which RDAs are responsible, while also clarifying RDA accountability towards both counties and the MRDEUF. This should be coupled with an outreach campaign, led by the MRDEUF, to ensure that the county leadership deepen their understands of the laws governing regional development and strategic planning, and how they apply to the counties and the RDAs. Such an outreach campaign could include organising briefings with county prefects, deputy prefects and county heads of department. Such meetings would ideally be conducted after county-level elections. Moreover, the MRDEUF and RDAs could prepare and disseminate briefing material that explains the value added of regional development strategic planning and the work of the RDAs to county leaders, including practical examples.

Croatia's RDAs operate more locally than many of their international peers

A further challenge that risks constraining the effectiveness of RDAs, and Croatia's regional development policy more broadly, is related to the territorial scale at which the RDAs operate. Counties in Croatia are geographically and demographically smaller than OECD Member countries on average (with the exception of Swiss cantons) (Figure 3.4). Moreover, in many OECD Member countries and EU Member States, RDAs operate at a TL2 level, serving areas with a larger average population and territorial size than those in Croatia (Table 3.4). There can be benefits to organising regional development planning and investment at the TL3 level. For example, the proximity of the RDAs in Croatia and Slovenia to local governments, civil society organisations, local businesses and citizens can help them design development plans and investment strategies that closely match local development needs, priorities and capacities.

Figure 3.4. Average population and area extension per region in OECD countries and Croatia

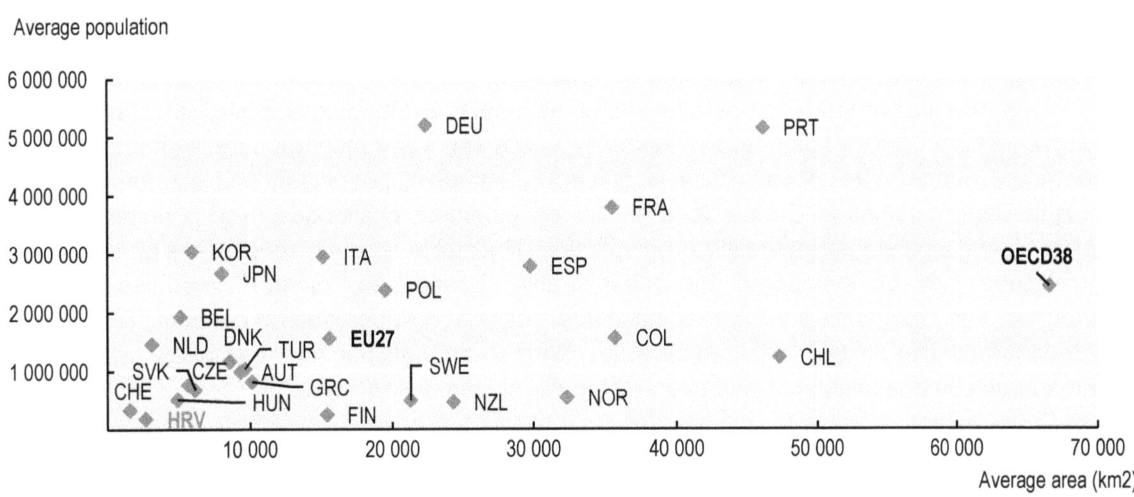

Note: Australia, Canada, Mexico and the United States are not shown on the graph because of the large average size of state governments. The UK is also not displayed due to the low number of regional governments (i.e. Northern Ireland, Scotland, Wales). In Türkiye, regional average sizes include the special administration provinces and the provincial metropolitan cities. The average regional size in France does not include the five overseas regions.
Source: Author's elaboration, based on (OECD/UCLG, 2022[45]; OECD, 2023[46]).

Table 3.4. RDAs and similar bodies in different EU and OECD countries

Country	Number of RDAs	Average population per RDA	NUTS/TL level at which RDAs operate	Average surface area in km2 per RDA
Costa Rica	6	860 506	TL 2	8 517
Croatia	**21**	**184 713**	**TL3**	**4 194**
Netherlands	9	1 948 156	TL2 and above	4 616
Romania	8	2 390 508	NUTS 2	29 800
Slovenia	12	175 584	TL3	1 707
Spain	19	2 491 134	TL2	26 630

Source: Population data (2021), except for Scotland: (OECD, 2022[47]). Population data for Scotland (2021): (UK Office for National Statistics, 2022[48]); Costa Rica: (OECD/UCLG, 2022[49]); Lithuania: (OECD/UCLG, 2022[49]) (OECD/UCLG, 2022[50]); Netherlands: (Netherlands Regional Development Corporations, n.d.[51]); Portugal: (EURADA, n.d.[52]); Romania: (ROREG, 2022[36]; EURADA, n.d.[37]); Slovenia: (Republic of Slovenia, 2023[53]); and Spain: (Foro ARD, n.d.[40]; EURADA, n.d.[54]).

Operating at the TL3 rather than the TL2 level can also present daunting challenges. First, it can lead to a suboptimal use or fragmentation of investment funds, as many small projects designed by and implemented at the county level might tackle similar issues that could benefit from inter-regional intervention (OECD, 2022[2]). In fact, small scale development projects can result in lower returns on public investment (OECD, 2019[55]). Small scale projects may even have an insufficient minimum scale for the investment to be eligible for financing (e.g. by the European Investment Bank) (OECD, 2023[18]).

Second, operating at the TL3 level comes with funding challenges. First, due to the relatively small populations and territories (in km^2) covered by RDAs operating at the TL3 level, the latter are more likely to have access to smaller pools of funding, directly affecting their ability to offer competitive salaries and benefits. In fact, interviews showed that many RDAs struggle to attract and retain highly skilled professionals (OECD, 2023[18]).

Third, having 21 TL3-level RDAs also risks disproportionate levels of spending on basic administrative functions. Each RDA needs its own administrative setup, including management, financial, and support staff. In countries where RDAs operate at the TL2 level, such roles and functions can be shared more efficiently, potentially freeing up funding to attract specialised professionals, for example with expertise in areas such as the green and digital transitions.

Fourth, having many RDAs operate at the TL3 level also implies important co-ordination costs. For example, RDAs may inadvertently compete for scarce national or EU funding or implement similar projects that would benefit from collaboration (e.g. in transport, waste and water management) without the benefits of collaboration. Furthermore, despite their significant geographic, population and economic diversity, many neighbouring counties in Croatia face similar development challenges (e.g. population decline, industrial transition) and can thus benefit from joint action. The ability of county-level RDAs to work together on such issues can be hampered by administrative boundaries, differing priorities of county administrations, and the complexities of managing inter-regional collaboration. In contrast, TL2 RDAs, by virtue of their larger scale, may facilitate more streamlined co-ordination in their territories, enabling more efficient resource use and alignment with overarching development strategies.

Croatia could consider the feasibility and benefits of RDAs working at a larger territorial scale

To address the challenges associated with RDAs operating at a relatively local scale, Croatia could consider conducting a cost-benefit analysis of establishing the RDAs at the TL2 level. In theory, such a reconfiguration could involve reducing the number of RDAs from 21 to four, one for each TL2 area. By covering larger areas, which often face similar socio-economic and development challenges, reconfigured

RDAs could facilitate Croatia's efforts to create territorial development strategies that address challenges facing multiple counties.

Furthermore, the reconfiguration could help the RDAs to pool financial and human resources. This would increase their capacity to carry out a broad set of tasks and responsibilities, going beyond their current set of activities. Indeed, their remit could be extended to include the design and management of a regional investment strategy. A reconfiguration could also enable them to allocate additional human and financial resources for various purposes such as engaging with the private sector, and academic and research institutions. Such non-governmental actors can make significant contributions to regional development, including in terms of productivity, innovation and digitalisation. Interviews with local stakeholders indicated that the RDAs currently have limited time available to engage systematically with non-governmental actors such as SMEs (OECD, 2023[18]).

Establishing the RDAs at the TL2 level could also help regions attract additional EU financing for macro-regional investment projects, for example from the European Investment Bank and the European Bank for Reconstruction and Development, which do not lend for relatively small projects (e.g. below EUR 25 million in the case of the European Investment Bank). The reconfiguration could, in time, open the door to the EU designating RDAs as Managing Authorities for European Union Cohesion Policy funds in the 2021-27 period, as was the case with the Romanian RDAs (Box 3.4). Operating at a broader scale could also reduce administrative overhead and duplication of efforts, as a smaller number of RDAs would require fewer administrative staff overall. Such personnel could be reskilled to support other RDA tasks or possibly be integrated into other parts of the county administration.

In addition to mapping potential benefits of establishing the RDAs at the TL2 level, the assessment should explore possible costs and legal and political challenges. For example, there may be resistance from current RDA directors and staff, who fear job losses or diminished influence. Moreover, county, cities and municipalities may have concerns over losing direct access to RDAs and the potential dilution of their local priorities. To mitigate these challenges, a phased transition plan could be developed, offering retraining and redeployment opportunities for affected staff within the new organisational structure. The establishment of satellite or liaison offices in major cities within each TL2 region could maintain the vital link between RDAs and local governments. These offices would ensure that cities and municipalities maintain easy access to their respective RDAs, and that local needs and insights could continue to inform regional development planning. Such measures would help preserve the benefits of proximity to local stakeholders while capitalising on the advantages of operating at a larger scale. In addition, the assessment should identify the different laws and regulations that would have to be modified to allow for the restructuring of the RDAs. This would also require the assessment of which actions are needed to ensure that counties maintain essential strategic planning capacity when RDAs are no longer part of their organisational structure.

Furthermore, the assessment should reflect on how the possible reconfiguration would impact the accountability structure for RDAs. For example, establishing the RDAs at the TL2 level could imply reconfiguring them as non-governmental actors that are supervised by regional boards composed of the representatives of county and local governments, as in Romania. Such a configuration could help the RDAs to become less vulnerable to political changes, both at the national and subnational levels. Another option would be to establish the RDAs as regional-level extensions of the MRDEUF. However, such a setup could result in a weakened link between RDAs and county and local governments and make the RDAs too dependent on central government funding and the political priorities of the national government.

Finally, this assessment should also consider an intermediate alternative that might achieve the benefits of scale without a full reconfiguration of RDAs. Exploring options for increased formal collaboration and co-ordination across the existing 21 RDAs could provide a pathway to realising some of the efficiencies and strategic advantages of operating at a larger scale. Such a step could include establishing formal partnerships among RDAs to share expertise, pool resources for larger projects, and jointly pursue funding opportunities. One way to encourage such co-operation would be through the MRDEUF, thus creating specific funding windows for projects that are prepared by more than one RDA. This approach could allow for a gradual transition, enabling stakeholders to adjust to new modes of operation and collaboration while preserving the local focus and expertise that RDAs currently offer. It would also provide valuable insights into the practical benefits and limitations of increased inter-RDA co-operation, informing future decisions on the optimal structure and scale of RDAs in Croatia. A final intermediate step could involve piloting the creation of a single macro-regional RDA for the next EU programming period. This pilot would test the feasibility, benefits and costs of consolidating RDAs at a larger territorial scale, providing a practical model and insights to guide the potential further reconfiguration of RDAs in Croatia.

Cities' and municipalities' planning capacities are strained

At the local level, the development of a medium-term development plan is optional for cities and municipalities. Both are, however, mandated to develop a short-term implementation programme, which identifies concrete measures that can help to meet their objectives (Official Gazette of Croatia No 151/22, 2022[17]). The local implementation plans need to be aligned with the county development plans (OECD, 2023[18]).

The fact that local governments are not mandated to design or adopt medium-term development plans is linked to their relatively high level of territorial fragmentation (e.g. in terms of their average population). The average local-level population in Croatia is nearly a third lower (30.3%) than in the OECD (Figure 3.5) with some having a population that is as small as 0.03% of the OECD average (OECD, 2023[46]; Croatian Bureau of Statistics, 2023[56]). Moreover, with 37% of municipalities having have fewer than 2 000 inhabitants and only 5% with have more than 20 000 (OECD, 2023[46]).

Figure 3.5. Average number of inhabitants per municipality in OECD countries and Croatia

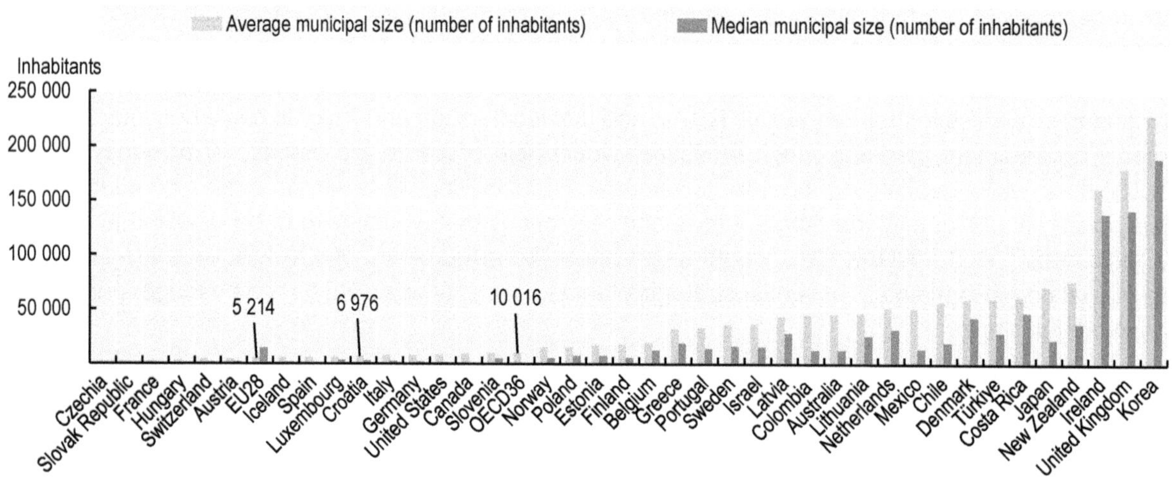

Source: Author's elaboration, based on (OECD, 2023[46]; Croatian Bureau of Statistics, 2023[56]).

As a result of the large number of small local government units and the shrinking local labour pool, many local administrations often lack the necessary human resource capacity to design a local development plan and support its implementation (OECD, 2023[18]). The high degree of territorial fragmentation also affects local service delivery, with many municipal administrations (as well as certain city administrations) lacking sufficient financial and human resources to fulfil the tasks and responsibilities that are assigned to them by law (Croatian Ministry of Justice and Administration, 2022[57]; OECD, 2023[18]).

To address the limited local capacity, cities and municipalities can enter into multiple inter-municipal co-operation agreements. This is supported by a financial incentive whereby local governments can obtain co-funding grants of up to 75%[2] from the national government when they co-operate on administrative tasks (e.g. a joint administrative department or sharing the remuneration of a civil servant working for both municipalities) (Official Gazette of Croatia No 88/2022, 2022[58]). In addition, city and municipal administrations that co-operate to deliver a public service can also secure national co-funding grants of up to 25%. Both grants are available to cities and municipalities for up to five years after they enter into a co-operation agreement. Interviews with local stakeholders indicated that since the grants were launched in 2022, the Ministry of Finance has approved inter-municipal co-operation agreements for 132 cities and municipalities, or nearly a quarter of the total number of cities and municipalities (OECD, 2023[10]).

The most generous financial incentives, however, are offered to city and municipal governments that choose to amalgamate with one or more neighbouring local governments. The incentives include, for example, a one-time grant to repay the debt obligations of the city or municipal government whose territory is being merged into another, coverage of the financial costs of the merger, and capital and operational grants for a five-year period (Official Gazette of Croatia No 88/2022, 2022[58]). Despite these incentives, no municipal mergers have taken place to date, in part owing to concerns around a loss of political control (OECD, 2023[10]).

Few cities and municipalities have a local development agency to support local development planning

Cities and municipalities are strongly encouraged to collaborate in the field of local development planning. For example, in order to help cities and municipalities develop and implement local development plans and projects, they can establish local development agencies (LDAs). LDAs can be created by one or more cities and municipalities. As such, cities and municipalities can pool resources to ensure they collectively have the necessary human resources to steward local development efforts.

The main strategic planning responsibilities of LDAs include co-ordinating the development of local strategic documents and action plans, as well as monitoring their implementation. They also support the development of local project proposals, and co-operate with other LDAs and RDAs to identify opportunities for joint projects (Official Gazette of Croatia No 147 et al., 2018[9]). In 2023, there were only 22 LDAs, which operated in 12 out of 21 counties. While twenty were established by cities alone, two were created by several cities and municipalities. Many local governments, and in particular municipalities, consider the costs to establish and run an LDA too steep (OECD, 2023[10]; MRDEUF, 2023[43]).

Additional incentives for inter-municipal co-operation may be needed to build local strategic planning capacities

To ensure cities and municipalities have the necessary capacity to support the design and implementation of regional development policy, it may be necessary for Croatia to adopt additional measures to support inter-municipal co-operation. For instance, Croatia could consider improving outreach to cities and municipalities about how the existing incentives for inter-municipal co-operation could be used to help support joint strategic planning activities or help set up joint planning departments.

In addition, collaboration among different municipalities (e.g. in the design of local development strategies) that currently do not have a local development strategy could be made a precondition to receiving competitive grant funding from the MRDEUF (see chapter 5). Furthermore, Croatia could consider exploring some of the policy measures adopted by Ukraine between 2014 and 2020, which drastically reduced municipal fragmentation. Key incentives offered to Ukraine's local governments willing to merge included expanding their mandate for service delivery and increasing their opportunities for generating additional own-source revenue. Merged local governments also gained access to additional regional development funding opportunities through the State Fund for Regional Development (OECD, 2022[2]).

Croatia could also consider increasing the capacity building support offered to cities and municipalities in areas related to regional and local development, including strategy design, EU and national funding and financing, as well as monitoring and evaluation. This could involve increasing the number of training sessions offered by the MRDEUF and the School of Public Administration for local civil servants (see chapter 4). These possibilities could be coupled with the development of a strategic planning toolbox, available online, to enable city and municipal staff to learn at their own pace.

Regional development co-ordination in Croatia

In Croatia, as in several OECD Member countries, the strategic planning cycle for regional development at all levels of government depends on co-ordination and communication mechanisms that dependably contribute to ensuring horizontal and vertical policy coherence. At the national level, for example, horizontal co-ordination mechanisms can include inter-ministerial bodies or committees for regional development, which help to align interests and priorities across ministries. With regard to vertical co-ordination among levels of government, mechanisms to align relevant public and non-governmental stakeholders can include dialogue platforms, inter-governmental consultation boards and contractual arrangements. At the subnational level, horizontal co-ordination mechanisms typically include inter-regional and inter-municipal co-operation arrangements, as well as metropolitan governance bodies (OECD, 2018[59]).

Croatia's vertical and horizontal mechanisms for regional development

In recent years, legislative developments in Croatia have established a diverse set of co-ordination mechanisms that can support the co-ordination of regional development policy.[3] Foremost among these is the national-level network of strategic planning co-ordinators, the Council for Regional Development, and the network of RDAs. Their work is supported by other co-ordination mechanisms, including county and local government associations, macro-regional partnerships (e.g. development councils), as well as partnership councils and local action groups. The current system provides a solid foundation for multi-level dialogue and consultation among national and subnational levels of government. At the same time, there is room for improvement, including by formalising mechanisms for the co-ordination of regional development policy across line ministries, and strengthening exchange and information sharing opportunities related to regional development among different levels of government.

National-level co-ordination mechanisms supporting regional development

There are a number of co-ordination mechanisms established at the national level to advance regional development. To support cross-sector co-ordination, there are strategic planning co-ordinators—specific units located within all central government bodies that perform and co-ordinate planning tasks, and their network is chaired by the MRDEUF (Official Gazette of Croatia No 151/22, 2022[17]). The strategic planning co-ordinators regularly report to the MRDEUF on the design and implementation of their ministry's planning documents (including sectoral and multi-sectoral strategies, national plans and implementation programmes) (Official Gazette of Croatia No 151/22, 2022[17]).

In turn, the MRDEUF provides comments to strategic planning co-ordinators on the planning documents that are developed and implemented by their line ministries. Such comments may include opinions on the alignment of strategic documents with Croatia's national planning framework, or recommendations on how to strengthen the design, monitoring and evaluation of such documents to improve their quality and impact (OECD, 2023[18]; OECD, 2023[10]).

A second mechanism for co-ordination among levels of government is the Council for Regional Development (Official Gazette of Croatia No 147 et al., 2018[9]). The Council was established by law as a platform for multi-level dialogue and consultation to help align strategic priorities and co-ordinate the implementation of policies, programmes and public investments for regional development (OECD, 2023[11]). Members include the MRDEUF, representatives of the Ministry of Physical Planning, Construction and State Assets, county and local government representatives, RDAs, a member of the Committee of the Croatian Parliament responsible for regional development and EU funds, representatives of the scientific and professional communities, as well as representatives of other ministries and public institutions of particular importance for regional development (Official Gazette of Croatia No 147 et al., 2018[9]; OECD, 2023[11]).

The Council, which was established in 2019, has never been operationalised. In practice, its work is carried out through meetings between the Prime Minister and relevant ministries, county prefects and representatives from the Croatian Association of Cities and the Croatian Union of Municipalities (hereafter the Prime Minister-led regional development co-ordination body). Such joint meetings have generally taken place on a biannual basis since 2016 (Karlovac County, 2023[60]; OECD, 2023[61]). They facilitate high-level political discussions on the co-ordination of territorial development between representatives from different levels of government, thereby carrying out similar tasks to those assigned to the Council for Regional Development.

Subnational co-ordination mechanisms, supporting exchange across jurisdictions and with the national government

A key subnational-level co-ordination mechanism is the network of RDAs that helps align policy objectives between national and county governments. The network is chaired by the MRDEUF and includes RDA representatives from all 21 counties. It meets once every three months and serves primarily as a platform for the MRDEUF to engage in downward communication with RDAs, including to outline new legislative or financial developments that are relevant for RDAs, counties, cities and municipalities (OECD, 2023[10]; OECD, 2022[28]).

Other vertical and horizontal co-ordination mechanisms play a supporting role in ensuring coherence in the design and implementation of regional development policy. In particular, the Organic Law on Regional and Local Self-Government allows counties and local governments to establish associations in order to promote and achieve common territorial interests (Official Gazette of Croatia No 151/22, 2022[17]). Currently, three such bodies exist: the Croatian County Association (comprising all 20 counties and Zagreb City), the Croatian Association of Cities (comprising 127 out of 128 cities) and the Croatian Union of Municipalities (comprising 327 out of 428 municipalities) (European Committee of the Regions, n.d.[62]). The Croatian County Association has particular relevance for the RDAs as they are allowed to participate, thus enabling them to receive regular updates on laws, regulations or funding calls (OECD, 2023[18]).

Moreover, certain vertical co-ordination mechanisms are in place to help manage specific macro-regional partnerships. For instance, strategic projects for macro-regional investment can be funded under development agreements between the national government and at least three county governments (Official Gazette of Croatia No 147 et al., 2018[9]). One such example is the 2017 Development Agreement of Slavonia, Baranja and Srijem (Government of Croatia, 2022[63]). A Council of Slavonia, Baranja and Srijem has been established to support the vertical (among the national government and counties) and horizontal (across counties) co-ordination of related investments. The Council, which meets biannually, is chaired by the Prime Minister, vice-chaired by the MRDEUF (which also acts as the Council's lead co-ordinator across government), and its members include line ministries, relevant county prefects, RDAs and associations (Official Gazette of Croatia No 21/2017, 2017[64]).

In addition, partnership councils have been created at the county and local levels to support the design and implementation of subnational development plans (e.g. county development plans, the plans for island development, Integrated Territorial Programme) (MRDEUF, 2024[1]). Partnership councils, which meet at least twice a year, typically function as advisory bodies that help the county, city and municipal administrations identify strategic priorities and projects for regional and local development and support their implementation. Partnership councils are generally composed of both governmental and non-governmental actors at the county and local levels. Their consultation is mandatory before county governments can adopt strategic plans, in order to ensure that the latter take local needs and priorities into account (OECD, 2023[10]). In several counties, the work of the partnership council is complemented by additional *ad hoc* co-ordination meetings. For example, in Osijek-Baranja, the county prefect meets the representatives of city and municipal authorities on a monthly basis to discuss relevant development challenges and needs. The RDA, through is ties with the county administration, can help shape the agenda of such meetings (OECD, 2023[10]).

Finally, guided by EU regulations, many cities and municipalities have established local action groups (LAGs) and fisheries' local action groups (FLAGs) (European Network for Rural Development, 2020[65]). Their territorial delineation is decided by their members (local authorities and private actors) according to functional, rather than administrative considerations. County authorities are not involved in these groups. Both types of action groups bring together public and private actors from at least five cities or municipalities. In particular, LAGs and FLAGs support the design, implementation and monitoring of local development plans that reflect the interests of the various socio-economic groups in their area, and include specific objectives for rural infrastructure development. LAGs can also develop proposals for projects to support the economic competitiveness of the area (e.g. local infrastructure), in order to be considered for sectoral grant funding by line ministries (OECD, 2023[10]; Croatian Network for Rural Development, n.d.[66]). There are 406 local governments in Croatia that are currently members of LAGs or FLAGs (OECD, 2023[11]). The 54 LAGs created during the EU programming period 2014-2020 spanned 90% of Croatia's total territory (OECD, 2023[10]).

Together, the aforementioned mechanisms complement one another in supporting place-based regional development at different levels of government. The RDAs and the regional development co-ordination body (led by the Prime Minister) can help align priorities among national and subnational levels of government (as do partnership councils between county and local levels of government). Simultaneously other mechanisms, such as Council of Slavonia, Baranja and Srijem, LAGs and FLAGs support macroregional and supralocal planning processes. Croatia's different associations of subnational governments, in turn, support learning and exchange between county and local governments, which can strengthen their ability to support strategic planning-related activities for regional development.

Challenges to the co-ordination of regional development in Croatia

There are a number of areas where existing co-ordination mechanisms could be reinforced in order to further improve the coherence of strategic planning for regional development across government. First, there are opportunities to further strengthen the Prime Minister-led regional development co-ordination body, in particular by ensuring effective inter-ministerial and inter-governmental co-ordination. For example, it lacks clearly formulated objectives for council meetings, which risks limiting its focus and impact. Moreover, the participation of key actors responsible for implementing regional development policy across government, including certain line ministries and RDAs that need to be a part of any such multi-level dialogue, in council meetings is not always guaranteed.

Second, co-ordination and exchange across RDAs needs to be institutionalised, including to support peer-to-peer learning. Third, there is a general sense among RDAs and local governments that relevant information on regional development (e.g. on legislative and regulatory changes, funding opportunities, development data) is often not shared consistently or in a timely manner by other levels of government.

The organisation of the Prime Minister-led regional development co-ordination body could be adjusted to improve its impact

There are a number of elements that could be adjusted to improve the impact of the Prime Minister-led regional development co-ordination body. First, it is recommended to establish formal objectives for the body. For example, its aim could be to support periodic reviews of Croatia's regional development policy priorities and funding mechanisms at different levels of government. Second, and relatedly, the body could be reorganised into two chambers: one to support inter-ministerial co-ordination of regional development policy and the other to support the policy's vertical co-ordination among different levels of government. This second body could include national-level line ministries and subnational actors such as county, city and municipal governments and RDAs.

Creating two chambers could allow for a specialised focus on different aspects of regional development. The separation into two chambers could ensure that one can concentrate on fostering high-level, inter-ministerial co-ordination of regional development policy and funding. Simultaneously, the other chamber could focus on the vital task of vertical co-ordination, bringing together a diverse range of stakeholders from national and subnational levels. This structure could enable targeted discussions and decision-making, addressing the specific needs and contributions of various public actors involved in regional development.

With regard to inter-ministerial co-ordination, the body's impact could be further strengthened by ensuring the systematic participation of ministers and/or state secretaries from all relevant line ministries (e.g. the ministries of Regional Development and EU Funds, Finance, Agriculture, Economy and Sustainable Development, Environmental Protection and Energy and Fisheries). Given that many ministries either directly or indirectly contribute to regional development, ensuring high-level ministerial participation in the Prime Minister-led regional development co-ordination body is important for two reasons. First, it can provide a forum for sectoral perspectives on regional development to be heard. Second, it can ensure that regional development is being incorporated as a cross-cutting issue within different line ministries. Given its remit in the field of regional development, the MRDEUF could be assigned the task of preparing the agenda for the meetings and co-ordinating follow-up on the meetings' outcomes.

Different OECD Member countries have set up similar inter-ministerial co-ordination bodies. Poland, for example, has established a Co-ordinating Committee for Development Policy to support decision-making related to the implementation of regional development policy across government. Members of the Committee include a representative of the Prime Minister's Office, as well as ministers and state secretaries from relevant line ministries. Various thematic subcommittees, which include representatives of subnational governments, academia and the private sector, support the committee's work by focusing on technical questions related to regional development policy (Government of Poland, n.d.[67]; OECD, 2019[68]).

With regard to supporting vertical co-ordination, the work of the Prime Minister-led regional development co-ordination body could be strengthened by guaranteeing the participation of RDAs, which are currently excluded from its activities. Supporting their participation in a second chamber on vertical co-ordination could create a forum for RDAs to act as a partner in policy discussions. Technical working groups could also be established, for example to assess different aspects related to regional development, including funding and financing, monitoring and evaluation, and engagement with non-governmental actors. Inter-governmental dialogue bodies in Poland and Sweden provide examples of how such arrangements can work (Box 3.5).

Box 3.5. Multi-level dialogue bodies in Poland and Sweden

Poland

Poland's Joint Central Government and Local Government Committee supports co-ordination, consultation and negotiation among levels of government. This body is composed of the minister responsible for public administration and 11 representatives appointed by the Prime Minister, together with representatives of national organisations of local government units (e.g. regions, counties, cities, metropolitan areas). National and local-level representatives work together in eleven 'problem teams' and three thematic working groups, and are supported by expert analysis.

The Committee aims to systematically support the development of common policy positions related to the functioning of local government. Key tasks performed by the Committee include:

- Developing a common position between national and local governments on subnational-level economic and social priorities;
- Conducting reviews and assessments of the legal and financial conditions that underpin local government;
- Analysing information about prepared draft legal acts, documents and government programmes regarding local government issues, in particular, the expected financial consequences;
- Giving opinions on draft legislation, strategic and other government programming documents that affect local governments.

Sweden

In Sweden, it is the job of regional development policy makers to convince other ministries that they should apply their 'territorial lenses' when planning and designing sector policies. The Forum for Sustainable Regional Development 2022-2030 is one important co-ordination platform that supports this objective. It is positioned to support the implementation of the National Strategy for Sustainable Regional Development throughout Sweden 2021-2030. The forum is chaired by the Secretary of State for Regional Development. It is divided into two groups: one that promotes dialogue between national- and regional-level politicians, and one that fosters dialogue between national- and regional-level civil servants (director-level).

Source: Author's elaboration, based on Poland (OECD, 2020[69]; Government of Poland, n.d.[70]; Government of Poland, n.d.[71]; Lublinska, 2017[72]); Sweden: (OECD, 2023[73]).

The existing network for strategic planning co-ordinators could play an important role in supporting the activities of the revamped Council for Regional Development. For instance, co-ordinators could support the preparation of the thematic working groups, summarise key findings and share them with the Council to support more informed, high-level regional policy making. Such activities could be complementary to their current work to support the design and implementation of planning documents. In particular, having greater exposure to the Council's work could help to improve their understanding of cross-cutting government priorities, such as balanced regional development. These priorities are required by law to be reflected in the strategic planning documents of their respective ministries and other national-level public bodies (Official Gazette of Croatia No 13/2021, 2021[21]).

Finally, to further institutionalise the work of the Prime Minister-led regional development co-ordination body, Croatia should consider incorporating the body into the Law on Regional Development, to formally replace the official Council for Regional Development. The revision of the Law could also be used to guarantee the participation of specific central government bodies, and the RDAs, as well as to establish the two-chamber structure proposed above.

Further institutionalising co-operation across RDAs can improve peer-to-peer exchange

At the subnational level, an important challenge relates to the limited formal mechanisms for exchange and dialogue among RDAs. In principle, the Croatian Association of Counties provides county government bodies, including RDAs with a forum for policy dialogue and peer-to-peer exchange, including on topics such as EU funds, economic development, agriculture, education, as well as health and social policy (OECD, 2023[10]). However, interviews indicated that the peer-to-peer exchange opportunities offered through the association are often more closely linked to the needs and priorities of county prefects rather than the RDAs (OECD, 2023[18]). While RDAs are established and partially funded by county governments, they also have some distinct needs and priorities that need to be articulated and shared. These include challenges related to aligning county development plans and programmes with national priorities, conducting monitoring and evaluating activities, and identifying funding and financing opportunities for regional development projects (OECD, 2023[18]).

For the above-mentioned needs and priorities to be met, the Croatian Association of Counties could consider setting up a forum or organisational unit that expressly aims to support knowledge exchange among RDAs. For example, it could provide opportunities for training and peer-to-peer learning on topics that are relevant to day-to-day RDA responsibilities in the strategic planning cycle, including: i) how to better support the implementation of planning documents; ii) how to enhance the quality of monitoring and evaluation (including data collection and analysis); iii) how to better identify funding and financing opportunities for programmes and projects, and iv) how to engage more effectively with cities, municipalities and the private sector.

An alternative to creating an RDA forum within the Croatian Association of Counties would be setting up an association of RDAs, following the example of other European countries (Box 3.6). Such an association of RDAs could have a rotating presidency and assign leadership for the development of training material (as well as lobbying and advocacy activities) to different RDAs, depending on their fields of expertise.

Box 3.6. Associations of regional development agencies in Europe

Associations of RDAs have been set up in several OECD Member countries and EU Member States. In general, the associations aim to strengthen regional development through co-operation among RDAs. They also constitute important platforms to amplify the voices of RDAs at the national and international levels. However, their objectives vary however (e.g. providing a space for exchange, lobbying for better regional development policies, securing EU funding). Consequently, the services they provide also vary. Furthermore, their organisational structures differ with certain associations operating under a more complex governance structure than others. The associations that operate in Bulgaria, Romania and Spain illustrate this diversity.

Bulgaria

The Bulgarian Association of Regional Development Agencies (BARDA) was established in 1997 at the behest of Bulgaria's RDAs. It is a legally independent, non-governmental umbrella organisation, acting as a network for RDAs and regional business centres. Its mission is to improve the economic environment in Bulgaria by promoting entrepreneurial initiatives in accordance with the strategies of its members. The association ensures capacity building for RDAs so that they can better support SMEs and are better informed about developments at the EU level, for example. The association facilitates information networks and partnerships with other countries to share good practices with its members. It also participates in several national and regional co-ordination bodies such as the working group for Bulgaria's National Development Plan.

Romania

The Romanian Association of Regional Development Agencies (ROREG) was established in 2005. Its members consist of the country's eight RDAs. ROREG plays an important role in ensuring that RDAs are represented at the national and international level. It lobbies to improve legislation for regional development in Romania and advocates for a favourable attitude towards regional development among citizens, public administration and other institutions of public interest. It also supports the capacity building of RDAs, hosts conferences and training sessions, and facilitates collaboration across regions through common work streams and communication mechanisms. The association is managed by a Board of Directors consisting of a president and two vice-presidents elected from among the RDA directors.

Spain

The Association of Spanish Regional Development Agencies (Foro ADR) was formally established in 2007. It is a co-operation network made up of RDAs, public companies and management centres of Spain's Autonomous Regions and the two autonomous cities of Ceuta and Melilla. Its main objective is to provide its members with a space for joint reflection and exchange. It holds an annual forum to address the main issues connected to entrepreneurship, as well as several events related to financing.

FORO ADR also includes working groups covering topics such as competition and cohesion policies, public policy evaluation and circular economy. It also publishes news items to keep RDAs up-to-date on relevant developments. It plays an important role in advocating for RDAs, as well as lobbying for business support policies. The work of the association is supported by a Board of Directors, and a Management Team composed of up to three representatives designated by each of the partner entities.

Source: Author's elaboration, based on Bulgaria: (Bulgarian Association of Regional Development Agencies, n.d.[74]); Romania: (Association of Regional Development Agencies of Romania, 2024[75]); and Spain: (Foro ADR, n.d.[76]).

Strengthening communication between the MRDEUF and RDAs

A further co-ordination challenge relates to the need for more timely and effective exchange and information-sharing among levels of government. For example, there could be scope to further improve the quality of upward exchange between the RDAs and the MRDEUF (OECD, 2023[10]). It should be noted that a number of government mechanisms already exist to support this process. For instance, RDAs have the right to respond to public consultations on draft laws or regulations during a prescribed 30-day period, like any other public body (Official Gazette of Croatia No 25/2013, 2013[77]). Moreover, on certain occasions, as part of the network of RDAs, the MRDEUF has proactively held meetings to discuss proposed amendments to the legislative framework (e.g. regarding the Law on the System of Strategic Planning and Development Management) (OECD, 2023[61]).

Nevertheless, interviewees indicated that RDAs do not always feel that they are consulted in a timely manner on adjustments to certain legislation, regulations or guidelines (OECD, 2023[10]). For instance, despite the Library of Indicators having been developed by the MRDEUF as a standardised system that would guide performance measurement among all levels of government, RDAs were not given the opportunity to provide feedback on the initial list of indicators (OECD, 2023[10]). Regulations are, however, in place that allow RDAs to propose the inclusion of new indicators (see chapter 4).

If they feel rushed, RDAs may not be able to process the information provided by the Ministry, consult with relevant stakeholders (e.g. cities and municipalities) or articulate regional priorities/needs to the MRDEUF (OECD, 2023[18]). In order to address this issue, and ensure that national-level policy making on regional development is more systematically informed by regional and local priorities, the MRDEUF could broaden its practice of proactive consultation with RDAs to cover a wider range of legislative and regulatory topics.

Conclusion

Through a series of legislative and regulatory reforms adopted by Croatia since 2014, the country has set up a robust regional and local development governance framework. In particular, the reforms resulted in the development of clear planning procedures at the national, county and local levels, and a clear assignment of responsibilities for regional development planning, implementation, monitoring and evaluation. Moreover, the reforms resulted in the creation of 21 RDAs—first as limited liability companies and later as regional co-ordinators—that were tasked with leading the design of subnational development plans and programmes that reflect local needs and capacities, while also contributing to national priorities. Several vertical and horizontal regional development co-ordination mechanisms (e.g. macro-regional development councils, LAGs and FLAGs) are in place to help ensure that relevant public actors at all levels of government can discuss territorial development challenges and support the design of place-based development plans, programmes and projects.

Despite the substantial progress that has already been made, Croatia needs to address several challenges to ensure that its regional development governance framework can support the government's objective of balanced regional development. Challenges identified in this chapter include the reported skills gaps within RDAs, including in relation to key planning-related activities such as policy implementation, and monitoring and evaluating development plans. Additional challenges requiring attention include the relatively local territorial level at which RDAs operate, as well as municipal fragmentation, both of which appear to spread financial and human resources for strategic planning too thinly.

References

Andalucía TRADE (n.d.), *Andalucía TRADE*, https://www.andaluciatrade.es/ (accessed on 1 February 2024). [39]

Association of Regional Development Agencies of Romania (2024), *Association of Regional Development Agencies of Romania*, https://www.roreg.eu (accessed on 5 Februay 2024). [75]

Bulgarian Association of Regional Development Agencies (n.d.), *Bulgarian Association of Regional Development Agencies*. [74]

Crescenzi, R. and M. Giua (2016), "The EU Cohesion Policy in context: Does a bottom-up approach work in all regions?", *Environment and Planning A: Economy and Space*, Vol. 48/1, pp. 2340-2357, https://doi.org/10.1177/0308518X16658291. [5]

Croatian Bureau of Statistics (2023), *Popis stanovništva, kućanstava i stanova 2021. - Stanovništvo [Census of population, households and apartments 2021 - Population]*, https://dzs.gov.hr/u-fokusu/popis-2021/88 (accessed on 4 March 2024). [56]

Croatian Ministry of Justice and Administration (2022), *Nacionalni plan razvoja javne uprave. za razdoblje od 2022. do 2027. Godine [National public administration development plan for the period from 2022 to 2027]*, https://mpu.gov.hr/UserDocsImages/dokumenti/Strategije,%20planovi,%20izvje%C5%A1%C4%87a/Nacionalni%20plan%20razvoja%20javne%20uprave%20za%20razdoblje%20od%202022_2027.pdf (accessed on 1 February 2024). [57]

Croatian Ministry of Science and Education (2022), *Savjetovanje o Prijedlogu nacrta Strategije pametne specijalizacije do 2029. (S3) [Consultation on the Draft Proposal of the Smart Specialization Strategy until 2029 (S3)]*, https://mzo.gov.hr/vijesti/savjetovanje-o-prijedlogu-nacrta-strategije-pametne-specijalizacije-do-2029-s3/5203 (accessed on 4 October 2023). [22]

Croatian Network for Rural Development (n.d.), *Što je LAG? [What is a LAG?]*, https://hmrr.hr/leader/sto-je-lag/ (accessed on 23 October 2023). [66]

EURADA (n.d.), *Regional Development Agencies in Portugal*, https://www.eurada.org/fileadmin/user_upload/docs/RDAs-Portugal-Study.pdf (accessed on 23 May 2023). [52]

EURADA (n.d.), *Regional Development Agencies in Romania*, https://www.eurada.org/fileadmin/user_upload/docs/RDAs-in-Romania.pdf (accessed on 12 May 2023). [37]

EURADA (n.d.), *Regional Development Agencies in Spain*, https://www.eurada.org/fileadmin/user_upload/docs/RDAs-Spain-study.pdf (accessed on 19 May 2023). [54]

European Commission (2023), *The Recovery and Resilience Facility*, https://commission.europa.eu/business-economy-euro/economic-recovery/recovery-and-resilience-facility_en (accessed on 21 September). [26]

European Committee of the Regions (n.d.), *Croatia - Systems of Multi-level Governance*, https://portal.cor.europa.eu/divisionpowers/Pages/Croatia-MLG.aspx (accessed on 6 February 2024). [62]

European Network for Rural Development (2020), *How to form a Local Action Group (LAG)?*, https://ec.europa.eu/enrd/leader-clld/leader-toolkit/implementing-lags-and-local-strategies-1_en.html (accessed on 2 April 2024). [65]

Foro ADR (n.d.), *Quienes somos [Who we are]*, https://www.foroadr.es/quienes-somos1 (accessed on 5 February 2024). [76]

Foro ARD (n.d.), *Agencias asociadas [Member Agencies]*, https://www.foroadr.es/agencias-y-colaboradores (accessed on 18 May 2023). [40]

Government of Croatia (2022), *Slavonia, Baranja and Srijem programme has reached HRK 20 billion in contracted assets*, https://vlada.gov.hr/news/slavonia-baranja-and-srijem-programme-has-reached-hrk-20-billion-in-contracted-assets/35792 (accessed on 25 August 2023). [63]

Government of Croatia (2021), *Nacionalni plan oporavka i otpornosti 2021. - 2026 [National Recovery and Resilience Plan 2021-2026]*, https://planoporavka.gov.hr/UserDocsImages/dokumenti/Plan%20oporavka%20i%20otpornosti%2C%20srpanj%202021..pdf?vel=13435491 (accessed on 21 September 2023). [27]

Government of Croatia (2020), *Programme of the Government of the Republic of Croatia*, https://vlada.gov.hr/UserDocsImages/ZPPI/Dokumenti%20Vlada/Program%20Vlade%20Republike%20Hrvatske%20za%20mandat%202020.%20-%202024..pdf (accessed on 20 September 2023). [20]

Government of Poland (n.d.), *Komisja Wspólna Rządu i Samorządu Terytorialnego [Joint Commission of the Government and Local Government]*, https://www.gov.pl/web/kwrist-mswia (accessed on 30 October 2023). [70]

Government of Poland (n.d.), *Komitet Koordynacyjny do spraw Polityki Rozwoju [Development Policy Co-ordination Committee]*, https://www.gov.pl/web/premier/komitet-koordynacyjny-do-spraw-polityki-rozwoju (accessed on 28 September 2023). [67]

Government of Poland (n.d.), *Unpublished documents*. [71]

IDETA (2023), *Nos missions [Our missions]*. [32]

IGRETEC (n.d.), *Who we are*, https://www.igretec.com/en/igretec/who-are-we/ (accessed on 2 February 2024). [33]

Karlovac County (2023), *Sastanak predsjednika Vlade sa županicama i županima [Meeting of the Prime Minister with prefects]*, https://www.kazup.hr/index.php/aktualno/sastanak-predsjednika-vlade-sa-zupanicama-i-zupanima (accessed on 23 October 2023). [60]

Lublinska, M. (2017), *Decentralisation and multi-level governance in Poland: Ensuring coherence between national and subnational development strategies/policies*, https://www.oecd.org/regional/regional-policy/Decentralisation-and-multi-level-governance-in-Poland.pdf (accessed on 2 October 2023). [72]

MRDEUF (2024), *Written comments received from the Government of Croatia in March 2024*. [1]

MRDEUF (2023), *PowerPoint presentation on strategic planning across levels of government in Croatia, prepared the MRDEUF for the OECD's benefit*. [31]

MRDEUF (2023), *Presentation given by the MRDEUF for the OECD during the 2023 Croatia accession mission.* [19]

MRDEUF (2023), *Register of regional coordinators and local development agencies*, https://razvoj.gov.hr/upisnik-regionalnih-koordinatora-i-lokalnih-razvojnih-agencija/4007 (accessed on 30 November 2023). [41]

MRDEUF (2023), *Upisnik regionalnih koordinatora i lokalnih razvojnih agencija [Register of regional coordinators and local development agencies]*, https://razvoj.gov.hr/upisnik-regionalnih-koordinatora-i-lokalnih-razvojnih-agencija/4007 (accessed on 2 December 2023). [43]

MRDEUF (2022), *Sustainable Social and Economic Development Programme of Assisted Areas*, https://razvoj.gov.hr/UserDocsImages//Dokumenti/BBP%20PP//Program%20odr%C5%BEivog%20dru%C5%A1tvenog%20i%20gospodarskog%20razvoja%20potpomognutih%20podru%C4%8Dja.pdf (accessed on 29 November 2023). [24]

MRDEUF (2021), *Nacionalni Plan Razvoja Otoka 2021.-2027. [National Plan for Islands Development 2021-2027]*, https://razvoj.gov.hr/UserDocsImages/O%20ministarstvu/Regionalni%20razvoj/Otoci%20i%20priobalje/2021/Nacionalni%20plan%20razvoja%20otoka%202021.-2027._28.12.2021..pdf (accessed on 20 September 2023). [23]

MRDEUF (n.d.), *Programmes of the Government of Croatia 2021-2027*, https://razvoj.gov.hr/istaknute-teme/eu-fondovi-2021-2027/operativni-programi-republike-hrvatske-2021-2027/4854 (accessed on 22 September 2023). [25]

Netherlands Chamber of Commerce (n.d.), *Regional Development Agencies (ROMs)*, https://business.gov.nl/running-your-business/business-location/establishing-or-relocating-a-business/regional-development-agencies-roms/#:~:text=ROM%20Nederland%20%2C%20the%20umbrella%20organisation,and%20have%20no%20profit%20motive. (accessed on 21 October 2022). [35]

Netherlands Regional Development Corporations (n.d.), *Wat is een ROM? [What is a Regional Development Corporation"?]*, https://www.rom-nederland.nl/ (accessed on 12 May 2023). [51]

OECD (2024), *Presentation by EURADA during the OECD-led study tour of Croatian RDAs to Charleroi and Brussels, Belgium.* [44]

OECD (2023), *Enhancing Strategic Planning and Innovation Services: Supporting Romanian Regional Development Agencies*, OECD Regional Development Studies, OECD Publishing, Paris, https://doi.org/10.1787/8d80ef62-en. [38]

OECD (2023), *Interviews with local stakeholders conducted as part of the "Enhanced Strategic Planning at the Regional and Local Levels in Croatia" project.* [18]

OECD (2023), *Interviews with local stakeholders conducted as part of the Croatia accession mission, under the auspices of the OECD Regional Development Policy Committee.* [10]

OECD (2023), *OECD Public Governance Reviews: Czech Republic: Towards a More Modern and Effective Public Administration*, OECD Public Governance Reviews, OECD Publishing, Paris, https://doi.org/10.1787/41fd9e5c-en. [73]

OECD (2023), *Recommendation of the Council on Regional Development Policy*, https://legalinstruments.oecd.org/en/instruments/OECD-LEGAL-0492 (accessed on 28 November 2023). [3]

OECD (2023), *Response the the OECD Regional Development Policy Committee Accession Background Questionnaire: Croatia*. [11]

OECD (2023), *Subnational governments in OECD countries: Key data (Brochure)*, OECD Publishing. [46]

OECD (2023), *Written comments provided to the OECD by the Government of Croatia*. [61]

OECD (2022), *OECD Statistics. Demography and Population. Population Statistics. Historial Population Data*, https://stats.oecd.org/ (accessed on 12 May 2023). [47]

OECD (2022), *Rebuilding Ukraine by Reinforcing Regional and Municipal Governance*, OECD Multi-level Governance Studies, OECD Publishing, Paris, https://doi.org/10.1787/63a6b479-en. [2]

OECD (2022), *Response to the project questionnaire "Enhanced Strategic Planning at the Regional and Local Levels in Croatia" addressed to Croatia's regional development agencies*. [42]

OECD (2022), *Response to the project questionnaire "Enhanced Strategic Planning at the Regional and Local Levels in Croatia" addressed to the Ministry of Regional Development and European Union Funds (MRDEUF)*. [28]

OECD (2020), *The Future of Regional Development and Public Investment in Wales, United Kingdom*, OECD Multi-level Governance Studies, OECD Publishing, Paris, https://doi.org/10.1787/e6f5201d-en. [4]

OECD (2020), "The Future of Regional Development and Public Investment in Wales, United Kingdom", *OECD Multi-level Governance Studies*, https://doi.org/10.1787/e6f5201d-en (accessed on 2 October 2023). [69]

OECD (2019), *Effective Multi-level Public Investment. OECD Principles in Action*, https://www.oecd.org/effective-public-investment-toolkit/Full_report_Effective_Public_Investment.pdf (accessed on 13 February 2023). [55]

OECD (2019), *Effective Public Investment Across Levels of Government: Implementing the OECD Principles*, https://www.oecd.org/effective-public-investment-toolkit/OECD_Public_Investment_Implementation_Brochure_2019.pdf (accessed on 28 September 2023). [68]

OECD (2019), *OECD Regional Outlook 2019: Leveraging Megatrends for Cities and Rural Areas*, OECD Publishing, Paris, https://doi.org/10.1787/9789264312838-en. [8]

OECD (2018), "Making Decentralisation Work: A Handbook for Policy-Makers", *OECD Multi-level Governance Studies*, https://doi.org/10.1787/g2g9faa7-en. [59]

OECD (2016), *OECD Regional Outlook 2016: Productive Regions for Inclusive Societies*, OECD Publishing, Paris, https://doi.org/10.1787/9789264260245-en. [7]

OECD/UCLG (2022), *2022 Report of the World Observatory on Subnational Government Finance and Investment - Country Profiles. Croatia*, https://www.sng-wofi.org/country-profiles/ (accessed on 7 April 2023). [29]

OECD/UCLG (2022), *2022 Report of the World Observatory on Subnational Government Finance and Investment - Key Findings*, OECD/UCLG. [45]

OECD/UCLG (2022), *2022 Report of the World Observatory on Subnational Government Finance and Investment. Country Profiles. Costa Rica*, https://www.sng-wofi.org/country-profiles/ (accessed on 22 March 2023). [49]

OECD/UCLG (2022), *2022 Report of the World Observatory on Subnational Government Finance and Investment. Country Profiles. Lithuania*, https://www.sng-wofi.org/country-profiles/ (accessed on 12 June 2023). [50]

Official Gazette of Croatia No 118/18 (2018), *Zakon o potpomognutim područjima [Law of assisted areas]*, https://www.zakon.hr/z/1767/Zakon-o-potpomognutim-podru%C4%8Djima (accessed on 2 October 2023). [13]

Official Gazette of Croatia No 118/2018 (2018), *Zakon o Brdsko-planinskim Područjima [Law on Hilly and Mountainous Areas]*, https://www.zakon.hr/z/754/Zakon-o-brdsko-planinskim-podru%C4%8Djima (accessed on 12 November 2023). [14]

Official Gazette of Croatia No 123/2017 (2017), *Zakon o lokalnoj i područnoj (regionalnoj) samoupravi [Law on Local and Regional Self-government]*, https://www.zakon.hr/z/132/Zakon-o-lokalnoj-i-podru%C4%8Dnoj-%28regionalnoj%29-samoupravi (accessed on 17 August 2023). [15]

Official Gazette of Croatia No 123/2017 (2017), *Zakon o sustavu strateškog planiranja i upravljanja razvojem Republike Hrvatske [Law on the System of Strategic Planning and Development Management]*, https://narodne-novine.nn.hr/clanci/sluzbeni/2017_12_123_2798.html (accessed on 12 October 2022). [12]

Official Gazette of Croatia No 13/2021 (2021), *Nacionalna razvojna strategija Republike Hrvatske do 2030. godine [National Development Strategy of the Republic of Croatia by 2030]*, https://narodne-novine.nn.hr/clanci/sluzbeni/2021_02_13_230.html (accessed on 12 October 2022). [21]

Official Gazette of Croatia No 144/2020 (2017), *Zakon o lokalnoj i područnoj (regionalnoj) samoupravi [Law on Local and Regional Self-government]*, https://www.zakon.hr/z/132/Zakon-o-lokalnoj-i-podru%C4%8Dnoj-%28regionalnoj%29-samoupravi (accessed on 17 August 2023). [16]

Official Gazette of Croatia No 147 et al. (2018), *Zakon o regionalnom razvoju Republike Hrvatske [Law on Regional Development of the Republic of Croatia]*, https://www.zakon.hr/z/239/Zakon-o-regionalnom-razvoju-Republike-Hrvatske (accessed on 2 July 2022). [9]

Official Gazette of Croatia No 151/22 (2022), *Zakon o sustavu strateškog planiranja i upravljanja razvojem Republike Hrvatske [Law on the System of Strategic Planning and Development Management]*. [17]

Official Gazette of Croatia No 20/2021 (2021), *Zakon o sustavu civilne zaštite [Law on Civil Protection System]*, https://www.zakon.hr/z/809/Zakon-o-sustavu-civilne-za%C5%A1tite (accessed on 2 April 2024). [30]

Official Gazette of Croatia No 21/2017 (2017), *Odluka o osnivanju Savjeta za Slavoniju, Baranju i Srijem [Decision on the Establishment of the Council for Slavonia, Baranja and Srijem]*, https://narodne-novine.nn.hr/clanci/sluzbeni/2017_03_21_492.html (accessed on 14 August 2023). [64]

Official Gazette of Croatia No 25/2013 (2013), *Zakon o pravu na pristup informacijama [Law on the Right of Access to Information]*, https://narodne-novine.nn.hr/clanci/sluzbeni/2013_02_25_403.html (accessed on 23 October 2023). [77]

Official Gazette of Croatia No 88/2022 (2022), *Odluka o kriterijima za dodjelu pomoći na ime poticaja za dobrovoljno funkcionalno odnosno stvarno spajanje jedinica lokalne samouprave [Decision on the criteria for granting assistance in the name of incentives for voluntary functional...]*, https://narodne-novine.nn.hr/clanci/sluzbeni/2022_07_88_1361.html (accessed on 18 August 2023). [58]

Republic of Slovenia (2023), *Regional development*, https://www.gov.si/en/policies/state-and-society/local-self-government-and-regional-development/regional-development/ (accessed on 17 May 2023). [53]

ROREG (2022), *Responses to an OECD questionnaire as part of the "Towards better regional strategic planning and innovation support services in Romania" project*. [36]

UK Office for National Statistics (2022), *Population estimates for the UK, England, Wales, Scotland and Northern Ireland: mid-2021*, https://www.ons.gov.uk/peoplepopulationandcommunity/populationandmigration/populationestimates/bulletins/annualmidyearpopulationestimates/mid2021 (accessed on 1 June 2023). [48]

University, H. (ed.) (2008), *Metropolitan areas and the challenges of competitiveness*, Inter-American Development Bank and David Rockefeller Center for Latin American Studies, https://publications.iadb.org/publications/english/document/Governing-the-Metropolis-Principles-and-Cases.pdf. [6]

Wallonie Developpement (n.d.), *Nos membres [Our members]*, https://www.wallonie-developpement.be/membres/ (accessed on 2 February 2024). [34]

Notes

[1] The Law on Local and Regional Self-Government defines specific criteria for the classification of a local government unit as a city or a municipality. Generally, local governments that serve as the county capital, and units with a population of more than 10 000 inhabitants are classified as cities. Those with fewer inhabitants are typically classified as municipalities (Official Gazette of Croatia No 123/2017, 2017[15]).

[2] City and municipal governments with fewer than 1 000 inhabitants can be awarded co-funding of up to 75%. City and municipal governments with 1 000 inhabitants or more can be awarded co-financing of up to 50% (Official Gazette of Croatia No 88/2022, 2022[58]).

[3] In addition to the co-ordination mechanisms identified and discussed in this report, a series of co-ordination mechanisms mandated by the EU also operate in Croatia, including the monitoring committees for the EU-funded Programme for Competitiveness and Cohesion and the Integrated Territorial Programme 2021-2027.

4 Regional Development Planning Instruments and Practices

This chapter examines how Croatia's mechanisms and processes for regional development planning, implementation, monitoring and evaluation work in practice, and assesses their effectiveness. First, it conducts an in-depth exploration of the key national-level planning documents guiding regional development in Croatia. It assesses the extent to which those documents embed balanced territorial development as a cross-cutting government priority. Second, the chapter explores recent advances and challenges related to the design and implementation of county- and local-level planning documents, while also considering the various incentives that could support implementation. Finally, the chapter assesses the monitoring and evaluation mechanisms supporting regional development, including how results from such processes are used to improve policy implementation.

Introduction

Since the adoption of the 2017 Law on the System of Strategic Planning and Development Management, all county governments in Croatia have designed new county-level development plans. These planning documents are aligned with the National Development Strategy 2030 (NDS), which identifies balanced regional development as a key priority. In addition, county, city and municipal governments have enacted implementation programmes for their development plans. The design of mid- and short-term planning documents at various subnational levels could support the coherent, place-based implementation of specific territorial development initiatives that meet local needs and capacities, while contributing to national priorities.

This chapter looks at how the strategic planning process for regional development works in practice and assesses its effectiveness. In doing so, it considers the different stages of the strategic planning cycle—from design and implementation to monitoring and evaluation. It is important to note, however, that most of the relevant planning documents supporting regional development were only recently adopted (i.e. in 2021 or 2022). Consequently, limited evidence is available regarding the quality of their implementation.

The chapter's analysis identifies several important strengths in Croatia's strategic planning system for regional development. Notably, there is a clear hierarchy between national-, county- and local-level plans, with regional development agencies (RDAs) playing a key role in ensuring that subnational plans are compliant with the NDS. Moreover, since 2018, the Ministry of Regional Development and EU Funds (MRDEUF) has developed comprehensive guidelines, regulations and instruction manuals related to the design of strategic planning documents, and their monitoring and evaluation. These documents provide a strong basis for guiding regional development policy making. In addition, strategic planning documents at all levels of government are developed through extensive consultation with different governmental and non-governmental stakeholders. Consequently, the planning documents reflect stakeholder needs and priorities. Furthermore, monitoring and evaluation has been embedded in the strategic planning processes at all levels of government, and clear processes for upward reporting on the implementation of county- and local-level development plans have been established.

To ensure the development plans and projects in Croatia are effectively implemented, however, there are five challenges that will need to be overcome. First, Croatia lacks a national-level regional development strategy that provides details on the country's specific regional development objectives and suggested lines of actions for addressing territorial disparities. Second, with the implementation of the county development plans being dependent on the collective efforts of a wide range of public and non-governmental actors, there is a risk that they will not be fully implemented. Third, at the local level, municipal fragmentation hampers local capacity to carry out strategic planning tasks. Fourth, a lack of local-level data and limited awareness of existing data among subnational actors constrains their ability to develop diagnostics of territorial development challenges and opportunities. It also constrains the ability of subnational policy makers to monitor county and local development plans. Fifth and finally, a lack of multi-level performance review mechanisms has reduced monitoring to a primarily procedural requirement, rather than a substantive exercise that can help to improve the implementation of subnational development plans.

This chapter begins by exploring the key national-level planning documents guiding regional development in Croatia. In particular, it assesses their design process and the extent to which they embed balanced territorial development as a cross-cutting government priority. Subsequently, the chapter explores issues related to the design of county-level planning documents, while also considering different incentives that could support implementation. Further to this, the chapter considers challenges related to the design and implementation of local-level planning documents and the need to enhance local strategic planning capacities. Finally, the chapter assesses the monitoring and evaluation mechanisms supporting regional development. In particular, it looks at how monitoring and evaluation activities have been institutionalised among levels of government, as well as the quality of monitoring and evaluation processes. Lastly, it evaluates the way in which results from such processes are used, for example to improve policy implementation.

Box 4.1. Recommendations to further strengthen the effectiveness of Croatia's regional development policy

To ensure progress towards Croatia's long-term strategic objective of balanced regional development, the country is advised to:

- Update the NDS, ensuring that balanced regional development is integrated as a cross-cutting priority. This could involve modifying strategic objectives and including indicators to track progress towards territorial development objectives.
- Ensure that a territorial perspective is incorporated into other high-level strategic documents, such as sectoral and multi-sectoral plans. This may require updating the guidelines for the development of such plans.

To clarify Croatia's regional development policy and help subnational policy makers design development plans that better align to national priorities, Croatia is advised to:

- Design a national strategy for regional development, as required by law and identified in the NDS. Building on the previous national regional development strategy, the new version should:
    - Clearly outline the specific contributions that relevant actors are expected to make towards the achievement of priority actions.
    - Devise a comprehensive performance measurement framework, including a range of output, outcome and impact indicators to track implementation progress.

In order to strengthen the design and implementation of county development plans, Croatia is advised to:

- Require that the draft development plans include an implementation feasibility assessment that provides information on: i) the actors involved in implementation, ii) the nature of their contribution to implementation; and iii) the mechanisms through which these actors can be engaged during implementation.

In order to improve the design and implementation of local development plans, Croatia is advised to:

- Produce and disseminate practical information on how existing inter-municipal co-operation incentives can support local strategic planning. For instance:
    - The MRDEUF could disseminate information on how the few local development agencies that were created by more than one local government have supported collective strategic planning.
- Introduce additional incentives for small cities and municipalities to develop joint local development plans in order to better address shared development challenges, for example by:
    - Making the design of a joint local development plan a precondition to receiving funding through one or more of the country's regional development grants.
- Strengthen the strategic planning skills and expertise of local civil servants, by:
    - Designing and delivering a local government capacity building plan, with tailored training activities for cities and municipalities.
    - Developing a practical guide or manual to help local governments as they design and implement their local development plan and/or implementation programme.

In order to strengthen the institutional framework for monitoring and evaluating regional development policy, Croatia is advised to:

- Develop a single set of non-binding methodological guidelines for evaluating the implementation of county and local development plans, which recaps the various legislative provisions in simple, action-oriented language.
- Adjust timelines for reporting on the implementation of county development plans, requiring county departments, city and municipal governments to share data with RDAs at an earlier stage than is currently the case, in order to improve reporting quality.

In order to improve the quality of regional development monitoring and evaluation, Croatia is advised to:

- Increase the availability of timely, local data on topics such as investment, economic development and innovation, by:
  - Ensuring that subnational governments and RDAs are systematically consulted by the Croatian Bureau of Statistics to identify local data needs and measures to address them.
- Invest in increased awareness by subnational governments, including RDAs, of existing local-level datasets, including by:
  - Encouraging the Croatian Bureau of Statistics to publish a newsletter that provides periodic updates on relevant data for county, city and municipal governments.
  - Organising periodic meetings run by the Croatian Bureau of Statistics, in order to apprise subnational governments of existing datasets.
- Update the Library of Indicators, in close collaboration with RDAs and the Croatian Bureau of Statistics, to ensure that for all indicators data are available to support monitoring and evaluation.

In order to improve the impact of regional development monitoring and evaluation, Croatia is advised to:

- Set up performance dialogue mechanisms within subnational governments to ensure monitoring results are systematically discussed by decision makers (e.g. the prefect or mayor) and staff supporting strategic planning, to facilitate policy learning.
- Ensure that evaluation reports include an executive summary, drafted in easy-to-understand language, to make evaluation findings more accessible for relevant stakeholders.
- Create an interactive online portal where relevant information on regional development, including monitoring and evaluation reports, can be published in an accessible format.

Croatia's national-level strategic planning guidelines and documents

Over the past decade, Croatia has made important strides towards consolidating its system of cross-government strategic planning. The 2017 Law on the System of Strategic Planning and Development Management has provided extensive guidance to policy makers at the national and subnational levels of government on the process of developing strategic plans, as well as their prescribed structure (Box 4.2). There are, however, a number of challenges that stem from the current national-level strategic planning documents as they relate to regional development. In particular, while the NDS successfully presented balanced regional development as a core long-term strategic priority, it is not fully integrated into the different pillars of strategy. This risks regional development being considered more a sectoral priority than a cross-sectoral one that is embedded across government. This could lead to regional development objectives not being considered in the strategic planning documents and policies of line ministries, which may limit the overall impact of the NDS. The government currently also lacks a national-level regional development strategy which, if supported by a strong evidence base, would enable it to articulate a more detailed vision for balanced territorial development.

Box 4.2. Guidelines for the development of Croatia's main planning documents

In line with the 2017 Law on the System of Strategic Planning and Development Management, the MRDEUF prepared regulations on and instructions for the development of the planning documents. These include:

- **National planning documents**, such as the NDS, sectoral and multi-sectoral strategies, national plans, the Government Programme and their implementation programmes; and
- **County and local planning documents**, such as county and local development plans, and their implementation programmes.

The MRDEUF developed a regulation outlining the elements that must be included when developing strategic planning documents (e.g. vision statement, analysis of development challenges and opportunities, objectives, performance measurement framework, financial costs). It also developed detailed instructions for government bodies regarding how the planning documents should be prepared (e.g. how to manage a stakeholder consultation process, how to design objectives and performance indicators). Finally, the Ministry developed a rulebook that prescribes the deadlines and procedures for monitoring and reporting on all national- and subnational-level plans. Together, these elements provide a strong basis for guiding national and subnational-level policy makers through the various stages of the strategic planning cycle (Figure 4.1).

Figure 4.1. Strategic planning cycle

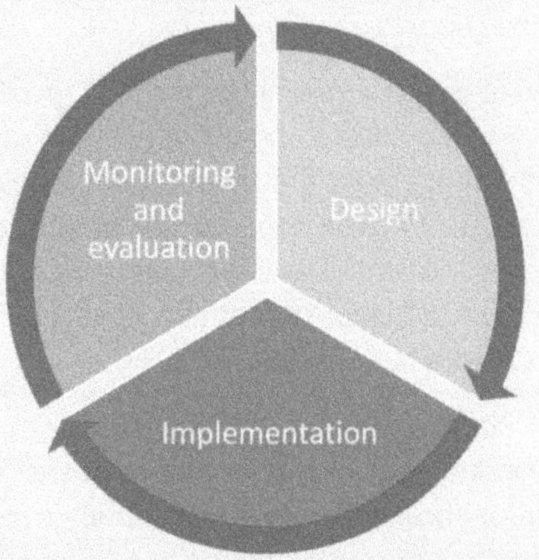

Source: Author's elaboration, based on (Official Gazette of Croatia No 151/2022, 2017[1]; Official Gazette of Croatia No 27/2023, 2023[2]; Official Gazette of Croatia No. 44/2023, 2023[3]; MRDEUF, 2021[4]).

The National Development Strategy 2030 guides Croatia's regional development policy

The NDS is the key planning instrument of Croatia's regional development policy framework. It was adopted in 2021, in order to articulate a high-level, long-term vision for Croatia's economic development. One of its strengths is the fact that it was designed based on extensive consultation with regional and local stakeholders. For example, a steering group, chaired by the Prime Minister and with representatives from line ministries, parliament, the Croatian County Association, the Croatian Association of Cities and the Croatian Union of Municipalities, was established to guide the NDS's design (Official Gazette of Croatia

No 13/2021, 2021[5]). By inviting such a wide range of actors, the government ensured that regional and local needs were taken into consideration at every stage of the strategy design process.

Furthermore, consultation with different stakeholders was pursued through a multi-level working group on territorial development, in which representatives from county, city and municipal governments, RDAs and other regional and local stakeholders all participated. The government also organised different development fora in order to identify urgent challenges, opportunities and help to define a long-term vision for territorial development. These were chaired by county prefects, with the participation of RDAs and other county-level representatives.

Non-governmental stakeholder participation was promoted through different actions, including the dissemination of an online survey. In addition, participatory workshops on the future of Croatia's development were organised in seven of the 21 counties. The workshops, in which representatives from academia, civil society and the private sector participated, were organised in consultation with RDAs (Official Gazette of Croatia No 13/2021, 2021[5]).

Balanced regional development is not fully integrated as a cross-cutting priority in the NDS

One challenge with the NDS relates to its structure. For the MRDEUF, the development of the NDS was regarded as an important opportunity to raise the visibility regarding Croatia's regional development objectives across and among levels of government (MRDEUF, 2024[6]). At the same time, however, despite establishing balanced regional development as a long-term priority, it makes few links between regional development and other strategic objectives (e.g. sustainable economy and society; and strengthening crisis resilience). Consequently, there is a risk that regional development will be seen as a sectoral priority, rather than an overarching one that should be considered in the design and implementation of policies in fields such as economic development, digitalisation and the green transition.

Of the 13 strategic objectives outlined in the NDS, six strategic objectives do not mention regional development at all, while a further five make only cursory references to possible regional development-related measures. The remaining two strategic objectives have a clear focus on regional development: i) Supporting the development of assisted areas[1] and areas with developmental specificities; and ii) Strengthening regional competitiveness. Progress towards each of these objectives is measured through a single indicator: levels of regional GDP per capita, in the case of the former, and regional competitiveness index values, in the case of the latter (Official Gazette of Croatia No 13/2021, 2021[5]).

Both indicators—regional GDP per capita and regional competitiveness index scores—are, however, insufficient to track performance towards their corresponding objectives, and would need to be complemented by additional economic, environmental and/or social indicators. For instance, regional GDP per capita, which measures the value-added created through the production of goods and services in a territory over a set period, is unable to track progress towards the creation of more sustainable islands and cities.

As a consequence of not having embedded balanced regional development as a cross-cutting issue within the NDS, other public bodies (e.g. those responsible for education, economic development, housing, transport) may not feel compelled to support the MRDEUF's territorial priorities. In a future iteration of the NDS, the government should ensure that all relevant national-level objectives adopt a territorial lens, which can inform the activities of relevant public bodies. It can also contribute to a sense of shared responsibility with respect to supporting balanced regional development. Croatia could also use the forthcoming mid-term review of the NDS to further integrate balanced regional development as a cross-cutting priority.

The need for a new national-level regional development strategy in Croatia

To support the government's articulation of territorial priorities and address NDS-related challenges the government could consider adopting a national-level regional development strategy, like the one it had between 2017 and 2020. According to the Law on Regional Development, it is a legal requirement for the MRDEUF to develop a regional development strategy, which should determine territorial goals and priorities, as well as means of achieving them (Official Gazette of Croatia No 147 et al., 2018[7]). However, no such document currently exists.

A national-level regional development strategy would provide an opportunity for the government to articulate its vision, strategic objectives and priorities for balanced territorial development in greater detail, all of which could be supported by a robust, evidence-based diagnostic. The greater detail enclosed in a regional development strategy could thereby serve as a bridge between the NDS—which some RDAs reported as being too high-level—and other, national and subnational planning documents, including sectoral and multi-sectoral plans and county development plans (OECD, 2023[8]).

Croatia's Regional Development Strategy 2017-2020 provides a starting point for designing a new national-level regional development strategy

The Regional Development Strategy for the period 2017-2020, developed and implemented during the previous parliament, could provide a starting point for a new strategy (Box 4.3). Although the Strategy covered a period of only three years, and even though the government's regional development priorities—as set out in the NDS—have shifted since then, there is a measure of continuity between the two documents. For instance, both strategies place a strong emphasis on strengthening regional competitiveness and supporting sustainable territorial development.

Box 4.3. Croatia's Regional Development Strategy 2017-20

The Regional Development Strategy of the Republic of Croatia 2017-20 was developed by the MRDEUF. It included three strategic objectives for balanced territorial development, each of which were supported by a series of priority actions:

1. **Increase quality of life by encouraging sustainable territorial development.** Priority lines of action to achieve this objective included enhancing quality of life of citizens through education and cultural development, improving regional and local infrastructure (e.g. for education and healthcare), and providing targeted support to areas with unique development needs (e.g. islands and 'assisted areas').
2. **Increase competitiveness of regional economies and employment**. Priority lines of action to achieve this objective included creating a supportive business environment, increasing regional attractiveness through regional branding, providing tailored support to entrepreneurs, and ensuring labour supply meets labour demand.
3. **Systematic management of regional development.** Priority lines of action to achieve this objective included improving strategic planning capacities at all levels of government, improving policy co-ordination across sectors and strengthening financial and administrative skills in subnational governments.

Source: Author's elaboration, based on (MRDEUF, 2017[9]).

The Strategy provided a wide-ranging background analysis of territorial challenges and opportunities in Croatia, which was supported by quantitative and qualitative data. It also set out a clear strategic framework for regional development, comprised of strategic objectives, operational objectives and lists of measures for policy action (MRDEUF, 2017[9]).

However, there were also a number of drawbacks to the Strategy's design, which would need to be addressed in a revised national-level regional development strategy. First, while the Strategy's diagnostic identified a range of functional territories (e.g. hilly and mountainous areas, islands) that should receive government support, it did not include a comprehensive list of the development challenges or comparative strengths of these territories. Developing this would enable the MRDEUF to articulate strategic and operational objectives that are more closely aligned with functional area needs.

Second, with regard to implementation and accountability, the strategy did not outline the specific contributions that governmental or non-governmental actors should make to support its implementation, financing, monitoring and evaluation (MRDEUF, 2017[9]). Ensuring clarity in the assignment of responsibilities is critical in order to limit duplication, overlap and co-ordination challenges during the strategic planning cycle (OECD, 2018[10]). For instance, to ensure more effective implementation, a new regional development strategy should include information regarding the specific contributions that relevant actors are expected to make towards the achievement of each priority action.

Third, performance measurement could be further improved. Given the wide range of measures proposed to support operational and strategic objectives, performance indicators need to capture their impact more holistically. For instance, many of the monitoring indicators listed are output indicators that assess whether or not a policy or process is being implemented, rather than whether it has been effective in delivering meaningful change (MRDEUF, 2017[9]). Ideally, output indicators should be coupled with outcome indicators, which demonstrate the real-world changes that policies or processes have delivered, and impact indicators, which illustrate the effects that they will have on society or economy in general.

Fourth, a future national-level regional development strategy should be supported by consistent monitoring and evaluation activities. Despite a requirement for the monitoring of regional development policy to take place annually, no reports or evaluation reports connected to the Regional Development Strategy appear to have been produced between 2017 and 2020. A more systematic submission of annual or multi-annual public reports is needed in order to improve transparency and accountability around the implementation of regional development policy.

Policy makers should also ensure that other high-level planning documents include a territorial perspective

In addition to a regional development strategy, the government should look to ensure that a territorial perspective is incorporated into other high-level strategic documents, such as sectoral and multi-sectoral plans. This is particularly important given the cross-sectoral nature of regional development policy. The government's decision to define balanced regional development as one of its four cross-cutting strategic dimensions demonstrates that it recognises the importance of territorial development as a transversal issue. In this regard, through their regular co-ordination with the MRDEUF, the strategic co-ordinators located within line ministries (see chapter 2) should play a key role in ensuring that regional development appears as a cross-cutting priority in policy design and is implemented across the entire government.

The guidelines for developing sectoral and multi-sectoral plans could be modified in order to ensure that a territorial lens is applied by line ministries. For instance, the government could explore the approach used by the Government of Mexico to ensure that the different six-year programmes with national-level public institutions for the period 2018-24 embraced various cross-cutting priorities (Box 4.4).

Box 4.4. Mexico's approach to integrating cross-cutting priorities into national-level planning documents

Mexico's federal planning law mandates the formulation of development programmes at various government levels, all of which must align with the overarching National Development Plan, which spans a six-year term, coinciding with the presidential administration. This plan sets the country's long-term objectives, strategies, and priorities across economic, social, cultural, and environmental spheres. Specifically, it requires the development of various programmes:

- **Institutional programmes** are developed by each of the national-level public bodies. They highlight organisational improvements, and specific actions each public body will undertake to contribute to national objectives.
- **Sectoral programmes** are developed by various sectors of the public administration (e.g. health, education, energy) and outline the objectives, strategies and actions to be undertaken within these specific sectors.
- **Special programmes** focus on specific thematic areas or target particular social, economic, or environmental issues that cannot be addressed by individual public bodies, and instead require cross-sectoral collaboration.
- **Regional programmes** address the development needs and priorities of specific geographic areas (that go beyond the administrative boundaries of federal states) within the country.

In 2019, the Ministry of Finance and Public Funds organised a series of meetings for the planning staff of Mexico's national-level public bodies to guide them through the programme design process. The meetings included workshops on how to integrate various cross-cutting priorities (e.g. sustainable development, equality and non-discrimination, territorial development, interculturality, gender, the natural environment) in all institutional, sectoral, special and regional programmes.

With the support of different national government bodies and international organisations, the Ministry of Finance and Public Funds also created a website that enabled policy makers to access supporting material on the different cross-cutting issues and how to integrate them in the different national-planning instruments. This material included factsheets on a series of key economic, social, environmental and governance indicators (e.g. education, healthcare, trust, insecurity) that reveal relevant development gaps across population groups and regions. They were to be used to help design the diagnostic for each programme.

Source: Author's elaboration, based on (Government of Mexico, 2023[11]; Ministry of Finance and Public Credit of Mexico, 2018[12]).

Croatia's subnational-level strategic planning guidelines and documents

Croatia's reforms to its strategic planning system have supported greater multi-level policy coherence, and ensured that county and local development plans align with higher-level planning documents. The government has also taken important steps to strengthen the capacity of subnational governments to develop plans and programmes. For example, it has disseminated regulations and guidelines on the design of development plans (e.g. who needs to be consulted) and their content (Box 4.2) (MRDEUF, n.d.[13]).

An OECD comparative analysis of several county development plans and implementation programmes suggests that this government guidance has helped strengthen county-level strategic planning processes. In particular, county-level plans are typically characterised by: i) an extensive, evidence-based diagnostic on territorial challenges and opportunities; ii) a results-oriented framework for the implementation of strategic objectives; and iii) an indicative financial framework to support budget transparency and accountability. They are also typically based on extensive consultation with external stakeholders.

At the same time, some important areas for improvement of the county-level strategic planning process have been identified. With regard to design, county-level planning documents need to provide additional clarity on the stakeholder consultation processes. Providing information on which actors were consulted during the plan's development, on what topics, and how responses were processed can help to build trust in the strategic planning process. These county-level plans also need to clearly demonstrate their alignment with relevant higher-level planning documents, in order to further reinforce regional development policy coherence across government. Policy makers could also benefit from further clarity regarding some of the proposed implementation measures, in order to strengthen accountability for different components of the plans. Finally, with regard to performance measurement, certain county-level monitoring and evaluation practices need to be strengthened in order to identify whether policy actions are leading to the desired results.

Some important areas for improvement have also been identified with respect to the local-level strategic planning process. In particular, local-level territorial fragmentation should be addressed as many city and municipal governments currently lack sufficient financial or human resource capacity to effectively carry out tasks requiring specialist expertise, such as strategic planning.

Strengths in the county-level strategic planning process

By preparing and disseminating practical guidelines and instructions, and organising regular meetings (mainly virtual due to the COVID-19 pandemic), the MRDEUF helped the RDAs to draft county development plans. In response to an OECD county-level survey[2], 95% of respondents felt they had the capacity to develop a county development plan that reflects realistic needs, is aligned with the NDS, and includes local government input (OECD, 2022[14]). In addition, 86% of respondents felt they had the capacity to develop a realistic monitoring and evaluation framework, and involve non-governmental actors when preparing county development plans (Figure 4.2).

Figure 4.2. Capacity of RDAs to carry out strategic planning tasks

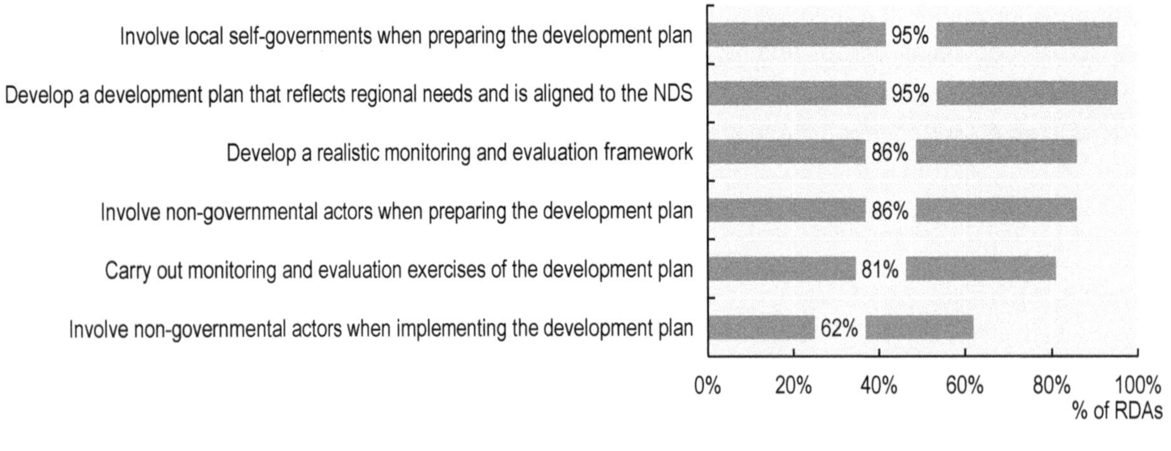

Note: Questionnaire question: Does your RDA have the necessary human resources (including expertise) to effectively carry out the following tasks related to the county development planning process? Full description of tasks: Involve the private sector, civil society or academia when implementing the county development plan; Carry out periodic monitoring and evaluation exercises of the county development plan; Involve the private sector, civil society or academia when preparing the county development plan; Develop a realistic monitoring and evaluation framework with clear objectives and indicators; Develop a county development plan that reflects regional needs and is aligned to the National Development Strategy 2030; Involve local governments (*općinas* and *grads*) when preparing the county development plan. N=21.
Source: Author's elaboration, based on (OECD, 2022[14]).

A comparative analysis of several county development plans and implementation programmes provides insight into the various strengths of county-level strategic planning in Croatia. First, the county development plans include an extensive diagnostic on territorial development challenges and opportunities, which are categorised by policy area (e.g. demography, education, economy and labour market). The diagnostic is based on a SWOT analysis framework that identifies strengths, weaknesses, opportunities and threats for each policy area. The diagnostics are backed by qualitative and quantitative data, thereby providing a solid evidence base that can support the identification of strategic objectives (Bjelovar-Bilogora County, 2022[15]; Koprivnica-Križevci County, 2021[16]; Osijek-Baranja County, 2022[17]).

It is notable, however, that 95% of the surveyed RDAs indicated that a lack of data was a challenge for developing county development plans (Figure 4.3). This is due in part to the limited availability of locally disaggregated data (in particular, economic, innovation and investment data on cities and municipalities) in Croatia, which, if available, could help to further clarify territorial needs and set priorities (OECD, 2022[18]). Establishing statistical offices in all counties, rather than solely in major cities, could help to improve the collection and analysis of relevant subnational data needed to support the design of county development plans.

Figure 4.3. Challenges to the design of the county development plans reported by RDAs

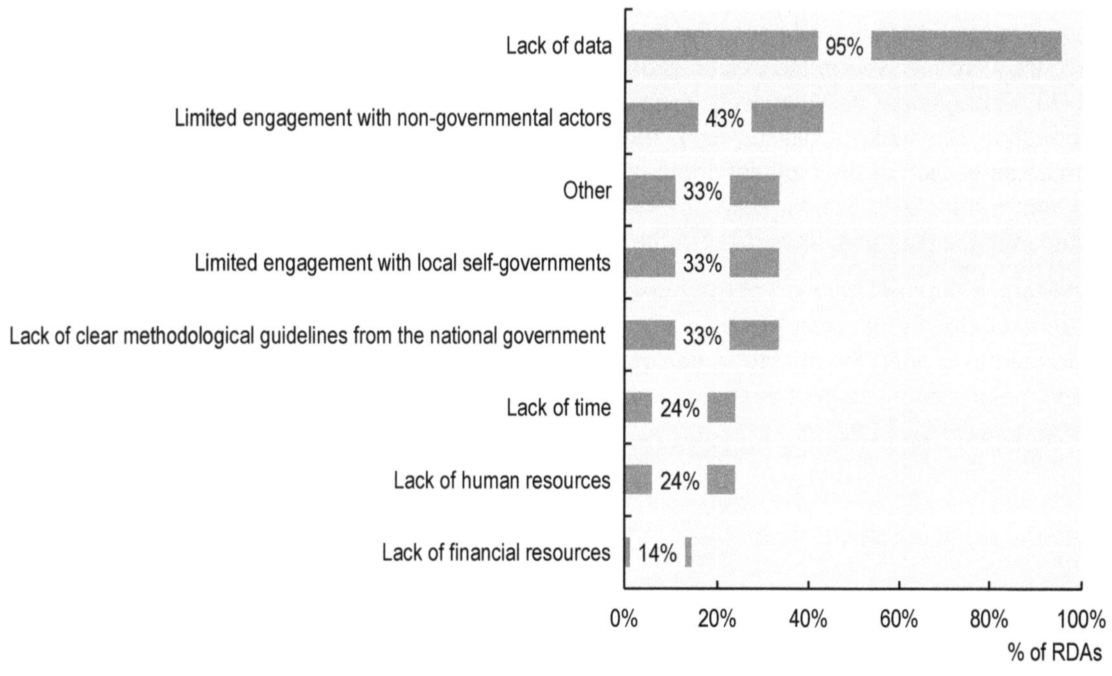

Note: Questionnaire question: What does your RDA consider to be the three main challenges for designing your county's regional development plan (whether completed or underway)? Full response options: Lack of financial resources; Lack of human resources (including expertise); Lack of time; Lack of clear methodological guidelines from the national government; Limited engagement with local governments; Limited engagement with non-governmental actors (academia, non-governmental organisations, the private sector, citizens); Lack of data; Other. N=21.
Source: Author's elaboration, based on (OECD, 2022[14]).

A second strength is that the plans include a logical framework that clearly links strategic objectives, operational objectives and proposed measures for implementation (Bjelovar-Bilogora County, 2022[15]; Koprivnica-Križevci County, 2021[16]; Osijek-Baranja County, 2022[17]). Such an approach can support more results-oriented implementation, and can also facilitate monitoring and evaluation activities. Third, the plans include an indicative financial framework for implementation, which also supports budget transparency and accountability. The frameworks typically set out cost estimates for achieving each strategic objective, along with planned sources of funding.

Finally, the plans analysed were developed on the basis of extensive consultation with relevant stakeholders. For example, per the national-level guidelines, a partnership council was established in each county to act as an umbrella body that could support the plan's development. Moreover, meetings and workshops were held with a range of actors (e.g. local public bodies, academia and the private sector) at the regional and local levels in order to help identify development challenges, opportunities and strategic priorities. These elements, in turn, informed the design of strategic objectives.

Areas for improvement in the design of the county-level strategic planning

Despite their strengths, several challenges related to the design of county-level strategic plans can be identified. For example, they sometimes fail to outline which actors will be responsible for implementing the actions identified in the plans. This can hamper effective implementation, for example by leading to a lack of ownership or commitment among involved parties, as unclear responsibilities can lead to disengagement.

Clarifying who contributed to the design of development plans, can increase a sense of ownership of regional development efforts

One design-related challenge relates to the fact that certain county development plans do not outline which stakeholders were involved in the design process (e.g. public bodies, academia, civil society), or which stakeholder engagement activities were organised (Bjelovar-Bilogora County, 2022[15]). The absence of this information can make it difficult to: i) establish whether the consulted stakeholders represent an accurate cross-section of the regional population and interests; and ii) understand how their inputs were used to inform the plan's design. Both of these elements are important to help foster a sense of broad ownership over the plan and create trust in the strategic planning process.

When designing the next iteration of their development plans, counties could follow the example set by Osijek-Baranja County. Its plan provides a comprehensive overview of all participants involved in the bodies formed to support the strategy's design. It also provides a detailed description and timeline of the consultation activities by each of these bodies, adding transparency about the design process of its plan (Osijek-Baranja County, 2022[17]).

Improving the alignment between county development plans and relevant higher-level strategic planning documents

A further challenge derives from the fact that the county development plans do not systematically demonstrate how they contribute to objectives set out in relevant higher-level planning documents. While all the plans analysed outline how they help to further the objectives that are set out in the NDS, only the Osijek-Baranja county development plan describes how it helps to further objectives that are laid out in other, higher-level plans (e.g. multi-sectoral strategies) (Osijek-Baranja County, 2022[17]). Clarifying such alignment is important for supporting the coherence of regional development policy across government. In addition, it can help pinpoint the central government bodies (e.g. ministries) that can contribute to the implementation of different parts of the county development plan (e.g. those related to housing, education or healthcare). Including such information could provide a basis on which the RDAs can co-ordinate with those bodies.

In order to further strengthen the vertical alignment among national and subnational development strategies and plans, there are a number of actions that the government could take. First, during the next round of county-level strategic planning, strategic planning co-ordinators from each line ministry could hold workshops for RDAs in which they: i) highlight the objectives that are included in their ministry's strategic plans; and ii) clarify how subnational governments can support their ministry's priorities.

In tandem, national-level strategic planning co-ordinators could upload background resources, containing synthesised information about strategic planning acts, onto an online portal. Such efforts would ease the burden on RDAs when verifying links between their county development plan and higher-level strategic planning. These actions could be taken when counties have to develop the next round of county development plans (i.e. in 2026-2027). However, outreach by the national-level strategic planning co-ordinators to the RDAs could potentially also be beneficial during the mid-term review of the county development plans (2024-2025). These reviews provide the RDAs with an opportunity to update their plans and ensure further continued alignment with national (incl. sectoral) and subnational development priorities.

Enhancing clarity about the actors involved in county development plan implementation

A third challenge with the design of the county development plans relates to clarity about who will support their implementation and how. It is notable that while certain county development plans reviewed by the OECD briefly list the actors responsible for implementation, none include an overview of the contributions that these actors are expected to make. The lack of detail on the contributions that public actors in particular can or are mandated to make—whether it be financial support, expertise, or material resources—means that stakeholders may not fully understand or commit to their roles. This can result in disjointed efforts, underutilisation of resources, and ultimately a lack of progress in reaching regional development objectives.

To address this issue, the government could amend the guidelines for designing county development plans and require them to provide additional information on implementation. For example, RDAs could be tasked with including a short implementation feasibility assessment in the draft plan, which could include:

- A mapping of public and non-governmental stakeholders that are mandated or can contribute to the implementation of each strategic objective, specifying the type of contribution they could make (e.g. financial, in kind, information).
- The mechanisms (e.g. co-ordination bodies) through which these stakeholders are or will be engaged in the implementation process.

Moreover, the MRDEUF, together with the RDAs, could design implementation guidelines along the above-mentioned lines to help ensure that subnational plans can be delivered effectively. For instance, the Local Government Association of England and Wales (UK) states that strategic plans should not only seek to identify all relevant local implementation partners, but also clarify expectations regarding the nature of their contribution (Local Government Association, n.d.[19]).

As Croatia considers the above-mentioned actions, it should pay particular attention to the ways in which non-governmental actors can support the implementation of county development plans. In response to the OECD survey, all RDAs indicated that city and municipal governments will be involved in implementing the plans (OECD, 2022[18]). However, only 52% mentioned private sector involvement, and only 29% noted the involvement of civil society actors (e.g. academia) (OECD, 2022[18]). This suggests that certain county governments may not be fully mobilising the knowledge and capacity of non-governmental actors. Academia and the private sector can play an important role in supporting regional development objectives. Through strategic investments, the private sector can create jobs, drive economic growth and spur innovation. By conducting targeted studies on local economic conditions, social challenges, and environmental issues, for example, universities and research institutions can provide data-driven policy recommendations. Further to this, by offering educational programmes that meet sector needs they can play a key role matching labour demand and supply (OECD, 2015[20]; OECD, 2019[21]).

More specific objectives and performance indicators can foster targeted policy action and facilitate monitoring and evaluation

A final design-related challenge concerns the indicators used to measure progress towards the counties' regional development objectives. In the Osijek-Baranja county development plan, for example, the measures on "reducing poverty and social exclusion" and "developing and improving of communal infrastructure" are relatively vague, with no indication of what implementation will concretely entail (Osijek-Baranja County, 2022[17]). This could lead to a lack of accountability for various implementation components, while also potentially undermining the strategy's ambitions. If the proposed measures for implementation are imprecise, box-ticking activities may suffice in order to fulfil them, rather than encouraging meaningful change. In order to avoid this issue, the national government should consider requiring plans and implementation programmes to outline concrete lines of action against which progress towards objectives can be measured, while placing special emphasis on which specific actor is responsible for the proposed actions.

Incentives for implementing county development plans

Effective implementation of the county development plans depends on more than strengthening their design. It also requires providing clearer political and financial incentives to counties, cities and municipalities to orient resources to meet regional development objectives.

Some political incentives already exist, such as the need to demonstrate results to local stakeholders. For instance, RDAs must submit an annual report on the implementation of the county development plan to the county government, which is also published online (Official Gazette of Croatia No. 44/2023, 2023[3]). In principle, therefore, local stakeholders have an opportunity to scrutinise these reports and hold the county government accountable by reviewing whether or not objectives are on track to be achieved.

In reality, however, there is no systematic process for involving local stakeholders in monitoring progress towards achieving the objectives set out in the county development plans. Only 43% of RDAs surveyed by the OECD indicated that private sector stakeholders were involved in monitoring the plan, while only 14% indicated that civil society stakeholders were involved in doing so (OECD, 2022[18]). This is partly by design, as monitoring reports in Croatia typically constitute the outcome of a technical reporting process, rather than a participatory process (MRDEUF, 2024[6]). At the same time, however, this means that local public scrutiny is unlikely to provide a particularly strong political incentive for the implementation of county development plans. Setting up a publicly accessible digital platform where citizens can track counties' performance towards meeting their regional development objectives could provide counties with an additional incentive for implementation. Such a platform could adopt a 'traffic' light system to provide users with a quick visual cue of the areas where performance has met targets and areas where process is lacking (Wandsworth County Council, 2024[22]).

A further political factor that complicates implementation is that while county prefects serve a four-year term, county development plans are mid-term planning documents, generally spanning six- to seven-year periods (Official Gazette of Croatia No 151/2022, 2017[1]). As such, prefects may be more inclined to prioritise development efforts that can materialise during their tenure than to pursue longer-term regional development objectives, which may have been identified by a previous administration. Indeed, interviews suggested that there is uncertainty regarding the interest among some county prefects to implement their plans in full (OECD, 2023[8]).

There is a lack of financial incentives for the implementation of county development plans

An additional issue is that counties currently lack: i) the financial means, and ii) clear financial incentives to implement their county development plans. For example, 95% of RDAs indicated that a lack of own-financial resources to fund activities was a key challenge to the implementation of county development plans (OECD, 2022[18]). This partly reflects the current composition of subnational funding and financing for territorial development in Croatia (see chapter 4). The perception that counties do not have the necessary financial means to fully implement their development plans may also be due to a lack of prioritisation of development needs and initiatives. Indeed, there are concerns that the breadth of development initiatives outlined in some county development plans far exceed the financial resources that can be mobilised (MRDEUF, 2024[6]). The implementation of territorial development projects depends heavily on EU programmes for their funding and financing (OECD, 2023[8]).

As such, there is a risk that the county and local priorities outlined in the county development plans will go unfunded if they cannot be covered by EU funding. This is a particular challenge given that EU funding is: i) linked to EU-level policy priorities, which may not fully cover regional and local development needs; ii) not unlimited and therefore unlikely to cover all county and local priorities; and iii) allocated on a competitive basis, which disadvantages county, city and municipal governments that do not have the necessary financial or administrative capacities to develop quality project proposals (Interreg Europe, n.d.[23]).

A possible solution could include setting up a dedicated territorial development fund at the national level to support the implementation of projects linked to county and local development plans. This would enable the national government to allocate additional funding to county and local priorities that are not covered by EU funding. The prospect of receiving such funding could create an additional incentive for the implementation of county and local development plans and, by extension, better support the achievement of NDS objectives at county and local levels.

Areas for improvement in the local-level strategic planning process

In tandem with the county-level strategic planning challenges highlighted above, there are also a number of elements that hamper the design and implementation of local development plans. For example, interviews have indicated that many local governments have opted not to adopt a local development plan (OECD, 2023[8]). Local development plans are, in fact, optional for cities and municipalities, which, depending on their human and financial resource capacity, can decide to only adopt short-term implementation programmes that link to the county development plans.

A key issue constraining the design and implementation of local development plans is the territorial fragmentation at the local level. Many city and municipal governments are small and have limited financial and/or human resource capacity to carry out tasks requiring specialist expertise, such as strategic planning and budgeting. While local governments may establish local development agencies (LDAs) to help carry out such tasks, only 22 LDAs, which support the activities of fewer than 30 cities and municipalities, have been established to date (Official Gazette of Croatia No 151/2022, 2017[1]; MRDEUF, 2023[24]).

In other cases, RDAs support city and municipal governments in their strategic planning tasks. However, given the significant range of other responsibilities with which RDAs are tasked (e.g. helping county and local governments develop project proposals for EU calls) their ability to support local-level strategic planning activities varies according to their own human resource capacity (OECD, 2023[8]). Based on these elements, the MRDEUF has actively encouraged municipalities with limited human and financial resources to focus on adopting short-term implementation plans (MRDEUF, 2024[6]).

There are, however, important benefits to having a local development plan. Unlike implementation programmes, for instance, development plans need to be supported by inputs from a consultation with local stakeholders and represent in greater detail the local development challenges, and the objectives to be achieved. Often this means that local development plans are likely to more closely reflect community needs and priorities and provide more guidance towards implementation. Given the limited resource capacity of many individual municipalities, Croatia could consider encouraging groups of municipalities to adopt joint local development plans. This would mean that development efforts in more local governments are guided through a robust strategic planning document.

Additional incentives for inter-municipal co-operation could strengthen local strategic planning

Enhancing inter-municipal co-operation is one way to strengthen strategic planning capacity at the local level. Since 2022, Croatia has provided city and municipal governments with a wide range of financial incentives to co-operate across jurisdictions. Existing incentives include securing co-funding grants of up to 75%[3] from the national government when city and/or municipal governments co-operate to jointly perform administrative tasks. Despite these efforts however, the vast majority have yet to establish inter-municipal co-operation agreements (OECD, 2023[25]). The limited uptake of inter-municipal co-operation may in part be due to a lack of understanding by local leaders of the potential benefits for inter-municipal co-operation, as well as fears of losing local influence in their communities (OECD, 2023[25]).

The government is currently developing a set of guidelines and tools that can help to demystify issues related to inter-municipal co-operation. In particular, an IT system is being developed that will help city and municipal governments assess their own capacities and identify areas of potential co-operation with other local governments (OECD, 2023[25]). The data will be collected from the Ministry of Justice and Public Administration's "Optimisation of the System of Local and Regional Self-government" and will provide a comprehensive picture of city and municipal governments' administrative, fiscal and human resource capacities (Croatian Ministry of Justice and Public Administration, n.d.[26]).

Helping local governments map their capacity gaps and identify potential opportunities for increased co-operation with their peers could spark local leaders' interest in adopting inter-municipal co-operation arrangements. Such partnerships could be used to enhance collective strategic planning capacity. For instance, resource-sharing could help to fund the establishment of additional LDAs, which could support strategic planning and implementation activities in neighbouring cities and/or municipalities.

Further to this, the government should consider disseminating information (e.g. through brochures or a dedicated website) about the experience of the few LDAs that were created by more than one local government. For instance, it could present examples of how the LDAs have supported collective strategic planning and quantify how many national and international grants have been mobilised thanks to the support of the LDA. In addition, the government could add to the brochure or website practical information on the other ways in which existing financial incentives for inter-municipal co-operation can support local strategic planning, e.g. setting up a joint strategic planning department.

The government could also introduce additional incentives for inter-municipal co-operation in order to support the design and implementation of joint local development plans. For instance, for local governments with weak fiscal and human resources capacities, access to a particular regional development grant could be made conditional on them developing joint development plans. This approach was adopted for Italy's National Strategy for Inner Areas, which aims to counteract marginalisation and enhance the territorial 'reactivation' of remote municipalities. Only development plans that are designed and adopted by multiple municipalities are able to obtain specific EU and national funding (Italy's Territorial Cohesion Agency, 2020[27]). Another example comes from Poland, which provides additional funding for municipalities of functional areas that prepare a joint strategic plan (OECD, 2021[28]). There are already examples that Croatia could build on. For example, the Primorje-Gorski Kotar RDA helped nine cities and municipalities design a joint local development plan for the 2022-2027 period (Primorje-Gorski Kotar RDA, 2022[29]).

An alternative measure would be to mandate that small local governments meeting certain criteria (e.g. those with fewer than 1 500 inhabitants) must collaborate with neighbouring cities and/or municipalities to develop a joint, local development plan. This would have a number of benefits. First, it would ensure that all Croatian territories would be covered by a development plan, which, as noted above, increases the likelihood that community needs will be more closely met than a short-term implementation programme. Second, pooling human resources through co-operative arrangements would enhance local government capacity for strategic planning by enabling the sharing of skills, expertise and good practices. In turn, this could lead to more sustainable development solutions that are tailored to the collective needs of the communities involved. When considering such measures, however, Croatia should ensure that they help municipalities build their strategic planning capacity to address local needs and priorities, and avoid significantly adding to their planning responsibilities. The latter would risk diverting already scarce human and financial resources away from implementation.

Opportunities to build the strategic planning skills of local governments

Efforts to increase local capacity for strategic planning and implementation will require more than pooling existing resources through increased inter-municipal co-operation. The strategic planning skills and expertise of local civil servants are also necessary. The MRDEUF, as the ministry in charge of ensuring coherent strategic planning across and among levels of government, should consider expanding its current efforts (e.g. through the National Recovery and Resilience Plan 2021-2026) to build the strategic planning capacity of local civil servants (Government of Croatia, 2021[30]). Its actions need to be supported by RDAs, whose mandate to guide county-level development planning and support local governments in areas such as mobilising EU funding leaves them well-positioned to develop the skills and expertise of local civil servants.

Interviews, however, indicated that several RDAs consider they lack the resources—in particular, time—and tools to support strategic planning at the local level (OECD, 2023[8]). In terms of tools and resources, the RDAs identify a need for practical guidelines or manuals on strategic planning to be developed, for the benefit of city and municipal governments. In the absence of clear tools and resources, or learning opportunities such as peer-to-peer knowledge-sharing sessions, local governments often rely on external consultants to support their strategic planning processes. However, the quality of external consultants is not always high, which can result in the development of strategic planning documents of sub-standard quality (OECD, 2023[8]). Moreover, by relying on external consultants, local governments fail to build up institutional planning capacity. When local authorities are too dependent on external support, it can prevent them from accruing the technical skills and experience of local civil servants that are needed to identify and refine poor-quality work by contractors (Wargent, Parker and Street, 2019[31]).

There are several complementary actions that the MRDEUF and RDAs could take to enhance the strategic planning capacity of local governments, as well as that of counties. First, the MRDEUF could assess the capacity building needs of subnational governments by conducting a national-level survey. The objective would be to develop a more robust understanding of the breadth of experience of county and local civil servants responsible for strategic planning, as well as map the challenges they face. The survey could be co-designed by the RDAs. The results of the survey could be complemented by county-level focus group meetings organised by the RDAs, with the objective of further pinpointing local capacity-building needs.

Second, based on the outcomes of the strategic planning capacity assessment, the MRDEUF could develop and lead the implementation of a local government capacity building plan. It would be important, however, to ensure that the timing and thematic focus of different training activities match the specific strategic planning tasks that city and municipal governments are engaged in or will be working on in the short term (e.g. drafting of an implementation programme or review of their local development plan). This could increase the value of participating in the training activities for local civil servants.

Some training sessions could be prepared and delivered by the MRDEUF, for example on the strategic planning, monitoring and evaluation responsibilities of county, city and municipal governments. Other capacity building initiatives might be delivered by the RDAs, local government associations, Croatia's School of Public Administration, or even external experts (OECD, 2023[25]). The training plan could also include peer-to-peer exchanges between Croatian county, city and municipal governments. These would provide an opportunity for civil servants to share good practices and lessons on how to design and implement their development plans, and report on progress.

Third, the MRDEUF, in collaboration with the RDAs, could create a practical guide or manual to help local governments design and implement their local development plan and/or implementation programme. The guide should build on the results of the strategic planning capacity mapping and could include sections on the following topics:

- **The legal and regulatory framework for (local) development planning**, specifying, for example, the planning responsibilities of local governments; how local development plans should align with higher-level planning documents; how they should be linked to local budgets; what local governments can expect from RDAs in terms of support; and what their obligations are to the RDAs in return (e.g. in terms of sharing data).
- **The strategic planning cycle**, highlighting, for example, its main stages (from drafting a diagnostic, to designing the plan, implementing it, and conducting monitoring and evaluation activities) and the specific responsibilities of local governments during each stage.

The guide should also include practical exercises, checklists and templates the local governments can use, for example to identify and engage with relevant stakeholders during the design process and conduct an implementation feasibility assessment. The Local Government Management Guide on Strategic Planning developed by the Office of the New York State Comptroller can serve as an example (Box 4.5).

Box 4.5. Local Government Management Guide on Strategy Planning

In 2003, the Office of the New York State Comptroller published a strategic planning guide for municipal decision makers. Its objective was to familiarise municipal staff with strategic planning, build their understanding of why strategic planning is beneficial, what applying strategic planning entails and which actors should be involved.

The guide consists of two distinct, but complimentary, parts. The first provides a theoretical explanation of strategic planning. The second is a "How-To" guide for municipal officials who have little to no prior experience in strategic planning. It also includes practical forms that municipalities officials can easily fill out, checklists for action and reference material.

Even though the guide was developed over two decades ago, it is still being used. In fact, it was used by the International City/County Management Association to support the design of a 2022 strategic planning manual for managers of small municipalities.

Source: Author's elaboration, based on (Office of the New York State Comptroller, 2003[32]; ICMA, 2022[33]).

To support the development of a strategic planning guide, and help ensure it meets the needs and capacity of local governments, the MRDEUF could set up an *ad hoc* working group consisting of RDAs and representatives from Croatia's three local government associations. This group could provide inputs for the guide, and review sections of the document drafted by the MRDEUF. Several measures can be taken to ensure officials take a broad interest in—and use—the guide. For example, making sure it is concise, easy to use, and written in easy-to-understand language. Furthermore, the MRDEUF and RDAs could organise a series of virtual or in-person meetings to present the guide and explain how the practical exercises and templates should be used.

Fourth, the MRDEUF, together with the RDAs, could also create an online strategic planning toolbox to enable local civil servants to learn at their own pace. This might be a cost-effective way to make resources and training materials easily accessible to county and local governments, and could be particularly beneficial given the limited capacity that MRDEUF and RDA staff have to organise frequent training sessions. In addition, it could provide local civil servants with the flexibility to access materials and resources at a time that is convenient for them. The online toolbox could include a variety of resources, such as the presentations prepared for the training and workshops mentioned earlier, the strategic planning manual, as well as reading material, and easy-to-adapt templates. The Territorial Portal (*Portal Territorial*) developed by the National Planning Department of Colombia could provide an example (Box 4.6).

Box 4.6. Colombia's online territorial portal

The Territorial Portal of Colombia was created by the National Planning Department to help municipalities improve municipal planning, administration and service delivery. The portal functions as a one-stop-shop for:

- Information on municipal planning and budgeting regulations and procedures.
- E-learning packages on topics such as: public investment, spatial planning, financial management, design of local development plans, and monitoring and evaluation. These packages include manuals, training videos, recommendations, examples of good practices, etc.
- Excel and PowerPoint templates that can be filled out by the local governments to help them carry out specific planning tasks. These include, for example, Excel spreadsheets for conducting ex-ante assessments of investment projects, and designing a development plan results framework.
- Contact information of territorial advisors located in different parts of the country.
- Access to all national, regional and municipal development plans.

Source: Author's elaboration, based on (Colombian National Planning Department, 2021[34]).

Finally, even if the MRDEUF and RDAs are able to increase their capacity-building support to local governments in the field of strategic planning, some may continue to contract external consultants, for example to help draft a local development plan or an implementation programme. To help those local governments, the MRDEUF and RDA can develop support material, such as practical guidelines on how to identify and contract well-qualified consultants. The support material, which can be published on the MRDEUF or RDA websites and disseminated through the relevant partnership councils, could include:

- Recommendations on how to define the objectives and scope of work for the external consultant. For example, it could recommend that cities and municipalities refrain from outsourcing the design of the full local development plan, but rather contract a consultant to support the development of specific sections. This would help the local civil servants create a sense of ownership of the plan and build up their strategic planning skills in the drafting process.
- Suggested qualifications, experience, and expertise that local governments should look for when selecting an external consultant.
- A template to help local governments draft terms of reference for external consultants tasked with supporting the development of local strategic planning documents.

Monitoring and evaluation of regional development in Croatia

Monitoring and evaluation are fundamental parts of a well-functioning strategic planning system. Monitoring can help assess progress made towards the implementation of strategic plans and identify potential bottlenecks during their implementation. Meanwhile, evaluation can help understand whether planning objectives have been achieved, what has been their impact and for whom and, consequently, improve learning for future plans. Monitoring and evaluation involve different methodologies, timelines and tools. Moreover, they require specific skill sets. However, they are also complementary practices. This section provides an overview of the monitoring and evaluation system in place to support Croatia's policy cycle, looking in particular at the monitoring and evaluation of subnational plans.

Institutional framework for monitoring and evaluation of regional development policy

Institutionalising monitoring and evaluation is essential to ensure that such activities are conducted on a systematic basis and feed decision-making and strategic planning. There is no uniform approach to the way in which governments have institutionalised monitoring and evaluation for strategic planning, and the specific setup in each country often depends on its overall institutional and legal culture. However, the OECD has identified several common elements that underpin sound institutional frameworks for the monitoring and evaluation of strategic plans, including (OECD, 2020[35]):

- A clear and shared understanding across government of what monitoring and evaluation is comprised of, in terms of different objectives, methods and tools;
- A framework that establishes high-level guidance on when and how monitoring and evaluation should be conducted;
- Specific actors that have an explicit mandate to conduct and/or co-ordinate monitoring and evaluation activities across government.

This section looks at the extent to which these three elements can be found at the county and local levels in Croatia. To reinforce the progress Croatia has made in institutionalising its strategic planning system, additional attention should be paid to performance measurement, and particularly to the attribution and alignment of responsibilities for monitoring and evaluation among levels of government.

Croatia has adopted a clear and shared definition of monitoring and evaluation

Establishing a clear cross-government definition for monitoring and evaluation is important for building a shared understanding of their respective objectives, tools and methods. While monitoring and evaluation pursue complementary objectives, they provide different types of evidence and mobilise different methods (Box 4.7).

Box 4.7. Differences between monitoring and evaluation

Monitoring can be defined as the systematic collection of performance data to assess the progress and achievement of objectives against set targets. It helps to identify and address implementation bottlenecks. As such, it is by nature an ongoing activity, which should be conducted with sufficient regularity so as to allow decision-makers to identify and correct issues related to the implementation of strategic plans. Unlike evaluation, monitoring is driven by regular and frequent data collection. Whereas policy evaluation studies the extent to which the observed outcome can be attributed to the policy intervention, monitoring provides descriptive information and does not offer evidence to analyse and understand cause-and-effect links between a policy initiative and its results.

Policy evaluation, which is defined by the *OECD Recommendation on Public Policy Evaluation* as the structured and objective assessment of the design (ex-ante evaluation), implementation and/or results of an ongoing (mid-term evaluation) or completed public intervention (ex-post evaluation) is more episodic in nature. Its primary purpose is to demonstrate or explain challenges regarding design, implementation challenges and/or results of strategic plans. Thus, while often conflated, monitoring and evaluation have very distinct aims and need to be supported by different tools.

Source: Author's elaboration, based on (OECD, 2021[36]; OECD, 2022[37]).

Croatia's Law on the System of Strategic Planning and Development Management distinguishes monitoring and evaluation as separate activities (Official Gazette of Croatia No 151/2022, 2017[1]). The law defines monitoring as"the process of collecting, analysing and comparing indicators that systematically monitor the success of the implementation of objectives and measures of strategic planning acts." The same law defines evaluation as an"independent comparison and assessment of the clarity and measurability of the established objectives, the adequacy of the selection of indicators for monitoring the achievement of the established objectives, planned costs and the expected and achieved results, outcomes and effects of the implementation of strategic planning acts" (Official Gazette of Croatia No 151/2022, 2017[1]). The above definitions capture the differences between the two practices.

Legislation provides high-level guidance but the monitoring methodology could be further clarified

Establishing clear, high-level guidance is the first step to ensuring that monitoring and evaluation is conducted systematically. It also helps the various actors involved in strategic planning to understand what should be monitored or evaluated, by whom, according to what timeline and for what purpose.

In Croatia, there is a solid legal framework for monitoring and evaluating regional and local planning documents. This helps to ensure that monitoring and evaluation of county- and local-level plans is being systematically conducted. For example, the Law on Regional Development (Official Gazette of Croatia No 147 et al., 2018[7]):

- Establishes monitoring and evaluation as key principles that should support the design and implementation of regional development policy;
- Tasks RDAs with monitoring and evaluating county development plans and implementation programmes;
- Provides guidance on how frequently RDAs should report to the MRDEUF on the implementation of the different planning documents;

- Establishes common rules for the monitoring and evaluation of all planning documents, including county and local development plans and implementation programmes.

Moreover, the law prescribes that county and local development plans should be supported by both monitoring and evaluation activities, while county and local implementation programmes only need to be supported by monitoring (Figure 4.4).

Figure 4.4. Different legal requirements for county and local planning documents in Croatia

	County level		Local level	
	Mid-term: development plans of counties	Short-term: implementation programs of counties	Mid-term (optional): development plans of cities and municipalities	Short-term: Implementation programs of cities and municipalities
Monitoring	✓	✓	✓	✓
Evaluation	✓	x	✓	x

Source: Authors' elaboration based on (OECD, 2023[8]; Official Gazette of Croatia No 151/2022, 2017[1]; Official Gazette of Croatia No 147 et al., 2018[7]).

In addition to the above-mentioned laws, high-level guidance on monitoring and evaluation at the subnational level in Croatia is complemented by secondary legislation (Annex Table 4.A.1). In 2023, the MRDEUF adopted three new ordinances that provide guidance on: i) how to structure the evaluation process for development plans; and iii) how to monitor the development plans (Box 4.8).

Box 4.8. Main ordinances guiding the monitoring and evaluation of development plans

The Ordinance on the Procedures for Monitoring and Reporting clarifies the timeline according to which RDAs and LDAs must prepare the monitoring reports for development plans. With regards to county-level plans, RDAs must submit an annual monitoring report on the implementation of the county development plan on the 31st of March to their county council. They must also submit the annual report to the MRDEUF within eight days of the county government's approval.

The Ordinance on the Implementation of the Procedure for Evaluation sets out rules on how to conduct evaluations of county and local-level plans. County, city and municipal governments must conduct an ex-ante evaluation, a medium-term evaluation and an ex-post evaluation of their respective development plans. The Ordinance indicates that the evaluations should assess the relevance, coherence, efficiency, effectiveness, impact and sustainability of the plans. It also provides guidance on how the evaluation process should be conducted (including the roles of relevant actors involved) and establishes follow-up mechanisms, while also clarifying how county, city and municipal governments should publish evaluation results.

Source: Author's elaboration, based on (Official Gazette of Croatia No 44/2023, 2023[38]; Official Gazette of Croatia No 44/2023, 2023[39]).

Through the above-mentioned documents, the government provides extensive high-level guidance on how the monitoring and evaluation of county- and local-level planning documents should take place. This provides actors (e.g. RDAs) with a clear outline of their monitoring and evaluation-related tasks and responsibilities. One area for potential improvement, however, is the way in which relevant monitoring and evaluation-related guidance has been embedded in various laws and ordinances. This limits the ease with which RDAs and other public bodies with monitoring and evaluation responsibilities are able to access relevant information. In order to address this issue, the MRDEUF could develop a single set of non-binding methodological guidelines to recap the legislative provisions in simple, action-oriented language. This same approach has been adopted in a number of OECD Member countries. For example, in the United Kingdom methodological guidelines play a role in clarifying monitoring and evaluation for all relevant actors across government, with several non-binding guidelines being used systematically. These include the following documents (HM Treasury, 2022[40]):

- **The Green Book**, which provides guidance on the appraisal and evaluation of policies, programmes and projects. It also provides guidance on the design and use of monitoring and evaluation before, during and after implementation.
- **The Magenta Book**, which offers guidance on evaluation methods. In particular, it provides material on the evolving approaches and methods used in evaluation, and emphasises the value of evaluation in providing evidence for the design, implementation and review stages of the public policy cycle.
- **The Aqua Book**, which focuses on the development of transparent, objective, evidence-based appraisal, evaluation and design of proposals, in order to inform public decision making.

Responsibilities for monitoring and evaluation across government are clearly defined in law, but may not always be fit-for-purpose

Clarifying roles and responsibilities for monitoring and evaluation is essential for ensuring effective co-ordination and communication among the different actors involved. Ensuring such clarity is particularly important in a regional development context, given that several national, county- and local-level actors may be involved in supporting such activities (Table 4.1). In Croatia, mandates for conducting monitoring and evaluation are clearly defined. Legislation establishes that the MRDEUF is responsible for monitoring the implementation of regional development policy at the national level, while at the county and local levels, such activities fall under the purview of RDAs and LDAs. Moreover, county, city and municipal governments are responsible for sharing data on the implementation of development plans with RDAs and LDAs (Official Gazette of Croatia No 151/2022, 2017[1]; Official Gazette of Croatia No 147 et al., 2018[7]).

Table 4.1. Institutions involved in the monitoring and evaluation of county plans and their responsibilities

Institution	Responsibilities for monitoring	Responsibilities for evaluation
MRDEUF	• Maintains Library of Indicators. • Monitors the status of implementation of the development plans, through the annual reports.	• Participates in the evaluation committee.
RDAs and LDAs	• Monitor and report on the implementation of regional and local plans. • Produce the annual monitoring reports.	• Develop an evaluation plan.
County and local governments	• Share data with RDAs and LDAs to support the preparation of annual monitoring reports. • Approve the monitoring reports.	• Initiate the evaluation process. • Approve an evaluation plan. • Appoint an evaluation team. • Establish an evaluation committee.

Source: Author's elaboration, based on (Official Gazette of Croatia No 151/2022, 2017[1]; Official Gazette of Croatia No 147 et al., 2018[7]).

The mandate for conducting evaluations, however, is not defined ex-ante. While the MRDEUF is mandated to set out common principles, criteria and standards for the evaluation procedures, the actors responsible for actually conducting the evaluations are not defined in law. Rather, the relevant legislation merely states that evaluations should be carried out by an evaluation team of internal or external experts who are "functionally independent" of the actors responsible for the design and implementation of planning documents. The evaluation team submits its evaluation reviews (be they ex-ante, mid-term or ex-post evaluations) to a temporary body called an evaluation committee, which is comprised of representatives from the MRDEUF, the RDA and other relevant stakeholders in charge of implementing the county, city or municipal development plan (Official Gazette of Croatia No 44/2023, 2023[39]; OECD, 2023[25]). The evaluation committee provides an opportunity for the MRDEUF to review challenges related to the implementation of development plans and issue recommendations to address them.

Other important actors involved in supporting the evaluation process include RDAs and LDAs, who are responsible for developing an evaluation plan (i.e. a timeline of evaluation reviews that need to be conducted in any given year). Finally, county, city and municipal governments are responsible for approving the evaluation plan, as well as appointing the evaluation team and the evaluation committee (Official Gazette of Croatia No 44/2023, 2023[39]).

While monitoring and evaluation responsibilities across government are clearly defined, there are opportunities to refine them. For example, RDAs are responsible for monitoring the implementation of county development plans but rely on data from county departments, cities and municipalities that are often delivered too late. This leaves them with limited time to process the information before having to submit a monitoring report to the county government and the MRDEUF (OECD, 2023[41]; OECD, 2023[8]). In order to improve the quality of reporting on the implementation of regional development policy, reporting timelines should be adjusted. In particular, county departments, city and municipal governments should be required to share data earlier than currently. This would provide RDAs with sufficient time to process local-level data and make requests for clarification or additional information before the monitoring reports must be submitted to the MRDEUF.

Quality of regional development monitoring and evaluation

While a clear assignment of tasks and responsibilities is a necessary pre-condition for ensuring that monitoring and evaluation takes place on a systematic basis, it does not, in and of itself, guarantee that the data and evidence being produced for monitoring and evaluation activities are of good quality. Yet, the quality of monitoring and evaluation is essential for ensuring that results can lead to policy learning, support improvements in the implementation of plans and be used by decision-makers with confidence. To be credible, monitoring and evaluation must be: i) technically and methodologically sound; and ii) well-governed. The first aspect can be ensured through sound data collection, rigorous methods and adequate resources (e.g. skills in monitoring and evaluation). At the same time, ensuring technical quality is not enough and it is important to make sure that monitoring and evaluation are well-governed, meaning that they are conducted in a way that can ensure both its independence and impact in decision making processes.

In Croatia, the quality of monitoring reports and evaluations is inconsistent at county and local levels. RDAs noted several challenges that constrain effective monitoring and evaluation of county development plans. These include limited technical infrastructure to support monitoring and evaluation activities (i.e. relevant IT tools), limited reliability and/or lack of relevant data, and a lack of mechanisms enabling the use of monitoring and evaluation results to adjust programming (Figure 4.5). Conversely, no RDAs indicated that a lack of clear guidelines is a key challenge to monitoring and evaluating the county development plans (OECD, 2023[8]). This may reflect the MRDEUF's efforts to create the wide range of ordinances, guidelines and instructions on monitoring and evaluation for national- and subnational-level policy makers.

Figure 4.5. Main challenges in monitoring and evaluating county development plans

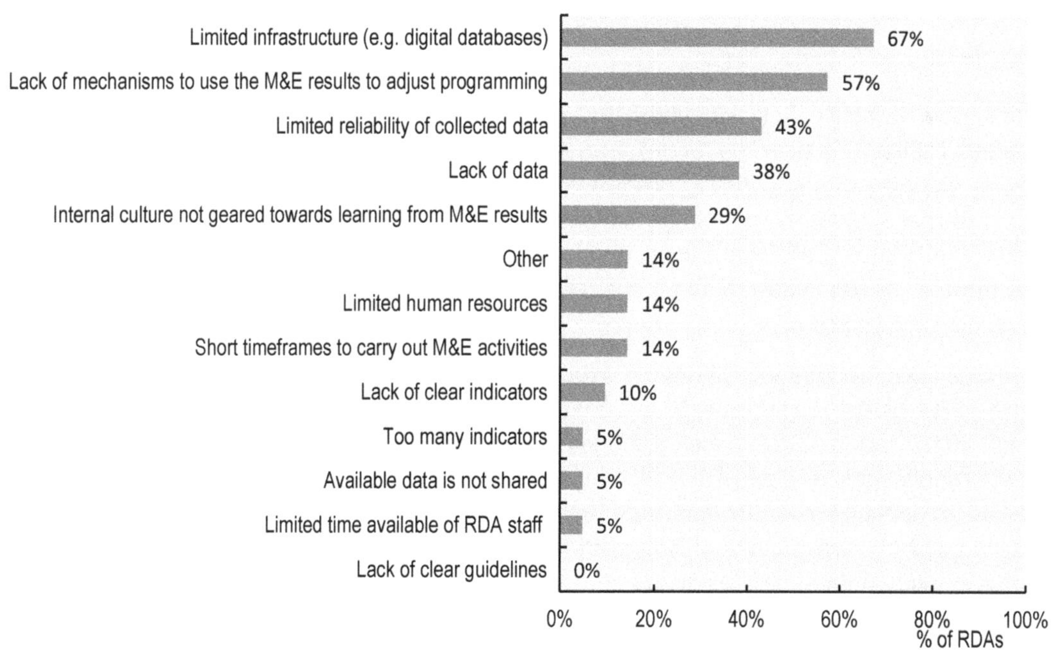

Note: Questionnaire question: What does your RDA consider to be the three main challenges to monitoring and evaluating your county's regional development plan? Full response options: Lack of clear guidelines; Limited time available of RDA staff; Available data is not shared (e.g. by the national government or local governments); Too many indicators (making monitoring and evaluation overly complex and/or time-consuming) Lack of clear indicators; Short timeframes to carry out monitoring and evaluation activities (including reporting); Limited human resources (including expertise); Internal culture not geared towards learning from monitoring and evaluation results; Lack of data; Limited reliability of collected data; Lack of mechanisms to use the monitoring and evaluation results to adjust programming; Limited infrastructure (e.g. digital databases, data analysis software); Other. N=21.
Source: Author's elaboration, based on (OECD, 2022[14]).

Ensuring that good-quality monitoring and evaluation can take place at all levels of government depends on having access to appropriate tools and data, and being equipped with appropriate skills. It also depends on clear methodological guidelines and quality control mechanisms being in place to support relevant actors in their monitoring and evaluation tasks. This section evaluates the extent to which the above-mentioned elements are in place at the county and local levels in Croatia.

Developing quality assurance and control mechanisms could improve the technical standard of evaluation reports

To be robust and trustworthy, and generate learnings that can improve the implementation of development plans, policy evaluations need to be both independent (i.e. free from undue political pressure or organisational influence) and methodologically sound (i.e. properly designed, using sound data collection practices and rigorous analytical methods).

A number of mechanisms can be adopted to support these objectives. These include quality assurance mechanisms, which seek to ensure credibility in the way in which the evaluation is conducted (i.e. the process). They can also include quality control mechanisms that focus on ensuring that the end product (i.e. the report) meets quality standards (OECD, 2020[35]). Across OECD Member countries, the most commonly used quality assurance mechanism is methodological guidelines (Box 4.9). Examples of quality control mechanisms are less common in OECD Member countries, but can include formal or informal peer reviews of the quality of evaluation products (e.g. in Portugal or Germany) (OECD, 2020[35]). Deploying a mix of quality assurance and quality control mechanisms may provide the best opportunity for policy makers to enhance the quality of their policy evaluations.

Box 4.9. The New South Wales Government's Evaluation Toolkit and the Better Evaluation website

In order to support quality policy evaluation, the Government of New South Wales, Australia, developed an Evaluation Toolkit. The toolkit is an online resource that provides government agencies with advice and tools for planning and conducting programme evaluations. It supports evaluation managers, and internal or external evaluators to manage an evaluation project, choose the appropriate methods, use them well, and meet the quality standards set out in associated guidelines. The toolkit provides concrete guidance through seven steps to ensure evaluation quality in terms of technical rigour, practical feasibility, utility and ethics.

A key resource that complements the toolkit is the Better Evaluation Website, through which actors from across the globe continuously provide information and guidance on evaluation. This platform was launched in 2012, and, in 2022, became the knowledge platform of the Global Evaluation Initiative, a coalition of organisations and experts working on monitoring and evaluation from various perspectives. More than 300 evaluation methods, tools and resources are currently accessible, on topics ranging from what data should be evaluated and how they should be synthesised, to how to conduct effective evaluation reporting and use the results to support improvements in the strategic planning cycle.

Source: Author's elaboration, based on (New South Wales Government, 2023[42]; BetterEvaluation, 2024[43]).

The Ordinance on the Implementation of the Procedure for Evaluation introduces a number of quality assurance provisions that aim to strengthen the independence and good governance of the evaluation process. For instance, as discussed above, it mandates that evaluation teams in county, city and municipal governments, which are responsible for evaluating county and local development plans, must be independent of those involved in the drafting process (Official Gazette of Croatia No 44/2023, 2023[39]). In principle, this prevents county and local-level officials from ‘marking their own homework’, thereby avoiding potential conflicts of interests. Interviews with local stakeholders indicated that, in practice, RDAs and LDAs often outsource their evaluations to external evaluators due to limited internal capacities (OECD, 2023[8]).

Moreover, in support of good governance, the Ordinance mandates the creation of an evaluation committee comprised not only of the MRDEUF, and RDAs or LDAs, but also other local public and non-governmental actors involved in supporting implementation. The committee’s composition can help increase the attention that different levels of government pay to the implementation of county and local development plans, including expected and achieved results. It also provides a forum where possible solutions to implementation challenges can be discussed by relevant actors.

Notwithstanding these elements, the methodological quality of evaluations in Croatia has varied. For instance, in some cases when evaluations were outsourced, limited flexibility in the selection of the external evaluators and value for money considerations have led to lower quality proposals (OECD, 2023[8]).

To promote evaluation quality, some counties have developed quality criteria, and included them in the Terms of References prepared for external evaluations. For example, in a tender to outsource the ex-ante evaluation of their draft county development plan, the Osijek-Baranja County indicated that interested evaluators need to possess specific skills and expertise (e.g. past experience in evaluating strategic plans, analytical and presentation skills) (OECD, 2023[8]).

Nevertheless, Croatian RDAs and LDAs could further strengthen the quality of evaluation reports by putting additional quality assurance and control mechanisms in place. One way to do so would be by establishing a network of evaluators across RDAs and LDAs to facilitate sharing good practices and providing an informal peer review of evaluation reports. Indeed, while RDAs and LDAs often do not perform evaluations themselves, they do play an important role in defining the scope of evaluations and assessing the quality of the end product. For this reason, sharing their experience in commissioning evaluations and managing evaluation teams could be beneficial for identifying potential obstacles and promoting the diffusion of good practices. In addition, a network of evaluators could offer opportunities for RDA staff to serve as informal peer reviewers for evaluations that are conducted by other RDAs.

A lack of access to, or awareness of, timely and granular data in Croatia constrains monitoring effectiveness

Ensuring access to high-quality and timely data is essential during the design stage of development plans, in order to ensure the latter adequately reflect local needs, priorities and capacities. High-quality and timely data are also critical for producing a results-based monitoring and evaluation system. Depending on the type of analysis being performed, different data sources (e.g. survey data, administrative data) or types of data (e.g. microdata, statistical data) may be needed.

The limited availability of subnational data is considered to be one of the most significant challenges to producing good-quality monitoring reports on Croatia’s county and local development plans and implementation programmes. RDA’s reported that the increased availability of economic, innovation and investment data in particular could help them improve evidence-based decision making (OECD, 2023[8]) (Figure 4.6).

Figure 4.6. Data needs, as reported by RDAs

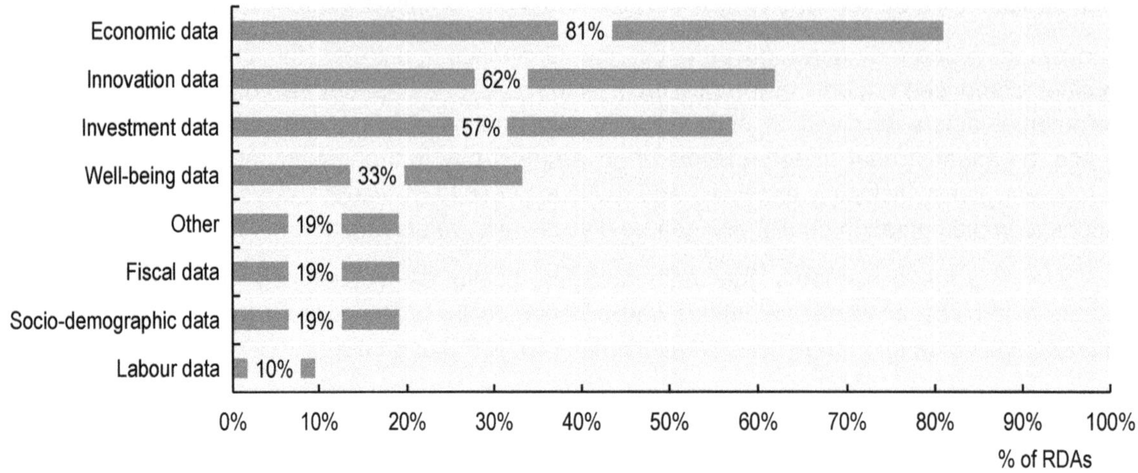

Note: Questionnaire question: Question: What type of territorially disaggregated data (data by region and/or local government) could help your RDA improve evidence-based decision making? Please select 3 options from the following list: Labour data (e.g. on productivity, (un)employment); Socio-demographic data (e.g. on population by age groups, migration); Fiscal data (e.g. expenditure, investment, revenue of counties and local governments); Well-being data (e.g. on education, healthcare outcomes, crime); Investment data (e.g. foreign direct investment at the subnational level); Innovation data (e.g. on patent applications, research and development expenditure in the business and public sectors); Economic data (e.g. on regional GDP, competitiveness); Other data. N=21.
Source: Author's elaboration, based on (OECD, 2022[14]).

The high demand for economic data may reflect a desire among RDAs to more closely track the effects of development initiatives on the local economy (e.g. on job creation). The demand for additional data on innovation may be explained by RDA efforts to foster regional competitiveness, and, in several counties, to advance work on industrial transition. Finally, obtaining increasingly-granular investment data can be essential for understanding the inflows of capital and their subsequent effects on regional and local development.

The scarcity of such data at the subnational level (in particular at the NUTS 3 level), poses a challenge for RDAs seeking to conduct thorough and accurate monitoring and evaluation exercises. Without timely and granular data, RDAs may struggle to pinpoint areas of progress or concern, potentially leading to an inefficient allocation of resources and delayed policy adjustments. Furthermore, as stated, the lack of granular data hinders the ability of policy makers to tailor development strategies to the unique needs and opportunities of specific regions.

To increase the evidence available to decision-makers involved in the design, monitoring and evaluation of county and local development plans, Croatia should invest in territorially-disaggregated data. Currently, subnational governments are not systematically consulted by Croatia's Bureau of Statistics on how to bridge local data gaps. For example, counties are not involved in supporting the annual planning of Croatia's statistical programme and only four out of 21 counties have local branches of the Croatian Bureau of Statistics. This runs counter to the experience in several OECD Member countries (e.g. Canada and the Netherlands), where the local government associations and national statistics institutes often strike strategic partnerships to increase the production and dissemination of local data (Federation of Canadian Municipalities, 2022[44]; Association of Dutch Municipalities, 2021[45])

Conducting surveys is one of the few ways in which counties, cities and municipalities are able to obtain additional data. However, skills and resources for data collection and analysis are limited at the subnational level (OECD, 2023[8]). In order to address this challenge, the MRDEUF should consider organising regular discussions between the network of RDAs and subnational government associations on the one hand, and the Croatian Bureau of Statistics on the other, in order to identify: i) subnational data needs; and ii) how additional data can be collected, analysed and disseminated.

The challenges experienced by subnational governments in terms of data availability cannot, however, be fully explained by the lack of local data being produced. They are also related to limited awareness among county and local governments regarding existing datasets. Interviews with local stakeholders have indicated that RDAs, LDAs and local governments are often unaware of existing local-level datasets, or where such data might be accessed (OECD, 2023[8]).

There are a number of options that the national government could consider to address this data issue. For instance, the above-mentioned meetings with the MRDEUF, Croatian Bureau of Statistics, network of RDAs and local government associations could also be used to perform a data-mapping exercise, in order to apprise subnational governments of relevant data and where such data might be accessed. In turn, RDAs could share such information during their meetings with local governments.

An alternative, or complementary approach could be for the Croatian Bureau of Statistics to launch a newsletter that provides periodic updates on data that are relevant for county, city and municipal governments, as well as training opportunities on how such data can be used by policy makers. This has been adopted in the Netherlands, where the Central Bureau of Statistics provides users with the chance to sign up for a series of free email subscriptions, which provide regular updates on the availability of key data (CBS Netherlands, n.d.[46]). An additional option would be for the Croatian Bureau of Statistics, the MRDEUF and RDAs to collaborate in the development of a publicly accessible portal to improve evidence-based decision making by local public officials. The Data Analysis Portal of the United Nations Development Programme (UNDP) in Mexico can provide some guidance on the components a publicly accessible portal could include (Box 4.10). Policy measures such as these can contribute to Croatia's efforts to strengthen its mechanisms for monitoring and evaluating regional development policy and plans, which is explored in more detail in the next section.

Box 4.10. Data Analysis Portal in Mexico

In order to improve evidence-informed decision making by public officials at the national, state and municipal levels, UNDP Mexico created the Data Analysis Portal (*Plataforma de Analysis de Datos*). It has three main components:

1. A databank that contains regional- and local-level data on over 600 indicators that are gathered by the National Institute of Statistics and Geography. The databank enables users to browse different datasets, generate charts and tables and make comparisons.
2. A databank with relevant analytical reports, development strategies and plans.
3. An application that enables users to download very concise information sheets for municipal government. The sheets present up-to-date information on a wide range of indicators (e.g. health, governance, education, crime) and compare municipalities' performance with that of the regional and national averages.

Source: Author's elaboration, based on (UNDP Mexico, 2023[47]).

Improving the quality of indicators can help policy makers track progress in meeting regional development objectives

Beyond the availability of timely, in-depth and high-quality data, effective monitoring also relies on a set of selected indicators that provide information on the state of implementation of development plans, programmes and projects. To be informative, indicators need to be well linked to the objectives of the strategic planning documents, and data need to be collected regularly enough to support the different monitoring goals (i.e. accountability, decision making and communication). In this regard, 71% of surveyed RDAs indicated that one of their greatest administrative capacity-related challenges was how to formulate effective performance indicators (OECD, 2022[18]). Different county development plans reviewed by the OECD also point to gaps in this area (Bjelovar-Bilogora County, 2022[15]; Osijek-Baranja County, 2022[17]).

In Croatia, the MRDEUF has developed guidelines to ensure that RDAs select suitable indicators to monitor development plans. The MRDEUF also set up a Library of Indicators, which serves as an exhaustive list from which RDAs can pick indicators to monitor regional and local development efforts (Official Gazette of Croatia No 151/2022, 2017[1]). Yet, some of the performance indicators developed for county development plans are insufficient to holistically monitor whether strategic objectives are being achieved. For instance, in the Bjelovar-Bilogora county development plan, one of the objectives is "demographic development of the county" for which measures are outlined to: i) support higher fertility rates, and ii) curb the emigration of young people (Bjelovar-Bilogora County, 2022[15]). At the same time, only one higher-level outcome indicator has been developed to track progress towards the objective "number of live births, by county". Given that the indicator does not take the emigration element into account, it provides an incomplete picture of progress towards the objective. In order to address this issue, policy makers should ensure that proposed implementation measures are systematically linked to performance indicators, with initial and target values.

The use of indicators such as these may be the result of the Library of Indicators containing several outcome and impact indicators, for which the underlying data are either not systematically collected at regional or local levels, or are not collected frequently enough to support the preparation of annual monitoring reports. A failure to address challenges linked to indicator quality risks RDAs producing monitoring reports that may not accurately or comprehensively reflect the progress made on meeting county or local development goals. This in turn, could lead to misguided policy adjustments and resource allocation. Additionally, reliance on incomplete or mismatched indicators can undermine the credibility of the monitoring process and diminishing stakeholder trust in the effectiveness of the development efforts. While RDAs can propose additional indicators for the Library, many consider it to be a complex process (OECD, 2023[8]). To help address this, the MRDEUF has developed a guide for the Library of Indicators, which also provides some instructions on how to submit new indicators to the library (MRDEUF, n.d.[48]).

In order to improve the quality of the indicators used in the county and local development plans, the MRDEUF may wish to update the Library of Indicators. However, such an effort should be the result of a close collaboration with the RDAs and the Croatian Bureau of Statistics. Such a partnership could help to ensure that the indicators chosen are both relevant and can be measured at regular intervals (i.e. that data are available to assess performance). Similar collaborative approaches to the definition of indicators for regional development have been adopted in several OECD Member countries (Box 4.11).

Box 4.11 Selecting indicators for regional development: using a participatory approach

The development of a robust set of indicators is a critical step to monitoring and evaluating regional development policy. Often however, a top-down approach is used. While a top-down definition of indicators (e.g. the MRDEUF in the case of Croatia) can help to ensure that indicators meet certain quality standards (commonly the R.A.C.E.R. criteria[4]) and maintain comparability across regions, it often lacks the flexibility required to adapt to specific regional contexts. To avoid this problem, a participatory approach to defining indicators involving both national and subnational stakeholders can be used to enhance their relevance and applicability. This collaborative method has been employed in the United Kingdom, Canada, Italy, and Austria to align indicators more closely with regional realities.

For instance, Austria's approach to selecting indicators for the 2007-2013 planning period involved a working group of both regional and national actors, who collectively chose 15 key indicators. In a similar exercise, Italy placed considerable emphasis on regional input to ensure the chosen indicators were backed by data that were actually accessible at the regional level. Such participatory approaches not only enhance the appropriateness of indicators for regional contexts, they also foster a sense of ownership among regional stakeholders, thereby enhancing the overall effectiveness of regional planning and development.

Source: Author's elaboration, based on (OECD, 2009[49]).

The impact of monitoring and evaluation evidence on regional development policy making

Monitoring and evaluation activities are not valuable unless their results are used to inform current and future strategic plans and their implementation. Indeed, without monitoring and evaluation results being used to inform the policy cycle, gaps will remain between what policy makers aim to achieve and real-world policy outcomes. However, just because monitoring and evaluation activities take place does not guarantee that their findings will be applied. The effective use of monitoring and evaluation results is multifaceted, and can be influenced by factors such as the governance system, institutional culture, and external demand (e.g. of non-governmental actors) for evidence-informed decision making. To enhance the impact of monitoring and evaluation, it is essential for governments to integrate their findings into the regional policy-making cycle, including strategy formulation and resource allocation. Moreover, clearly communicating monitoring and evaluation results can ensure that they guide regional development initiatives and stakeholder engagement effectively.

In Croatia, 57% of RDAs cited the use of monitoring and evaluation results to adjust planning and programming as the second most important hurdle they face related to effective monitoring and evaluation (OECD, 2023[8]) (Figure 4.5). Nevertheless, some interesting follow-up mechanisms already exist at the local level. This section explores the extent to which these mechanisms are effective, and suggests ways to increase the impact of monitoring and evaluation results and ultimately their use.

Creating feedback loops through decision-making processes

Effective monitoring and evaluation is particularly important for helping county and local governments identify whether their actions are leading to desired results, or whether programming changes may be necessary. Monitoring and evaluation evidence can be used to pursue three main objectives:

- **It contributes to operational decision making**, by providing evidence to help measure performance and identify implementation delays or bottlenecks;

- **It can strengthen accountability** related to the use of resources, the efficiency of internal management processes, or the outputs of a given policy initiative;
- **It contributes to transparency**, providing citizens and stakeholders with information on whether the efforts carried out by the government are producing the expected results.

Each of these goals are supported to varying degrees through Croatia's strategic planning, monitoring and evaluation system (Official Gazette of Croatia No 44/2023, 2023[38]). For example, RDAs and local governments are mandated to provide a formal response to the recommendations set out in ex-ante evaluations and provide an assessment of the degree to which they are able to implement these recommendations (Official Gazette of Croatia No 44/2023, 2023[39]). This is, therefore, an important instrument to ensure the use of evaluations and their impact on strategic planning.

Interviews with local stakeholders, however, also indicate that while subnational actors (e.g. RDAs) seek to comply with the formally established reporting guidelines and periods, the impact of the monitoring and evaluation reports produced is limited. For example, some stakeholders highlighted the difficulty in using evaluation results, as they are often finalised after the development of the next cycle of plans (OECD, 2023[8]). As a consequence, the evaluation reports mainly serve as an accountability tool rather than as one that can inform and improve the design of the next generation of strategic planning documents.

In a similar vein, the monitoring reports prepared by the RDAs and LDAs are primarily seen as accountability tools. While the system in place for preparing monitoring reports are well-defined, the monitoring information itself offers limited value to counties and local governments. This limitation arises because the methodology primarily focuses on reporting the monitoring information upwards. In fact, monitoring reports prepared by RDAs and submitted to the MRDEUF are rarely discussed by both actors (OECD, 2023[8]). This suggests that reporting is typically viewed as a procedural requirement rather than a substantive exercise that can help to improve the implementation of county and local development plans, including their contribution to the NDS.

For monitoring and evaluation evidence to serve as a management tool (i.e. for operational purposes), it must be embedded in a performance dialogue that is conducted regularly and frequently. This approach enables practitioners and decision makers to identify implementation issues in a timely manner, determine resource constraints, and adapt their efforts and resources in order to resolve such issues. Such an exercise should be closely tied to the implementation of plans. In the case of Croatia, a performance dialogue should be conducted within the county, city or municipal government, ideally between the highest level of the executive (e.g. the prefect or mayor) and the team involved in strategic planning. Moreover, such performance dialogues should take place at regular intervals (e.g. quarterly). The results of the performance dialogues could also be presented and discussed in the partnership council meetings.

To ensure that the monitoring and evaluating activities implemented at the county and local levels help policy makers to adjust and improve programming, several additional actions can be taken. For example, the MRDEUF could develop guidelines to suggest how performance dialogues should be organised and which actors should participate at the relevant levels (e.g. prefects, heads of county departments and the RDAs at the county level, and the MRDEUF). Moreover, the MRDEUF may wish to organise annual meetings with the RDAs to exchange on the implementation progress and challenges they have identified at the county and local government levels. Such performance dialogues could enable the MRDEUF to identify measures to address implementation challenges identified by the RDAs. As inviting 21 RDAs to participate in an annual performance dialogue meeting with the Ministry may limit the depth of the exchange, the MRDEUF could consider organising one meeting per NUTS 2 region. This would enable the Ministry to also determine whether region-specific implementation challenges have arisen.

In addition, Croatia could also reconsider the role of RDAs as the public body in charge of monitoring the implementation of the county development plans. Ideally, monitoring should be conducted by actors that have decision making power over implementation, as they can directly use the monitoring evidence to adjust and improve policy action. Following this logic, the responsibility for monitoring could be shifted towards other parts of the county administration (e.g. specific county departments). Such a change could have multiple benefits. First, it could enhance the awareness in the county administration of its responsibility for supporting the implementation of the county development plan. Second, it could help build ownership of the county development plans and their results at the county leadership level. Third, it could improve the impact of the monitoring evidence on policy outcomes, as county leadership could directly incorporate the monitoring results to adjust programming. For example, monitoring results could prompt the county leadership to modify the allocation of county resources aimed at regional and local development projects.

Communication of monitoring and evaluation results can be improved through the creation of a web searchable platform

Greater public awareness of monitoring and evaluation results can increase the pressure on decision-makers to support implementation and create the conditions for a more systematic follow-up of evaluation recommendations, while providing accountability to citizens concerning the impact of public policies and the use of public funds. Currently, RDAs are mandated to share monitoring and evaluation reports on county websites (Official Gazette of Croatia No 44/2023, 2023[38]; Official Gazette of Croatia No 44/2023, 2023[39]). However, not only are monitoring and evaluation reports difficult to find on such websites, they are also not presented in a format that is easy to read or understand. Several opportunities therefore exist to increase the visibility of monitoring and evaluation results.

First, the evaluations could benefit from having an executive summary, drafted in easy-to-understand language. This could make the evaluation findings more accessible for decision makers and non-government officials alike. Second, the MRDEUF should consider creating a dedicated online portal where relevant information on regional development, including monitoring and evaluation reports, could be published. The platform, which could be used to publish links to relevant laws, ordinances, and other material related to regional development, could also include interactive dashboards and maps. These represent interesting tools to engage with a larger public and increase their awareness of Croatia's regional development policy, its results and how it can benefit citizens. In this regard, Croatia could build on experiences from national and subnational governments across OECD Member countries. For example, in France, the Barometer on Public Action enables citizens to gain a quick view of their department's results on a set of key performance indicators (Box 4.12).

Box 4.12. Making performance information visually friendly: France

The French Barometer on Public Action (*Baromètre des Résultats de l'Action Publique)* is a good example of effectively communicating performance results. The Barometer was developed in 2021 by the Ministry of Transformation and the Civil Service, with the support of the Inter-ministerial Directorate for Public Transformation and the Government Information Service. The Barometer keeps track of the progress of priority projects at the national, regional and departmental levels through interactive maps and advanced filters. For example, Figure 4.7 shows the share of classrooms in different regions that contain fewer than 24 students, which is a target set by the government.

Figure 4.7. France performance information communication

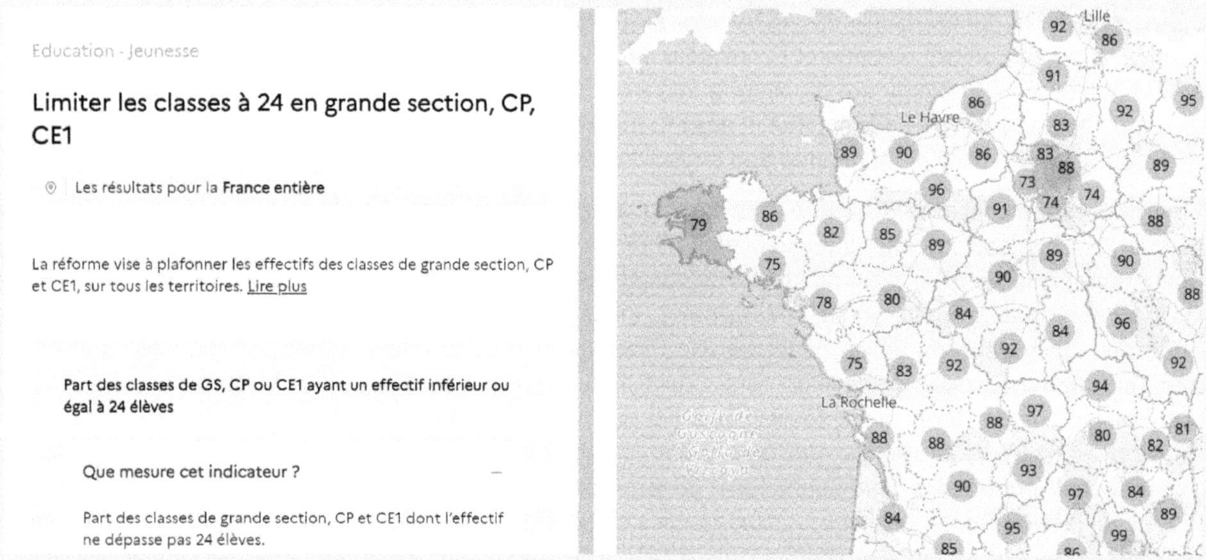

Source: Author's elaboration, based on (French Ministry of Transformation and the Civil Service, n.d.[50]).

Other examples come from Scotland and Mexico. For example, Scotland set up the National Performance Framework to communicate the country's high-level development goals (Government of Scotland, n.d.[51]). The National Performance Framework was created in 2007 to communicate the country's high-level development goals. The Framework and its online portal were designed to help citizens and other stakeholders track Scotland's progress across 11 priority dimensions (e.g. economy, poverty, health, education). Each dimension is associated with a vision statement, linked to the Sustainable Development Goals (SDGs), as well as 80+ indicators that citizens can consult to see progress over time (Government of Scotland, n.d.[51]).

Several elements contribute to the success of the National Performance Framework and its online platform as tools to communicate Scotland's progress towards development targets. For example, the framework enjoys high-level support from all political parties. This has been facilitated by the fact that it does not present the policy objectives of a single party or administration, but rather a set of long-term goals. Furthermore, the front-end of the portal is very simple, which means that users do not require advanced technical skills or knowledge of programming languages to use the platform. However, the portal also includes features for those users who have an interest in conducting more complex data analysis.

Another good practice includes the platform of the 2030 Strategic Plan of the Government of the State of Nuevo León, Mexico, which presents information on its long-term objectives, as well as the State's progress in meeting the goals of the plan. An interesting element of this platform is that two goals were defined per indicator, one optimistic and one conservative (OECD, 2021[52]; Nuevo León Council, 2021[53]).

Generating a similar publicly accessible performance monitoring platform may help Croatia's national government, as well as subnational authorities, communicate both internally and externally their progress towards reaching territorial development objectives. At the same time, it could enrich the public debate on the effectiveness of regional development policy, and how such policy affects, for example, local economic development, job creation and citizen well-being. However, keeping such platforms up to date over time requires continued effort on the part of the involved government institutions and may imply substantial investment in terms of staff time and technical infrastructure.

Conclusion

Over the past five years, Croatia has made important steps in putting into practice the legislative and regulatory framework for regional development described in chapter 2. For example, it adopted the NDS, which includes balanced regional development as one of the country's core strategic objectives. Moreover, county, city and municipal governments enacted new development plans and implementation programmes that are aligned with the NDS. The national government has also provided comprehensive regulations and guidelines related to the design of strategic planning acts, as well as their monitoring and evaluation. Furthermore, building on support material provided by the MRDEUF, extensive consultation with different governmental and non-governmental stakeholders has become a regular feature of strategic planning at all levels of government. Similarly, monitoring and evaluation processes have been clearly defined and embedded across the strategic planning system.

Despite these strengths, a number of challenges need to be addressed to ensure progress in meeting Croatia's regional development objectives. For example, Croatia should ensure that balanced regional development is adequately embedded as a cross-governmental priority across national-level public institutions. This can help foster a more unified approach to regional development, ensuring that different ministries and other national-level bodies understand how their actions impact regional and local development and how they can allocate resources more effectively to support these initiatives.

Furthermore, Croatia should address the planning gap between the high-level NDS and county and local development plans, for example by adopting a national-level regional development strategy, as prescribed in law. Such a planning document could provide national and subnational level policy makers with further guidance on Croatia's strategic priorities for regional development and how they could contribute to them. Moreover, there may be a need to expand the functional and financial incentives for county and local governments to support the implementation of their development plans. This should be coupled with efforts to ensure baseline capacities for strategic planning (including design, implementation, monitoring and evaluation) exist at the county, city and municipal levels.

The lack of territorially-disaggregated data and limited awareness of existing datasets by subnational governments are additional factors that hinder strategic planning at the subnational level. This has a marked impact on the monitoring and evaluation of county and local development plans. Challenges associated with local data are compounded by the limited quality and relevance of some of the indicators used to measure county and local development. Finally, the absence of performance dialogue mechanisms—for example between the MRDEUF and RDAs—risks monitoring serving mainly for upward accountability, rather than as a tool to inform and improve policy implementation.

The analysis presented in this chapter sets the stage for chapter 4's assessment of how Croatia's regional development policy has been funded and financed over the past decade. Building on the assessment of the strengths and capacity challenges faced by subnational governments in terms of policy implementation, the next chapter will, among other elements, explore how the funding for RDAs and concrete regional and local development initiatives can be put on a more solid footing.

References

Association of Dutch Municipalities (2021), *Agenda Special General Assembly VNG [AGENDA Buitengewone Algemene Ledenvergadering VNG]*, https://vng.nl/sites/default/files/2021-01/complete-vergaderset-alv-12-februari-2021.pdf (accessed on 27 February 2024). [45]

BetterEvaluation (2024), *About BetterEvaluaiton*, https://www.betterevaluation.org/about. [43]

Bjelovar-Bilogora County (2022), *Plan Razvoja Bjelovarsko-Bilogorske Zupanije [Bjelovar-Bilogora County Development Plan 2022-2027]*, https://jurabbz.hr/plan-razvoja-bjelovarsko-bilogorske-zupanije/ (accessed on 9 November 2023). [15]

CBS Netherlands (n.d.), *Available subscriptions*, https://www.cbs.nl/en-gb/subscriptions (accessed on 17 November 2023). [46]

Colombian National Planning Department (2021), *Portal Territorial de Colombia [Territorial Portal of Colombia]*, https://portalterritorial.dnp.gov.co/ (accessed on 21 August 2021). [34]

Croatian Ministry of Justice and Public Administration (n.d.), *Optimisation of the local and regional self-government system*, https://mpu.gov.hr/highlights/projects/eu-projects/optimisation-of-the-local-and-regional-self-government-system/25413 (accessed on 23 August 2023). [26]

Federation of Canadian Municipalities (2022), *Statistics Canada and the Federation of Canadian Municipalities: a collaboration to improve local level data*, https://fcm.ca/en/news-media/news-release/statistics-canada-and-the-federation-canadian-municipalities-collaboration (accessed on 28 February 2024). [44]

French Ministry of Transformation and the Civil Service (n.d.), *Le baromètre des résultats de l'action publique [The barometer of public action results]*, https://www.modernisation.gouv.fr/transformer-laction-publique/le-barometre-des-resultats-de-laction-publique. [50]

Government of Croatia (2021), *Nacionalni plan oporavka i otpornosti 2021. - 2026 [National Recovery and Resilience Plan 2021-2026]*, https://planoporavka.gov.hr/UserDocsImages/dokumenti/Plan%20oporavka%20i%20otpornosti%2C%20srpanj%202021..pdf?vel=13435491 (accessed on 21 September 2023). [30]

Government of Mexico (2023), *Ley de Planeación [Planning Law]*, https://www.diputados.gob.mx/LeyesBiblio/pdf/LPlan.pdf (accessed on 1 December 2023). [11]

Government of Scotland (n.d.), *National Performance Framework | National Performance Framework*, https://nationalperformance.gov.scot/. [51]

HM Treasury (2022), *The Green Book, Central Government Guidance on Appraisal and Evaluation*. [40]

ICMA (2022), *Strategic Planning in Small Communities. A Manager's Manual*, https://icma.org/sites/default/files/2022-09/Strategic%20Planning%20in%20Small%20Communities%20Final_1.pdf (accessed on 23 June 2023). [33]

Interreg Europe (n.d.), *Next call for projects*, https://www.interregeurope.eu/next-call-for-projects (accessed on 19 November 2023). [23]

Italy's Territorial Cohesion Agency (2020), *The National Internal Areas Strategy moves from the experimental phase to a true structural policy*, https://www.agenziacoesione.gov.it/news_istituzionali/aree-interne/ (accessed on 19 November 2023). [27]

Koprivnica-Križevci County (2021), *Plan Razvoja Koprivničko-Križevačke Županije za Razdoblje 2021. Do 2027. Godine [Koprivnica-Križevci County Development Plan 2021-2027]*, https://www.kckzz.hr/hr/dokumenti-kckzz/1459-plan-razvoja-koprivnicko-krizevacke-zupanije-za-razdoblje-od-2021-2027-godine/file (accessed on 9 November 2023). [16]

Local Government Association (n.d.), *Considerations for effective strategic planning*, https://www.local.gov.uk/pas/plan-making/strategic-plans/considerations-effective-strategic-planning (accessed on 25 January 2024). [19]

Ministry of Finance and Public Credit of Mexico (2018), *Enfoques transversales [Cross-cutting approaches]*, https://www.transparenciapresupuestaria.gob.mx/es/PTP/Enfoques_transversales (accessed on 3 December 2023). [12]

MRDEUF (2024), *Written comments received from the Government of Croatia in March 2024*. [6]

MRDEUF (2023), *Upisnik regionalnih koordinatora i lokalnih razvojnih agencij [Register of Regional Co-ordinators and Local Development Agencies, November 2023]*, https://razvoj.gov.hr/upisnik-regionalnih-koordinatora-i-lokalnih-razvojnih-agencija/4007 (accessed on 25 January 2024). [24]

MRDEUF (2021), *Upute za Izradu nacionalnih planova [Instructions for Making a National Plan]*, https://razvoj.gov.hr/UserDocsImages/Istaknute%20teme/Sustav%20strate%C5%A1kog%20planiranja%20i%20upravljanja%20razvojem%20Republike%20Hrvatske/Upute%20za%20izradu%20Nacionalnog%20plana%20i%20pripadajuceg%20akcijskog%20plana.pdf (accessed on March 2023). [4]

MRDEUF (2017), *Indeks razvijenosti [Index of Development]*, https://razvoj.gov.hr/o-ministarstvu/regionalni-razvoj/indeks-razvijenosti/112 (accessed on 25 January 2024). [57]

MRDEUF (2017), *Strategija Regionalnog Razvoja Republike Hrvatske za Razdoblje do Kraja 2020. Godin [Regional Development Strategy of the Republic of Croatia for the Period until the end of 2020]*, https://razvoj.gov.hr/UserDocsImages/O%20ministarstvu/Regionalni%20razvoj/razvojne%20strategije/Strategija%20regionalnog%20razvoja%20Republike%20Hrvatske%20za%20razdoblje%20do%20kraja%202020._HS.pdf (accessed on 17 November 2023). [9]

MRDEUF (n.d.), *Upute za dopunu biblioteke pokazatelja [Instructions for supplementing the Library of Indicators]*, https://razvoj.gov.hr/UserDocsImages//Istaknute%20teme/Sustav%20strate%C5%A1kog%20planiranja%20i%20upravljanja%20razvojem%20Republike%20Hrvatske/Ispravci%202022//UPUTE%20za%20dopunu%20Biblioteke%20pokazatelja%20v%201.0.pdf. [48]

MRDEUF (n.d.), *Upute za izradu planova razvoja jedinica područne (regionalne) samouprave [Instructions for Creating Development Plans (Regional Unit of Self-Government)]*, https://razvoj.gov.hr/UserDocsImages/Istaknute%20teme/Sustav%20strate%C5%A1kog%20planiranja%20i%20upravljanja%20razvojem%20Republike%20Hrvatske/Ispravci%202022/3/Upute%20za%20izradu%20planova%20razvoja%20jedinica%20podru%C4%8Dne%20(regionalne)%20samouprav (accessed on 10 January 2024). [13]

New South Wales Government (2023), *Evaluation Toolkit guide*, https://www.nsw.gov.au/departments-and-agencies/premiers-department/evaluation-toolkit/evaluation-toolkit-guide. [42]

Nuevo León Council (2021), *Plan Estratégico Consejo Nuevo León 2030 [Nuevo León Council Strategic Plan 2023]*, https://planestrategico.conl.mx/. [53]

OECD (2023), *Discussions with participants during the 1st knowledge-sharing forum, which was held as part of the "Enhanced Strategic Planning at Regional and Local Levels in Croatia" project*. [41]

OECD (2023), *Interviews with local stakeholders conducted as part of the "Enhanced Strategic Planning at the Regional and Local Levels in Croatia" project*. [8]

OECD (2023), *OECD interviews conducted with local stakeholders as part of the Croatia accession mission (RDPC)*. [25]

OECD (2022), *OECD Project Questionnaire: Enhanced Strategic Planning at the Regional and Local Levels in Croatia - questionnaire addressed to Croatia's regional development agencies*. [14]

OECD (2022), *OECD survey of Croatian RDAs conducted in 2022*. [18]

OECD (2022), *Recommendation of the Council on Public Policy Evaluation*. [37]

OECD (2022), *Response to the project questionnaire "Enhanced Strategic Planning at the Regional and Local Levels in Croatia" addressed to Croatia's regional development agencies*. [55]

OECD (2022), *Response to the project questionnaire "Enhanced Strategic Planning at the Regional and Local Levels in Croatia" addressed to the Ministry of Regional Development and European Union Funds (MRDEUF)*. [56]

OECD (2021), *Better Governance, Planning and Services in Local Self-Governments in Poland*, OECD Publishing, Paris, https://doi.org/10.1787/550c3ff5-en. [28]

OECD (ed.) (2021), *Monitoring and Evaluating the Strategic Plan of Nuevo León 2015-2030*, OECD, https://doi.org/10.1787/22190414. [52]

OECD (2021), *Monitoring and Evaluating the Strategic Plan of Nuevo León 2015-2030: Using Evidence to Achieve Sustainable Development*, OECD Public Governance Reviews, OECD Publishing, Paris, https://doi.org/10.1787/8ba79961-en. [36]

OECD (2020), *Improving Governance with Policy Evaluation: Lessons From Country Experiences*, OECD Public Governance Reviews, OECD Publishing, Paris, https://doi.org/10.1787/89b1577d-en. [35]

OECD (2019), *OECD Skills Strategy 2019: Skills to Shape a Better Future*, OECD Publishing, Paris, https://doi.org/10.1787/9789264313835-en. [21]

OECD (2018), "Making Decentralisation Work: A Handbook for Policy-Makers", *OECD Multi-level Governance Studies*, https://doi.org/10.1787/g2g9faa7-en. [10]

OECD (2015), *OECD Skills Outlook 2015: Youth, Skills and Employability*, OECD Publishing, Paris, https://doi.org/10.1787/9789264234178-en. [20]

OECD (2014), *Measuring and managing results in development co-operation. A review of challenges and practices among DAC members and observers*, https://www.oecd.org/dac/peer-reviews/Measuring-and-managing-results.pdf (accessed on 12 February 2024). [58]

OECD (2009), *Governing Regional Development Policy: The Use of Performance Indicators*, OECD Multi-level Governance Studies, OECD Publishing, Paris, https://doi.org/10.1787/9789264056299-en. [49]

Office of the New York State Comptroller (2003), *Local Government Management Guide. Strategic Planning*, https://www.coldspringny.gov/sites/g/files/vyhlif416/f/uploads/osc-lgmg_strategic_planning.pdf (accessed on 2023 February 23). [32]

Official Gazette of Croatia No 13/2021 (2021), *Nacionalna razvojna strategija Republike Hrvatske do 2030. godine [National Development Strategy of the Republic of Croatia by 2030]*, https://narodne-novine.nn.hr/clanci/sluzbeni/2021_02_13_230.html. [5]

Official Gazette of Croatia No 147 et al. (2018), *Zakon o regionalnom razvoju Republike Hrvatske [Law on Regional Development of the Republic of Croatia]*. [7]

Official Gazette of Croatia No 151/2022 (2017), *Zakon o sustavu strateškog planiranja i upravljanja razvojem Republike Hrvatske [Law on the System of Strategic Planning and Development Management]*, https://www.zakon.hr/z/975/Zakon-o-sustavu-strate%C5%A1kog-planiranja-i-upravljanja-razvojem-Republike-Hrvatske (accessed on 2 November 2023). [1]

Official Gazette of Croatia No 27/2023 (2023), *Uredba o smjernicama za izradu akata strateškog planiranja od nacionalnog značaja i od značaja za jedinice lokalne i područne (regionalne) samouprave [Regulation on guidelines for drafting strategic planning acts...]*, https://narodne-novine.nn.hr/clanci/sluzbeni/2023_03_37_622.html (accessed on 2 November 2023). [2]

Official Gazette of Croatia No 37/2023 (2023), *Uredba o smjernicama za izradu akata strateškog planiranja od nacionalnog značaja i od značaja za jedinice lokalne i područne (regionalne) samouprave [Decision on guidelines for the preparation of strategic planning acts of national importance...]*, https://narodne-novine.nn.hr/clanci/sluzbeni/2023_03_37_622.html. [54]

Official Gazette of Croatia No 44/2023 (2023), *Pravilnik o provedbi postupka vrednovanja akata strateškog planiranja od nacionalnog značaja i od značaja za jedinice lokalne i područne (regionalne) samouprave [Ordinance on the implementation of the procedure for evaluation of acts...]*, https://narodne-novine.nn.hr/clanci/sluzbeni/2023_04_44_771.html. [39]

Official Gazette of Croatia No 44/2023 (2023), *Pravilnik o rokovima i postupcima praćenja i izvješćivanja o provedbi akata strateškog planiranja od nacionalnog značaja i od značaja za jedinice lokalne i područne (regionalne) samouprave [Ordinance on deadlines and procedures for monitoring...]*, https://narodne-novine.nn.hr/clanci/sluzbeni/2023_04_44_772.html. [38]

Official Gazette of Croatia No. 44/2023 (2023), *Pravilnik o rokovima i postupcima praćenja i izvješćivanja o provedbi akata strateškog planiranja od nacionalnog značaja i od značaja za jedinice lokalne i područne (regionalne) samouprave [Rulebook on deadlines and procedures...}*, https://narodne-novine.nn.hr/clanci/sluzbeni/2023_04_44_772.html (accessed on 2 November 2023). [3]

Osijek-Baranja County (2022), *Plan Razvoja Osječko-Baranjske Zupanije Ra Razdoblje do 2027. godine [Osijek-Baranja County Development Plan for the Period until 2027]*, https://www.obz.hr/index.php/plan-razvoja-osjecko-baranjske-zupanije-do-2027-godine (accessed on 9 November 2023). [17]

Primorje-Gorski Kotar RDA (2022), *Plan Razvoja Gorskog Kotara [Gorskog Kotara Development Plan]*, https://prigoda.hr/plan-razvoja-gorskog-kotara/ (accessed on 2 April 2024). [29]

UNDP Mexico (2023), *Plataforma de Análisis de Datos*. [47]

Wandsworth County Council (2024), *Performance indicators*, https://www.wandsworth.gov.uk/the-council/open-data-and-transparency/council-datasets/performance-indicators/ (accessed on 28 February 2024). [22]

Wargent, M., G. Parker and E. Street (2019), “Public-private entanglements: consultant use by local planning authorities in England”, *European Planning Studies*, Vol. 28/1, pp. 192-210, https://doi.org/10.1080/09654313.2019.1677565. [31]

Annex 4.A. Legislation guiding the monitoring and evaluation of regional development in Croatia

Annex Table 4.A.1. Main legal acts establishing monitoring and evaluation of regional and local strategic planning acts

Name of legislation	Articles relevant for monitoring and evaluation	Content
Law on Regional Development of the Republic of Croatia (2014)	8, 13(5), 15(6), 16, 25, 47, 48 and 49	8: Regional development policy should be monitored and evaluated 13(5) and 15(6): the MRDEUF should provide guidelines on monitoring. and evaluation at the county and local levels. 16: Establishment of a central electronic database. 25: Sets the mandate of regional co-ordinators (RDAs). 47: Sets the mandate of the MRDEUF. 48: Planning documents are subject to ex-ante, mid-term and ex-post evaluations. 49: Sets reporting periods.
Law on the System of Strategic Planning and Development Management of the Republic of Croatia 123/17 and 151/2022	15, 33, 45, 47, 48 and 49	33: Mandate of the co-ordination body 45: Regional and local co-ordinators are responsible for monitoring and reporting 47: Publication of reports 48: General rules on evaluation 49: Use of evaluation results for new planning documents
Regulation on Guidelines for the Drafting of Acts of Strategic Planning from National Importance and Importance for Local and Regional Self-government Units (37/2023)	8 and 20	8: Mandatory content of medium-term strategic planning acts 20: Compulsory to select indicators from the Indicator Library to monitor
Ordinance on Deadlines and Procedures for Monitoring and Reporting on the Implementation of Strategic Planning Acts of National Importance and of Importance for Local and Regional Self-government Units (44/2023)	All	General reporting rules
Ordinance on the Implementation of the Procedure for the Evaluation of Strategic Planning Acts of National Significance and of Relevance to Local and Regional Self-government Units (44/2023)	All	General evaluation rules

Source: Author's elaboration, based on (Official Gazette of Croatia No 37/2023, 2023[54]; Official Gazette of Croatia No 44/2023, 2023[38]; Official Gazette of Croatia No 44/2023, 2023[39]; OECD, 2023[8]; OECD, 2022[55]; OECD, 2022[56]).

Notes

[1] The Government of Croatia uses the Regional Development Index to identify regional and local governments lagging behind the national average according to their level of development. The index is a composite weighted indicator based on an adjusted average of standardised values of socio-economic indicators (Official Gazette of Croatia No 147 et al., 2018[7]). In accordance with the regulation, the following indicators are used for the calculation of the Regional Development Index: a) average income per capita, b) average primary income per capita, c) average unemployment rate, d) general movement of the population, e) level of education of the population (tertiary index), and f) ageing index. County, city and municipal governments with an index below average (i.e. below 100%) are considered assisted areas (MRDEUF, 2017[57]).

[2] An OECD survey was disseminated among Croatia's 21 RDAs in September 2022. The OECD received responses from all RDAs.

[3] City and municipal governments with fewer than 1 000 inhabitants can be awarded co-financing of up to 75%. City and municipal governments with 1 000 inhabitants or more can be awarded co-financing of up to 50% (OECD, 2023[25]).

[4] The R.A.C.E.R. acronym stands for: i) relevant (the indicator must measure what is intended to measure and be pertinent to the objectives of the policy, plan or project); ii) accepted (the indicator needs to be accepted and understood by all stakeholders involved in the process); iii) credible (the indicator should be reliable and based on available data, ensuring that it accurately reflects the issue being measured; iv easy (the indicator should be easy to use, not overly complex, and easy for stakeholders to interpret and apply; and v) robust (the indicator must be methodologically sound, with clear definitions and a consistent data collection process to ensure comparability over time and across different regions or contexts) (OECD, 2014[58]).

5 Regional development funding and financing

This chapter examines how regional and local development is funded and financed in Croatia. First, it assesses the changes in subnational public finances in Croatia between 2010 and 2022, while outlining the implications for the country's regional development. Second, it identifies the main EU and national government funding mechanisms supporting the implementation of Croatia's regional development policy. Finally, the chapter proposes policy solutions to address five key challenges Croatia faces in mobilising and using funding and financing mechanisms.

Introduction

A necessary pre-condition for regional development policy to meet its objectives is having sufficient financial resources to support policy implementation. For instance, governments need to ensure that the tasks and responsibilities assigned to levels of government are matched with sufficient sources of funding and financing (e.g. to support local businesses, provide healthcare or invest in key public infrastructure) (OECD, 2019[1]). However, the effectiveness of funding and financing mechanisms for regional development also depends on other elements, including whether subnational governments have: i) appropriate levels of fiscal autonomy to make spending and revenue-raising decisions; and ii) the capacity to access and deploy available financial resources in a productive way.

Over the past two decades, Croatia has gradually engaged in a process of administrative and fiscal decentralisation, granting counties, cities and municipalities crucial competencies and financial resources for regional development. This has resulted, for example, in a 26% increase in total revenue at the subnational level (in real terms) between 2016 and 2022.

At the same time, despite small increases in the share of tax revenue as part of total subnational government revenue between 2010 and 2022, counties cities and municipalities continue to rely heavily on grants and subsidies. This was mainly driven by a significant uptick in European Union (EU) funding in the wake of Croatia's accession to the EU in 2013. The influx of EU funding has resulted in an increase of 82.7% of subnational government investment in real terms between 2010 and 2021, with cities and municipalities as the primary drivers. This has directly supported the implementation of regional and local development projects across the country (OECD, 2023[2]). In parallel, Croatia's national government has established numerous mechanisms to help fund regional development. These include a co-funding programme that helps subnational governments compete for EU funding, as well as grants for subnational governments performing below the national average across a series of economic, well-being and demographic indicators.

An examination of the financial resources available to Croatian subnational governments for implementing regional development policy suggests that there are several areas of improvement. First, Croatia should ensure that the increased access to and use of EU funding by its subnational governments is spent effectively to tackle regional and local development needs and priorities. Moreover, in order to prevent an increasing reliance on EU funding over time, it is important for Croatia to ensure that subnational governments maintain diversified revenue streams.

Second, and relatedly, there is a need to increase the fiscal autonomy of subnational governments (i.e. their capacity to raise own-source revenue) without widening inter-regional or intra-municipal inequalities. This would increase their ability to orient revenue to meet specific local needs and priorities, while also helping to lower subnational government's reliance on grants.

Third, it would be relevant to review the effectiveness of the way in which the Regional Development Index has been set up, which the government uses to identify those subnational governments that are in need of special financial support. The allocation of funding based on a subnational government's Index score may inadvertently encourage counties, cities and municipalities to underperform in order to receive funds.

Fourth, Croatia should address the funding- and financing-related challenges associated with county- and local-level fragmentation (e.g. a scattering of financial resources across a large number of small-scale projects, thus limiting their impact). Strengthening existing horizontal and vertical co-ordination mechanisms would help to improve the targeting of development funding to meet regional needs.

Fifth, Croatia should consider revisiting the financing model of regional development agencies (RDAs) in order to ensure their long-term operational sustainability. Their reliance on EU Technical Assistance funding, which ends in December 2025, along with the limited fiscal space of county governments to bolster RDA budgets, has placed the RDAs in a difficult financial position. Finding a more sustainable approach to ensure that RDAs can continue to support regional development efforts should be a priority for all stakeholders involved.

This chapter begins by analysing the current state of Croatia's public finances at the subnational level by highlighting primary fiscal indicators and the specific funding and financing sources for regional development available to subnational governments. Subsequently, the chapter assesses the five key challenges faced by subnational governments when seeking to mobilise resources for regional development in a sustainable manner.

Box 5.1. Recommendations to strengthen Croatia's subnational finances for funding regional development

In order to prevent subnational governments from becoming heavily reliant on EU funding to implement regional development plans and projects in the long term, Croatia could:

- Explore options to further diversify subnational government revenue streams, including by:
  - Devolving existing national taxes to lower levels of government (green taxes or fees). This needs to be based on a careful assessment of how the proposed changes to the tax system affect the fiscal capacity of citizens, businesses and different levels of government, and consider mechanisms to mitigate any negative impacts.
- Strengthen the capacity of subnational authorities to set up and manage public-private partnerships (PPPs) effectively, including by providing them with information and training on: i) how to assess the value added and risks of PPPs, ii) how to manage PPPs, and iii) how to establish a transparent system that can track the use of public funding through PPPs.

In order to ensure that the 2023 personal income tax reforms do not exacerbate regional and local disparities, Croatia should:

- Monitor the effects of the reforms on county and local budgets, in order to ensure that the new rate-setting powers of cities and municipalities do not lead to large fiscal disparities at the subnational level.

In order to strengthen the ability of the Regional Development Index to encourage balanced territorial development, Croatia is recommended to:

- Adjust the way in which regional development funding is provided to counties and local governments based on their Index scores, in order to encourage them to improve their performance, for instance by:
  - Ensuring that county and local governments that recently left the 'assisted areas' category in the Index receive funding that decreases over a set period (e.g. three years). This would help to reduce the incentive for local leaders to deliberately seek an 'assisted area' designation, while also providing them with financial means to consolidate their recent developmental gains.
  - Using the Index as a foundation to support a more performance-based funding model for regional development, i.e. one in which socio-economic progress yields certain additional rewards, such as tax breaks or increased investment opportunities.

In order to further strengthen the vertical and horizontal co-ordination of regional development funding and financing, Croatia is advised to:

- Conduct an assessment of national budget funds allocated to initiatives that support regional and local development. This could help to determine:
  - Which public bodies, because of their funding for regional and local development, should be part of the Prime Minister-led regional development co-ordination body; and
  - Whether the funding provided through the national budget aligns with the country's long-term development objectives and whether there are funding gaps or possible inefficiencies that need to be addressed.

- Consider expanding the use of macro-regional co-operation instruments such as development agreements between county governments and RDAs on the one hand, and the national government on the other, including by:
  - Helping county administrations and RDAs identify funding and financing opportunities to support the implementation of development agreements, e.g. by developing framework agreements with international financial institutions to ensure that macro-regional development councils can borrow from such institutions.

In order to shore up the financial sustainability of RDAs, Croatia needs to:

- Consider complementary options to fill the funding gap that will be created when EU Technical Assistance funding for RDAs expires after 2025, including by:
  - Providing direct funding to the RDAs through the national budget, complementing the funding provided by the RDA founders (counties and cities).
  - Expanding the membership base of RDAs to include (more) cities and/or municipalities. Their financial contribution could enhance the RDAs' financial sustainability, while also strengthening the collaborative ties between the RDAs and local governments.

Sources of regional development funding and financing in Croatia

Regional development efforts in Croatia are funded and financed at the subnational government level (counties, cities and municipalities combined) through a wide range of mechanisms, including inter-governmental transfers, shared and own-source tax revenues, non-tax revenues and loans from national and international financing institutions. Regional development funding also comes from the EU.

This section illustrates the evolution of subnational public finances in Croatia between 2010 and 2022, while outlining the implications for the country's regional development. This section considers specific indicators related to the volume and composition of subnational revenue, expenditure and debt. In addition, information is provided on specific EU and national funding and financing mechanisms that support regional development initiatives.

Croatia's performance on selected fiscal indicators

Drawing on recent historical data, a number of trends in Croatia's subnational fiscal performance can be identified. With regard to revenues, county- and local-level budgets have grown steadily in real terms between 2010 and 2022 (OECD, 2023[2]). The composition of subnational budget revenues, however, has been heavily weighted towards inter-governmental transfers. A marked reliance on transfers, which are often earmarked for specific functions, risks limiting the ability of subnational governments to allocate spending to meet specific local needs. At the same time, levels of subnational tax autonomy have slowly increased, with city and municipal governments (but not county governments) able to set rates on a number of subnationally-levied taxes.

With regards to expenditures, between 2010 and 2022, total subnational expenditure in real terms increased gradually (OECD, 2023[2]). Despite this increase, subnational government spending as a share of total public expenditure in Croatia has remained low compared to the OECD38 and EU27 averages. One notable finding is that the country's subnational governments allocate a significantly higher share of their budgets to staffing costs than the OECD38 and EU27 averages, which may suggest a need for county and local-level functions to be further streamlined.

The most pronounced expenditure-related change over the past decade has been a substantial rise in subnational public investment in Croatia between 2010 and 2021 (OECD, 2023[2]). While public investment has risen in real terms in counties, cities and municipalities respectively, growth has been particularly strong in the latter two. This might reflect the fact that own-source revenue makes up a larger share of total revenue in cities and municipalities than in counties, providing them with greater flexibility to allocate a larger portion of their budgets towards capital investment. Finally, subnational government investment capacity has been supported by its relatively low level of debt compared to the OECD average.

Subnational governments continue to rely heavily on grants and subsidies, despite increasing tax revenue

Between 2010 and 2022, Croatia reported a 26% increase in total revenue at the subnational level in real terms, rising from EUR 5.3 billion in 2010 to over EUR 6.5 billion in 2022. Despite this upward trend, subnational government revenue now accounts for 27.5% of total revenue in Croatia, which is significantly lower than the OECD38 and EU27 averages (44.9% and 38.1%, respectively) (OECD, 2023[2]; OECD, 2023[3]). This means that compared to the OECD and EU, Croatia collects and manages a larger share of revenue at the national level, leaving subnational entities with a smaller portion of the revenue pie.

A key driver of the growth in subnational government revenues has been an increase in inter-governmental transfers. Since 2010, the value of inter-governmental grants and subsidies—the main source of subnational revenues—has increased by roughly 30%, reaching over EUR 3.5 billion in real terms in 2022 (Figure 5.1). In parallel, tax revenues rose by nearly a third over the same period, reaching EUR 2.5 billion in 2022, while user charges and fees decreased by 10%.

Figure 5.1. Subnational revenue by category in real terms for Croatia, 2010-2022

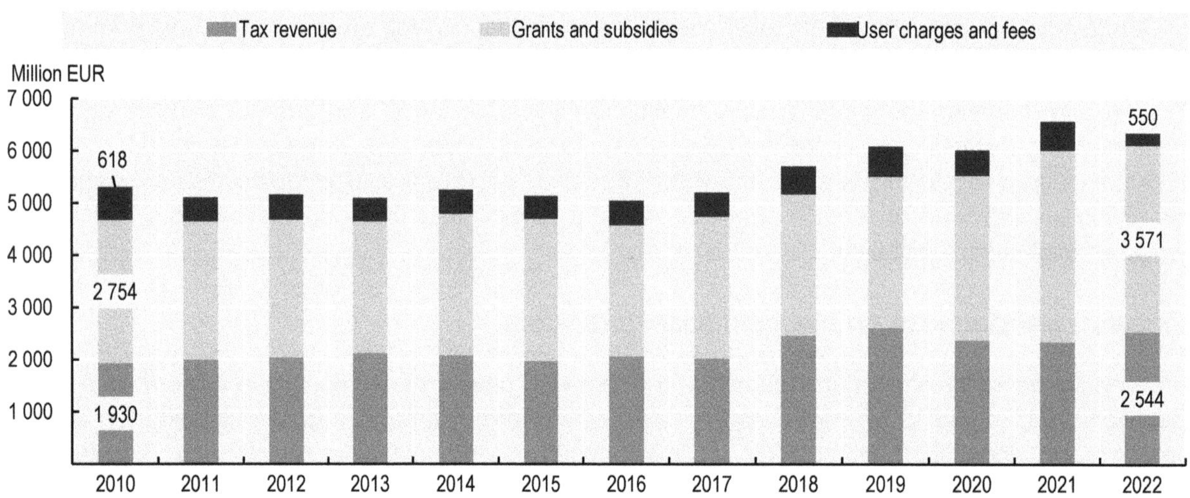

Note: User charges and fees include income generated from the use of a public service (i.e. public transport), as well as administrative fees, donations from outside the general budget and administrative fines or penalties.
Source: Author's elaboration, based on (OECD, 2023[2]).

A significant finding was that between 2010 and 2022, the share of grants and subsidies as part of total subnational revenues grew 3.4%. This mean that, in 2022, grants and subsidies accounted for 53.6% of total subnational revenues. This level surpassed the EU27 and OECD38 averages (of 45.6% and 52.8%, respectively) (OECD, 2023[3]). As such, inter-governmental transfers make up an increasing large majority of subnational budget revenues, while own-source revenues (tax revenue and user charges and fees combined) account for a reduced share. This means that subnational governments' fiscal autonomy has slightly decreased since 2010. Moreover, as grants are often earmarked and may attach stringent conditions to public expenditure, an increased reliance on intergovernmental transfers can limit the flexibility that governments have to target spending in a way that best addresses territorially-diversified development needs (Council of Europe, 2007[4]; World Bank, 2021[5]).

An analysis of subnational revenue distribution by government level, based on data from Croatia's Ministry of Finance[1], shows that the reliance on grants and subsidies is significantly greater at the county level than at the local level. In 2020, inter-governmental transfers accounted for a 54.6% share of county budgets, compared with 14.8% of city budgets and 26% of municipal budgets (see Annex Figure 5.A.1; Annex Figure 5.A.2 and Annex Figure 5.A.3, respectively) (Ministry of Finance, 2023[6]). By the same token, cities and municipalities have a more diversified revenue structure than counties, with own-source revenues (i.e. tax revenues, and user charges and fees) accounting for over two-thirds of their budgets (79.6% and 67.3%, respectively). This, in part, reflects differences in the assignment of responsibilities among subnational governments (see chapter 3) (MRDEUF, 2024[7]). The relative weight of user charges and fees in city and municipal budgets (20.8 and 21.1%, respectively) reflects the wide array of services they provide (e.g. utility services, transportation, disposal of municipal waste, public area maintenance, funeral services and public lighting)[2].

The more balanced composition of revenue sources of cities and municipalities, combined with their limited reliance on transfers, compared to that of counties, has different implications for regional development. In addition to giving local authorities more flexibility to allocate resources based on local needs, it can reduce their vulnerability to economic downturns associated with a single revenue stream (OECD, 2021[8]). For instance, local governments that are highly reliant on inter-governmental transfers may be severely affected when, during an economic downturn, the national government decides to reduce spending for subnational governments (Blöchliger et al., 2010[9]). It should be noted, however, that some of this risk is mitigated by the fact that wages related to education and healthcare delivery comprise a significant portion of inter-governmental transfers. Although such wages are paid from the central government, they are formally registered as inter-governmental transfers (Ministry of Finance, 2024[10]).

Cities and municipalities receive most of their transfers from EU funds

Grants account for a significant share of subnational transfers, the majority of which come from the Ministry of Regional Development and EU Funds (MRDEUF), the Ministry of Science and Education, as well as international donors. In 2020, subnational governments received most grant funding from the national government ("other budgets", 35%), from the EU (31%) and from the equalisation mechanism (25%), the latter of which is allocated for decentralised functions (e.g. primary and secondary education, healthcare, social services and firefighting) (Figure 5.2) (Ministry of Finance, 2023[6]).

Figure 5.2. Subnational transfers by sub-category, 2020

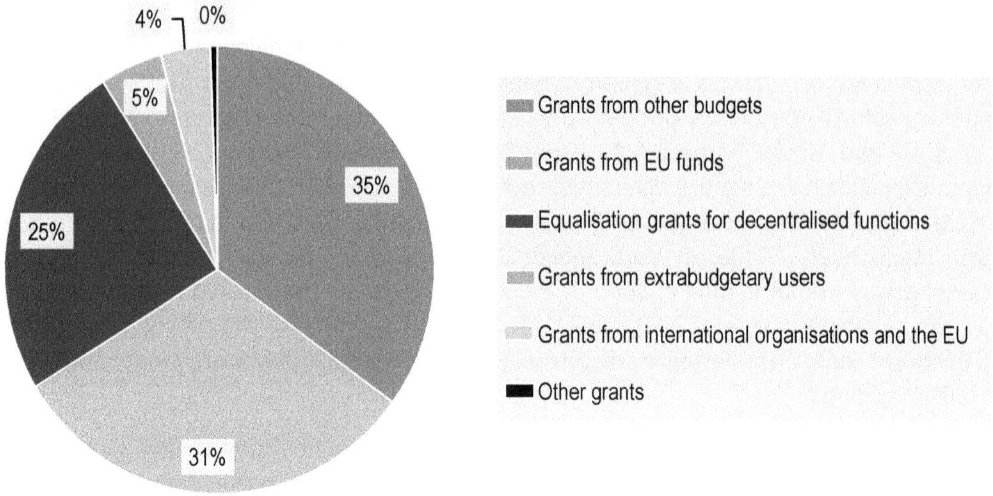

Note: 'Other transfers' include the items 'transfers between budget users of the same budget', 'aid from foreign governments', and 'help to budget users from a budget not under their responsibility'.
Source: Author's elaboration, based on (Ministry of Finance, 2023[6]).

There were important variations by level of government. In 2020, grants from EU funds accounted for a particularly large share of city and municipal transfer revenue (39% and 44%, respectively) when compared with county transfer revenue (16%). By contrast, equalisation grants for decentralised functions accounted for nearly half (45.1%) of county transfer revenue, compared to 17% and 2% in the case of cities and municipalities, respectively. As noted above, these variations reflect differences in the assignment of responsibilities among subnational governments. They also point to the relative dependency of counties, cities and municipalities on different funding sources (e.g. counties on equalisation grants). This can mean, for example, that counties' ability to fund public service delivery and/or to make strategic investments (e.g. in transport infrastructure) may be particularly affected if Croatia decided to change its equalisation system. By the same token, cities and municipalities are more vulnerable to possible changes in EU funding volumes and priorities.

Subnational tax autonomy has gradually increased in Croatia

Despite the growing dependence on grants and subsidies at the subnational level in Croatia, the share of tax revenues in subnational budgets has increased slightly over the past decade, from 36.4% in 2010 to 38.2% in 2022 (OECD, 2023[2]). PIT has been the primary source of subnational tax revenue in recent years, accounting 90.1% of the total in 2020 (Ministry of Finance, 2023[6]). Beyond PIT revenues, counties, cities and municipalities have the ability to levy several other taxes (Table 5.1). For example, counties can levy taxes on inheritance and gifts, motor vehicles, vessels, and gambling machines, while city and municipal governments can collect taxes on local consumption of alcoholic beverages and certain non-alcoholic ones, holiday homes, tourism, and the use of public land (Official Gazette of Croatia No 127 et al., 2017[11]; World Bank, 2021[5]). While the rates for all taxes levied by county governments are nationally-defined, city and municipal governments can set rates on a number of locally-levied taxes, albeit sometimes within a band defined by the national government.

Table 5.1. Subnational tax by type and autonomy to set tax rates in 2024: Croatia

Tax	Type			Autonomy to determine tax rates		
	Shared among subnational governments	County	City and municipal	Central government determined	Local governments determine rates	Local governments determine rates within range set by central government
Personal income tax	✓					✓
Inheritance and gift tax		✓		✓		
Tax on motor vehicles		✓		✓		
Tax on vessels		✓		✓		
Tax on gambling machines		✓		✓		
Local consumption tax			✓			✓
Tax on holiday houses			✓			✓
Tax on the use of public land			✓		✓	

Source: Author's elaboration, based on (Official Gazette of Croatia No 127 et al., 2017[11]; World Bank, 2021[5]).

The ability of cities and municipalities to set rates on certain taxes can be an important mechanism to help tailor fiscal policy more closely to local development needs. For instance, local governments can strategically adjust tax rates to encourage or discourage certain economic activities, attract new investment, or fund local infrastructure projects. For example, a city may lower taxes on local consumption of beverages to boost the hospitality sector, making it an attractive location for new bars and restaurants, thereby stimulating local employment. Conversely, municipalities could increase taxes on the use of public land for commercial purposes, aiming to discourage overdevelopment in ecologically sensitive areas, thus preserving local natural resources.

Driven by EU accession, subnational investment increased by 82.7% over the last decade

Between 2010 and 2021, Croatia saw a significant increase, in real terms, in subnational public investment. During this time, public investment spending by subnational governments rose 82.7%. As a result, subnational public investment as a share of GDP reached 2.05% in 2021 (nearly double its share in 2010), which exceeded the 1.8% average for both the EU27 and OECD38 (OECD/UCLG, 2022[12]; Eurostat, 2023[13]; OECD, 2023[3]). Driven in part by the influx of EU funding linked to Croatia's EU accession, direct investment by subnational governments increased from 26.1% of total public investment in 2013 to 42.3% in 2021 (Figure 5.3).

Figure 5.3. Subnational public investment as a share of total public investment, 2010-2021

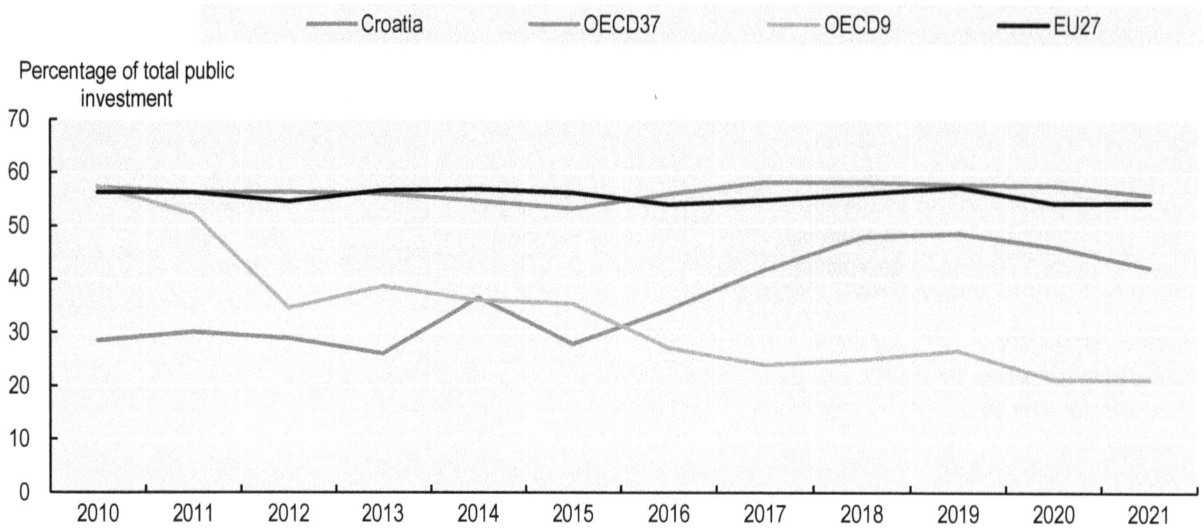

Note: Colombia is excluded due to lack of data. OECD37, EU27 and OECD9 averages are unweighted. OECD9 includes Estonia, Greece, Hungary, Poland, Portugal, Slovak Republic, Slovenia, Spain and Türkiye, which are all countries that had a similar average GDP per capita as Croatia in 2023. The slight decline in direct investment between 2019 and 2021 (from 48.6%) reflects a reallocation of budget resources in response to the COVID-19 pandemic crisis, as has been the case in other countries (IFC, 2021[14]; OECD, 2021[15]).
Source: Author's elaboration, based on (OECD, 2023[2]).

A detailed examination of public investment by county, city and municipal governments shows that subnational public investment is unevenly distributed (Ministry of Finance, 2023[6]) (Figure 5.4). Most subnational investment is undertaken by cities. However, both cities and municipalities have borne witness to substantial growth in investment spending between 2014 and 2020, increasing 25% in the case of the former and more than doubling in the case of the latter. Although counties also somewhat increased their investment spending over the period, they did so from a very low base. As such, cities and municipalities are the main drivers of subnational public investment, having accounted for nearly 90% of total subnational investment spending in 2020.

Figure 5.4. Subnational public investment by subnational government category in real terms, 2014-20

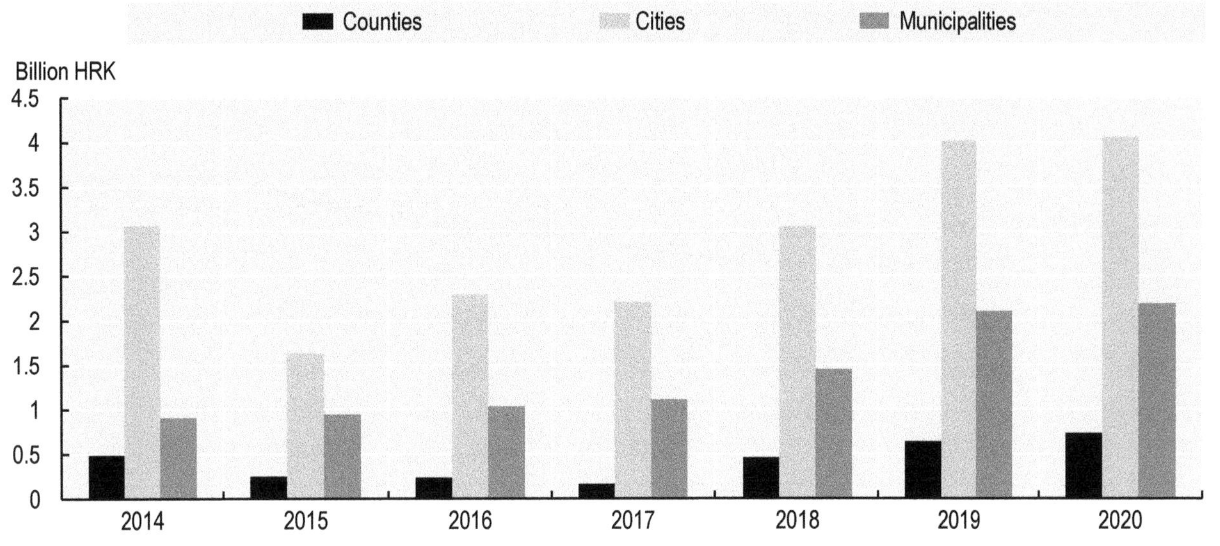

Note: Units in million HRK, base year is 2014. The chart is based on financial reports disaggregated by level of subnational government. It does not include possible additional investments that are presented in consolidated financial reports to which the OECD did not have access.
Source: Author's elaboration, based on (Ministry of Finance, 2023[6]).

The disparity in public investment suggests that cities and municipalities have greater flexibility to allocate a larger portion of their budgets to capital investments, potentially enabling a more targeted approach to addressing local infrastructure needs and development initiatives. Notwithstanding differences in the assignment of responsibilities among subnational governments, the lower percentage of capital investment by counties may also reflect their more constrained financial capacity, which could be tied to a relatively high reliance on earmarked grants compared to cities and municipalities.

Subnational governments have maintained sound fiscal health during crises thanks to national government support

Between 2010 and 2022, total subnational revenues grew slightly faster than subnational expenditures, (26% vs. 19.2% in real terms, respectively). This has helped limit subnational debt levels. In fact, in 2022, subnational debt in Croatia accounted for only 3.0% of public debt, well below the EU27 and OECD38 averages of 13.2% and 12.9% of public debt in 2020 (latest year available), respectively (OECD, 2023[3]).

As shown in Figure 5.5, transfers from the central government have also helped to limit subnational debt by acting as a buffer against economic shocks (e.g. the global financial crisis in 2008 and the COVID-19 pandemic in 2020). The cyclicality of deficits is noticeable almost exclusively at the national government level (e.g. in 2020 and 2021 when the COVID-19 pandemic led to reduced government revenue). This stems from the fact that transfers from the national to subnational governments during this period helped balance the latter's budgets.

Figure 5.5. Total government expenditure and revenue by sector of government in real terms, 2010-22

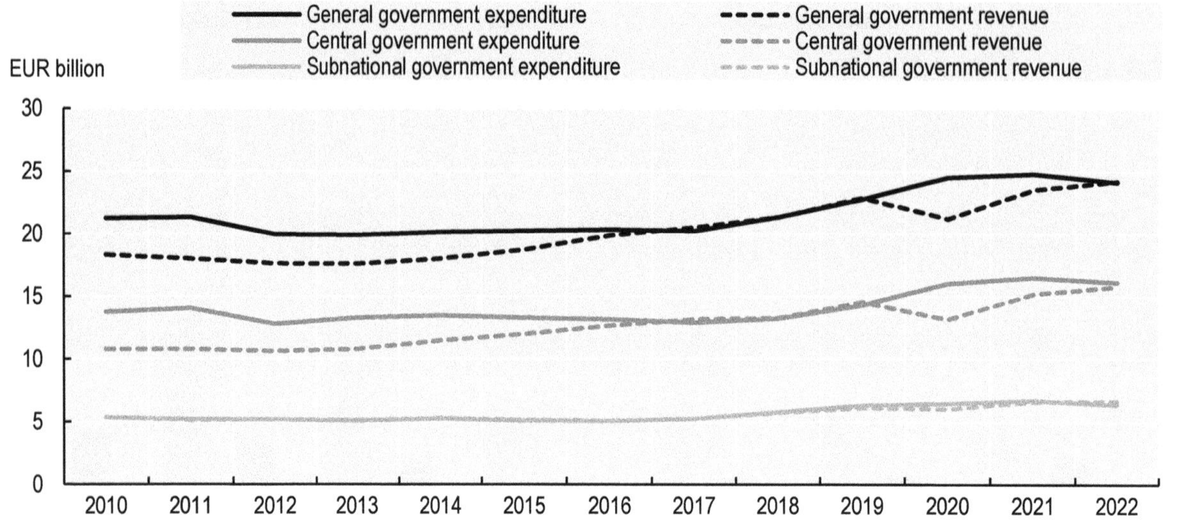

Note: In real terms.
Source: Author's elaboration, based on (OECD, 2023[2]).

The fiscal health of Croatian subnational governments also reflects their application of the "golden rule", a regulation that limits their borrowing to cover capital expenditure (Figure 5.5) (Official Gazette of Croatia No 144/2021, 2021[16]; OECD/UCLG, 2022[12]). Given the substantial responsibilities that subnational governments have for capital investment spending, the golden rule has played an important role in discouraging budget deficits and fostering fiscal discipline at the subnational level.

Box 5.2. Borrowing by Croatia's subnational governments

Croatia's subnational governments can only borrow to finance capital investment (the "golden rule"). Borrowing is subject to prior approval by the national government. In addition, there are two main prudential rules: a general limit on the aggregate borrowing of all subnational governments (5% of current revenues of the previous year) and an individual limit (20% of current revenues of the previous year). Both limits include guarantees and borrowing approvals issued by local governments, including to their utility companies.

Source: Author's elaboration, based on (Official Gazette of Croatia No 144/2021, 2021[16]; OECD/UCLG, 2022[12]; Ministry of Finance, 2024[10]; Official Gazette of Croatia No 149/23, 2023[17]).

Croatia's subnational governments also appear to have a stable debt-to-revenue ratio (Figure 5.6). This suggests that, in principle, subnational governments have sufficient capacity to service their debt obligations, which are not particularly burdensome, without compromising their ability to fund essential public services and infrastructure projects (Figure 5.6). Additionally, by keeping the debt-to-revenue ratio stable, subnational governments may have more flexibility and space for borrowing when they seek to finance new development projects.

Figure 5.6. Subnational debt-to-revenue ratio, 2010-22

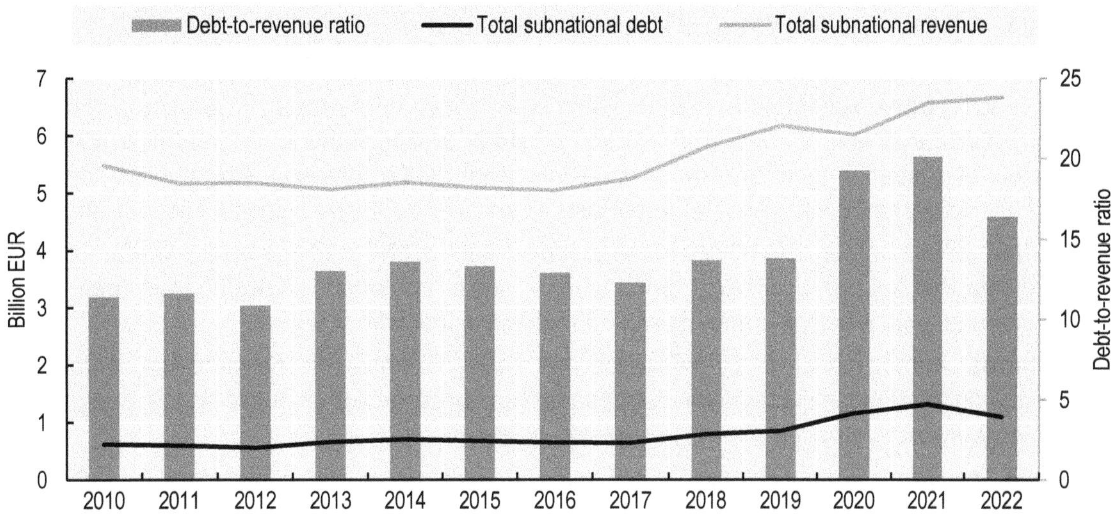

Note: In real terms.
Source: Author's elaboration, based on (Eurostat, 2023[13]; Eurostat, 2023[18]).

EU and national funding and financing mechanisms for regional development

This section focuses on the specific EU and national funding and financing mechanisms that have become central to Croatia's regional development policy. These mechanisms include, among others: i) funds from the Programme for Competitiveness and Cohesion and the Integrated Territorial Programme, ii) funds from the national Recovery and Resilience Plan, iii) funding for regional and local development projects from the national government, iv) funding for the operations of RDAs, and v) financing options for regional development.

Taken together, funding and financing mechanisms established in recent years underscore Croatia's commitment to place-based development. Most of the mechanisms are designed to cater to the specific challenges and needs of distinct territories, e.g. islands, hilly and mountainous areas, and 'assisted areas'. Furthermore, the diverse territorial scope (i.e. local, regional or macro-regional) of funding and financing mechanisms reflects the fact that some development challenges are best addressed through local investment (e.g. maintenance of a school), while others are more effectively and efficiently implemented at a larger territorial scale (e.g. upgrading of transport infrastructure).

Integrated Territorial Investments

The Integrated Territorial Investments (ITI) mechanism stands out as one of the key instruments for regional development funding in Croatia. It facilitates the design and implementation of territorial strategies that extend across local administrative boundaries by pooling investments from different EU structural funds across different priority areas.

In Croatia, the first ITIs were implemented as part of the Operational Programme on Competitiveness and Cohesion during the 2014-20 EU programming period. They involved the eight largest cities in the country, which accounted for almost half of the Croatian population (OECD, 2023[19]). Strategies developed under this initiative had a broad thematic focus. Among other elements, they aimed to strengthen the role of cities in developing business infrastructure, promoting cultural heritage for tourism and enhancing the offer of clean urban transport. In total, ITI funding over the 2014-20 period amounted to EUR 1.5 billion.

For the 2021-2027 EU programming period, an Integrated Territorial Programme (ITP) targets 22 urban centres. ITI funding over the period amounts to EUR 1.5 billion, of which 88.2% and 11.8% has been allocated through the European Regional Development Fund (ERDF) and the Just Transition Fund (JTF), respectively. Investments within the ITP are classified into four main types (MRDEUF, 2022[20]):

1. **Industrial transition**: More than EUR 550 million (about 35% of total ITP funding) will be allocated to projects that aim to support innovation clusters, broker strategic partnerships for innovation, boost the creation and growth of start-ups and SMEs, develop smart skills, and improve infrastructure for companies. These projects also cover territories classified as 'assisted areas'.
2. **Cities**: Approximately EUR 680 million (just over 43% of ITP funding) will be allocated to cities for projects that support brownfield development, clean and smart city traffic, business incubators, tourism, energy efficiency, and green and multifunctional infrastructure.
3. **Islands**: Approximately EUR 150 million has been earmarked to promote island development, including through the sustainable management and preservation of public space, and encouraging energy efficiency and the use of renewable energy sources.
4. **Just Transition Fund**: Close to 12% of total ITP investments will be funded by the Just Transition Fund in fields related to the green and digital transitions. These investments will be made in two counties with highly-polluting industries that account for a significant share of greenhouse emissions: Istria and Sisak-Moslavina (European Commission, 2022[21]).

National Recovery and Resilience Plan

Following the economic upheaval caused by the COVID-19 pandemic, the government developed a Recovery and Resilience Plan to support Croatia's economic recovery, while addressing challenges and opportunities that stem from the green and digital transitions. Funding for the Recovery and Resilience Plan amounts to approximately EUR 10 billion.

Seventy-seven projects being implemented through the Recovery and Resilience Plan will affect regional and local development. For example, 30 projects are located in the Pannonian Croatia macro-region (TL2), and include a wide range of initiatives, including the retrofitting of public buildings with new, energy-efficient technologies, renovating kindergartens, and food distribution centres (European Commission, 2023[22]).

Regional development funding from the national government

There are a variety of national-level funding mechanisms that support regional development in Croatia, many of which have been set up by the MRDEUF. These mechanisms range from place-targeted funds (e.g. assisted areas, mountainous areas and islands) to line ministry or sector grants that indirectly advance development.

The MRDEUF provides funding to assisted and mountainous areas, comprising 12 counties and 304 city and municipal governments, which represent one-third of Croatia's population. The MRDEUF launches periodic public calls for development projects, with a total annual budget of approximately EUR 34 million (MRDEUF, 2023[23]). Through this funding mechanism, the MRDEUF has launched calls aimed at specific territories, such as one for the economic revitalisation of Slavonia, Baranja and Srijem counties. Funding for assisted and mountainous areas has included initiatives to support demographic revitalisation, economic regeneration, connectivity and mobility and the construction of housing developments.

In addition, the MRDEUF allocates funding for Croatian islands through the Island Development Programme. The Programme aims to support the development of local island communities, in particular by funding projects that facilitate access to and the quality of local public services and business infrastructure, and support the green transition (MRDEUF, 2024[24]). For instance, in early 2024, a call was launched for projects that aim to support the development of civil society organisations on islands. The call has an envelope of EUR 300 000, which can be spent on projects worth between EUR 4 000 and EUR 10 000 (MRDEUF, 2024[24]).

Furthermore, the government created a specific fund for the reconstruction and development of Vukovar, following Croatia's war of independence. Among other areas, the funds can be used to support local economic development projects and SMEs, as well as for the construction and maintenance of communal infrastructure (MRDEUF, 2024[7]). In 2023, planned spending through the fund amounted to EUR 9.83 million (MRDEUF, 2023[25]).

It is worth noting that other ministries, such as the Ministry of Science and Education and the Ministry of Agriculture, offer sectoral grants that can indirectly promote regional development (OECD, 2023[26]). At present, however, there is no publicly accessible overview of national government grants supporting regional and local government. Given this lack of a comprehensive perspective, county, city, and municipal governments may face challenges identifying and applying for funding opportunities that most closely align with their specific development objectives.

The national government can enter into development agreements with three or more county governments, through which a partnership for macro-regional investment is formed. In the case of the Slavonia, Baranja and Srijem Development Agreement, for example, 67 projects were foreseen across a wide range of sectors, from agriculture, wood and metal processing industries, to tourism and infrastructure. To support the implementation of the development agreement, the Council of Slavonia, Baranja and Srijem, which comprises the five counties of Virovitica-Podravina, Požega-Slavonia, Slavonski Brod-Posavina, Osijek-Baranja and Vukovar-Srijem, secured EUR 1.56 billion in EU funding, as well as additional funds from the national budget (MRDEUF, 2023[25]). As of 2024, counties within the agreement have spent EUR 2.4 billion in total, out of which a relatively small share (EUR 269 million) are labelled as joint projects involving several different counties (Council of Slavonia, Baranja and Srijem, 2024[27]). To date, eight projects have been completed, while an additional 18 are currently being implemented (MRDEUF, 2024[7]).

Funding for the operation of RDAs

As discussed in chapter 3, RDAs were established as limited liability companies that provided paid services. However, following legislative changes in 2017, they were re-established as public regional co-ordinators and are now funded exclusively by the public sector. National government funding accounts for roughly two-thirds of RDA revenues, with the remainder allocated through county budgets (and Zadar City in the case of the Zadar County RDA). Two EU funding calls, paid through the Operational Programme on Competitiveness and Cohesion, sustained RDA activities between 2017 and 2023 (MRDEUF, 2024[7]). A new grant worth EUR 15.2 million will be made available to the RDAs over 2024 and 2025 (OECD, 2023[26]).

Financing options for regional development

Besides funding through national and international programmes, Croatia can also seek financing from domestic financial institutions (e.g. the Croatian Bank for Reconstruction and Development, HBOR) or international financial institutions, such as the World Bank, the International Monetary Fund (IMF), the European Investment Bank (EIB) and the European Bank for Reconstruction and Development (EBRD) (Box 5.3). These international financial institutions (IFIs) mobilise funds through member contributions, borrowing from capital markets, and other financial instruments. They offer loans to support regional development projects, providing national and subnational governments with the necessary capital to invest in infrastructure, human and institutional capacity building programmes.

Box 5.3. Financing regional development through the HBOR and the EIB

Beyond EU funding, the Croatian Bank for Reconstruction and Development (HBOR) and the EIB provide several financing products that can be used to encourage sustainable regional development. HBOR offers loans with interest rates ranging from 3.1-4% per annum, with repayment periods extending up to 15 years and the possibility of including a grace period of up to five years. A key criterion for these loans is their allocation to capital investments that support green or net-zero initiatives. HBOR also provides incentives such as reduced interest rates for projects that further the green and digital transitions or contribute to the development of lagging regions. HBOR also allows for the reduction of interest rates of up to 75% over loans that support the green and/or digital transition. It is therefore essential for regional and local authorities to build their expertise and skills related to the green or digital transitions, in order to maximise funding and financing from HBOR.

At the international level, the EIB offers a diverse portfolio of financing products tailored to the investment needs of national and subnational governments. These include investment loans designed for large-scale individual projects related to water, waste, or energy infrastructure. For smaller or medium-sized projects, the EIB provides multi-beneficiary intermediated loans, which support smaller-scale projects for subnational governments through national promotional banks and institutions (e.g. the HBOR in Croatia).

Additionally, structural programme loans are available, specifically aimed at co-financing investments managed by public authorities within their Operational Programmes. These are aligned with EU economic and social cohesion objectives and are often supplemented by EU grants. The EIB's financial instruments extend to equity, hybrid bonds and guarantees. Countries can also entrust the implementation of financial instruments (e.g. European Structural and Investment Funds) to the EIB, thereby benefitting from its professional fund management expertise. Finally, the EIB facilitates framework loans targeting multi-annual investment programmes executed by national and subnational governments. Such loans can also provide co-financing alongside EU funds.

Source: Author's elaboration, based on (EIB, 2023[28]; EIB, 2017[29]; EIB, 2024[30]; EIB, n.d.[31]).

Loans from IFIs generally have concessional terms, including lower interest rates and longer repayment periods, which help reduce the financial burden on recipient countries. However, subnational governments in Croatia may confront two issues in accessing IFI financing. First, financing from IFIs is not available for projects below a certain size, since very small and local projects are not considered reliable and/or secure enough for investors. For instance, financing from the EIB generally starts at about EUR 25 million (OECD, 2023[26]). Second, applying for a loan requires technical expertise (e.g. with preparing documentation) that may be scarce at the subnational level. Given the limited fiscal and human resource capacity of many subnational governments, and the limited territorial scale at which they operate, only Croatia's largest cities tend to successfully access financing from IFIs.

Public finance-related challenges to regional development in Croatia

Croatian subnational governments have seen a gradual rise in revenues and expenditures, in real terms, over the past decade. Revenue growth has sustained their ability to deliver basic public services that contribute to regional and local development (e.g. healthcare, education, transport). Moreover, Croatia reported a slight increase in the share of tax revenues as part of total subnational budgets, reflecting a very modest improvement in fiscal autonomy and flexibility to orient spending to meet local needs. In addition, counties, cities and municipalities saw a marked increase in public investment, which was supported by the influx of EU funds and the creation of several regional development grants. Each of these elements have helped Croatia's subnational governments support the implementation of county and local development plans and contribute to Croatia's long-term strategic objective of balanced regional development.

Despite these developments, five key challenges regarding the funding and financing of regional and local development in Croatia can be identified. First, subnational governments rely heavily on grants. Second, subnational governments, counties in particular, continue to have relatively limited fiscal autonomy compared to their peers in the OECD. Third, Croatia's Regional Development Index, created to identify subnational governments in need of particular financial support, potentially provides perverse incentives to subnational governments. Fourth, the uptake of macro-regional development agreement has been limited, despite their potential to mobilise and allocate funding and financing for development projects that span multiple counties. Fifth, the funding model of Croatia's RDAs is precarious. Addressing these challenges could increase Croatia's ability to ensure that regional development strategies and plans are properly funded and financed, and can be effectively implemented.

Making the most of EU funding for regional development

Since joining the EU in 2013, Croatia's county, city and municipal governments have increasingly been able to mobilise and use EU funding to support the implementation of county- and local-level development plans and projects. The increasing proportion of EU funding within subnational revenues can be clearly seen when looking at grants from EU funds received by subnational governments. While in 2014, Croatia reported that subnational governments did not receive revenue from EU grants, by 2020 close to 8% of subnational revenue (EUR 273 million) came from EU funds (Ministry of Finance, 2023[6]). This trend points to the increasing opportunity for Croatian subnational governments to receive transfers from the EU, primarily to support capital investment spending (IFC, 2021[14]; OECD, 2021[15]). As shown in Figure 5.7 there are sizeable variations by level of government. Municipalities have been able to mobilise EU funding more extensively than cities and counties, the latter of which tend to rely more extensively on decentralisation equalisation funds. In 2020, 11% of city revenue came from EU funds, compared to 6% for municipalities and 2% for counties.

Figure 5.7. Grants from EU funds as a share of total county, city and municipal revenue in Croatia (2014-20)

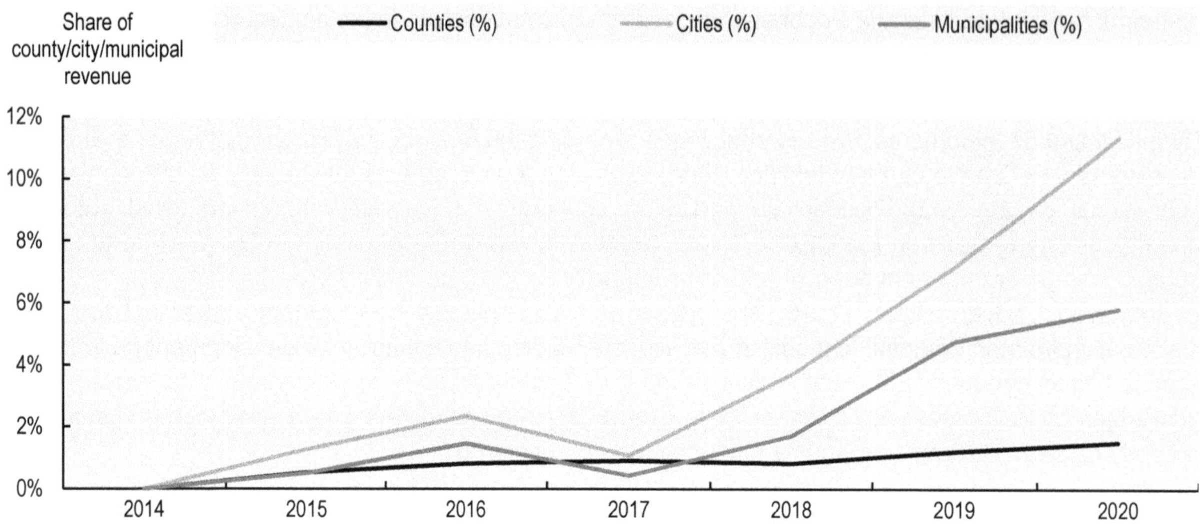

Source: Author's elaboration, based on (Ministry of Finance, 2023[6]).

The increasing use of EU funding by subnational governments has two main advantages. First, it has opened up various opportunities for subnational governments to invest in regional development priorities. Second, it has helped subnational governments hone their strategic planning and investment skills and expertise. In particular, it has helped subnational governments to gain experience in identifying funding opportunities, preparing competitive proposals and conducting monitoring and evaluation activities (OECD, 2023[26]). Skills developed as a result of applying for and managing EU funding are also transferrable to non-EU funding sources, as the processes of application, implementation and evaluation do not vary widely.

The increasing use of EU funding, however, comes with a number of risks. First, EU funding calls may not always be suitable to address specific local needs and priorities. Second, not all county and local governments may have the human and fiscal capacity to meet the requirements (e.g. for co-funding) associated with EU funding opportunities. Third, if the proportion of EU funding as part of total subnational revenues continues to increase significantly, subnational governments, and cities in particular, may risk becoming vulnerable to possible changes in the volume and sectoral priorities of the EU.

An increasing use of EU funding may pose challenges for policy makers to effectively address local needs

While a gradual increase in the use of EU funding by subnational governments, and cities in particular, is normal given the country's relatively recent accession to the EU, it is crucial to ensure that EU funding be used to help meet specific needs. In other words, Croatian subnational governments should invest their resources in obtaining EU funding that matches their regional and local priorities. Interviews with local stakeholders have pointed to concerns that some local leaders may be chasing EU funding opportunities regardless of whether or not the funding call is closely linked to local priorities (OECD, 2023[26]). When subnational governments aggressively pursue EU funding opportunities, it could lead to a misalignment between the projects that receive funding and the actual needs of the local population. For instance, a local government might allocate significant resources to develop a high-tech innovation park because it will attract EU funding, even though the area has more pressing needs, such as improving public transportation or healthcare services. This phenomenon can result in investments that do not directly contribute to the well-being or economic development of the local community, and it highlights the importance of strategic alignment between funding and local priorities.

Resource disparities across cities and municipalities can affect equal access to EU funding opportunities

Competitive EU funding can ensure that funds are allocated to the authorities that are in the best position to spend them effectively on regional or local development priorities. However, not all subnational governments have the same capacity to prepare robust project proposals. For example, wealthier cities have generally been able to create Local Development Agencies (LDAs), which in turn have helped them to identify funding opportunities and support the drafting of project proposals (OECD, 2022[32]). By contrast, other city and municipal governments need to compete for the attention of already thinly stretched RDAs to secure comparable technical support.

The co-funding requirements that accompany many, if not most, EU funding opportunities present another challenge for subnational governments. In order to help address subnational government co-funding needs, in 2015, Croatia set up a national co-funding programme for the implementation of EU projects at the regional and local levels. In particular, the programme helps county, city and municipal governments (including any legal entities owned by them and institutions established by them) to meet EU co-funding requirements (typically 15% of the total project value). Through the programme, subnational governments can receive a maximum of 50% co-funding for EU projects, or 80% in the case of specific disadvantaged areas (i.e. 50-80% of the 15% that subnational governments generally have to provide as co-funding). This approach renders funding mechanisms sensitive to differences in the fiscal capacity of Croatia's subnational governments, thereby supporting the ability of subnational governments with a weak fiscal capacity to compete for EU calls.

Under the auspices of this programme, the MRDEUF has so far launched nine public co-funding calls during the 2014-20 EU programming period and one public co-funding call for the 2021-27 EU programming period. For instance, the last 2023 call for co-funding published by the MRDEUF amounted to EUR 50 million and received 323 applications from subnational beneficiaries (MRDEUF, 2023[33]). To date, 2 109 co-funding contracts have been signed, with a total value of EUR 303.72 million, and covering all 20 counties and Zagreb City. In total, national co-funding amounted to over EUR 2 billion during the 2014-2020 programming period and EUR 1.5 billion during the current period, both of which represent just under 15% of the total funding linked to EU projects (European Commission, 2023[34]).

Despite the existence of the MRDEUF-managed co-funding programme, the current levels of co-funding may be insufficient to meet local needs. All 21 Croatian RDAs cited a lack of co-funding resources as the primary challenge to accessing and managing EU funding (OECD, 2022[32]). Smaller county, city or municipal governments in Croatia appear to face a particularly acute challenge in this regard. Their limited size often means that they struggle to raise the necessary own-source funds or access loans to apply to an EU funding call (Rodríguez-Pose and Garcilazo, 2015[35]). The MRDEUF hopes to address this challenge through the latest iteration of the EU co-funding programme covering the 2021-27 period, as part of which annual calls will be launched (MRDEUF, 2024[7]).

Subnational governments should diversify their revenue streams

In order to address the increasing reliance of subnational governments on EU funding to implement regional development plans and projects over time, it is important for Croatia to diversify subnational government revenue streams. This could include measures to: i) boost subnational fiscal autonomy; and ii) strengthen their capacity to enter into financing arrangements that can leverage private sector resources and expertise (i.e. public-private partnerships, PPPs).

In order to enhance subnational government fiscal autonomy, the revenue streams of subnational governments can be diversified through new fiscal decentralisation arrangements, for instance by devolving existing national taxes to lower levels of government or by exploring the introduction of new locally-levied taxes. With regard to the former, Croatia could consider devolving some existing green taxes or fees (i.e. to deter activities that are environmentally-damaging) to subnational governments. For instance, local taxes or fees could be levied on landfill use, on the environmental damage wrought by companies and on the sale of disposable plastic products. With regard to the latter, Italy and Sweden have adopted new taxes on the sale of disposable plastic products, which support local government budgets (Normattiva, 2023[36]; Rödl & Partner, 2022[37]). The assignment of such revenue-raising powers to subnational governments could help to diversify their revenue streams further while also supporting policy action on the green transition. For example, subnational governments with green credentials could generate interest from investors, potentially attracting investment capital, stimulating the local economy, and further increasing subnational tax revenues. Levying such subnational taxes may, however, require Croatia to invest data-gathering tools at the local level (e.g. to track the sale of disposable plastic products). Further to this, any possible adjustments to Croatia's subnational taxes need to be based on a careful assessment of how the proposed changes to the tax system would affect the fiscal capacity of citizens and businesses.

Under certain conditions, subnational public-private partnerships could mobilise funding for regional development initiatives

Another way for subnational governments in Croatia to further enhance the diversity of their revenue streams is by increasing their use of alternative financing arrangements for public investment, including public-private partnerships (PPPs). PPPs involve collaboration between the public and private sectors to finance, develop, operate, and maintain infrastructure projects or services. Under the right conditions, PPPs can enable subnational governments to leverage private sector expertise, innovation, and resources to deliver projects more efficiently and effectively. This can be particularly beneficial for infrastructure projects that require significant upfront investment, such as transportation networks, energy systems and medical centres (OECD, 2022[38]).

While Croatia has a comprehensive legal framework for PPPs, they are rarely used at the subnational level (Official Gazette of Croatia No 78 et al., 2018[39]; Official Gazette OG No 88/12 15/15, 2015[40]; Official Gazette of Croatia No 16/13, 2013[41]). A large majority of RDAs (86%) felt that one of the primary obstacles to the successful use of PPPs at the county level was public distrust of the mechanism, while a further 43% cited a lack of guidance from the national government and regulatory uncertainty as important barriers (OECD, 2022[32]) (Figure 5.8).

Figure 5.8. Main obstacles to successful PPPs at the county level according to RDAs

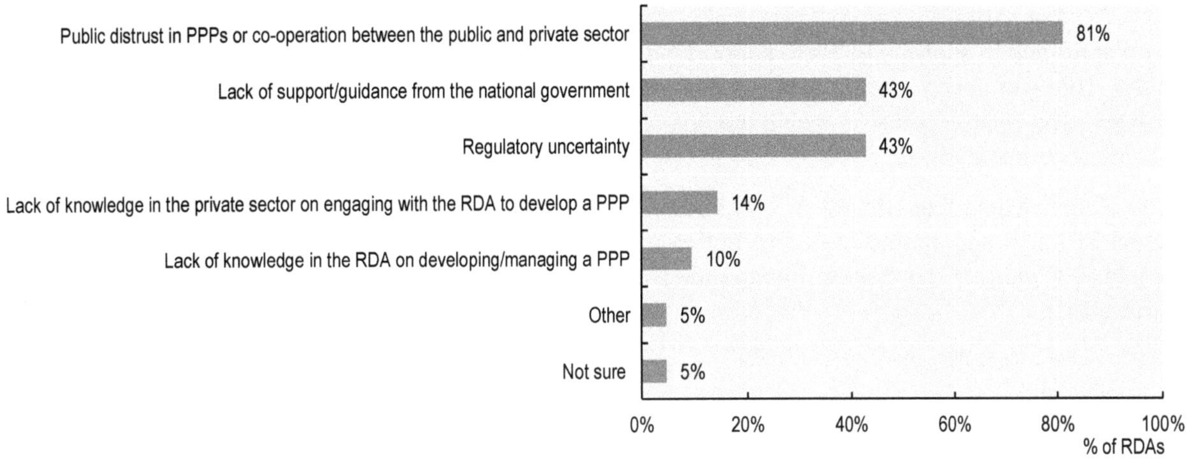

Note: Questionnaire question: What does your RDA consider to be the two largest obstacles to successful PPPs in your county?
Full response options: Public distrust in PPPs or co-operation between the public and private sector, in general; Lack of support/guidance from the national government; Regulatory uncertainty; Lack of knowledge in the private sector on engaging with the RDA to develop a PPP; Lack of knowledge in the RDA on developing and/or managing a PPP; Not sure; Other. N=21.
Source: Author's elaboration, based on (OECD, 2022[32]).

Only under certain conditions and strict control mechanisms can PPPs contribute to diversifying funding for regional and local development projects. Without strict control mechanisms, PPPs can lead to regulatory capture, conflicts of interest and corruption, potentially resulting in long-term impacts on government fiscal capacity and trust in government. In sum, PPPs should be used only when they can produce greater value for money than would be provided by the delivery of public services or investment through traditional means. In practice, this means that they should primarily be directed towards large-scale projects in priority infrastructure sectors (OECD, 2022[42]).

Moreover, the government should also recall that, ordinarily, only larger cities have the fiscal and institutional capacities necessary to make PPPs work. This means that PPPs are generally not appropriate for small local governments. They are typically also not appropriate for small projects, where value for money can be limited. Small PPP projects do not necessarily imply small liabilities, underscoring the need to also consider the full extent of contingent liabilities created through guarantees to PPPs (OECD, 2022[38]). In addition, small PPPs are not always commercially viable. To overcome this challenge, governments in some OECD Member countries (e.g. the United States) have introduced provisions to bundle PPPs across sectors or jurisdictions in order to encourage economies of scale (Box 5.4). Exploring opportunities to bundle subnational PPPs could be of particular value for Croatia, given its high degree of territorial fragmentation.

Box 5.4. Bundled subnational public-private partnerships, an example from the United States

One approach to applying PPPs to support many small projects is to bundle smaller projects into larger ones. This can improve scale and viability thus making them more attractive to larger private sector players, and enable better financing options, including PPPs. In some cases, governments in multiple jurisdictions are involved.

The Pennsylvania Department of Transportation, in the United States, took a bundling approach to small PPPs. It aggregated the construction and maintenance of a few hundred small bridges into a single PPP project. This helped manage the limited viability of individual PPP projects arising from their small size.

Source: Author's elaboration, based on (OECD, 2021[43]).

In order to increase the responsible use of PPPs to mobilise funding for regional development initiatives, Croatia could take several complementary actions. For instance, the national government could provide support and guidance to ensure that subnational governments are well-informed regarding the potential benefits and risks of PPPs, and the provisions of Croatia's regulatory framework. It should also aim to strengthen the capacity of subnational authorities to administer PPPs and deliver investment projects effectively, while managing risks. For instance, the government could provide information and training to subnational governments regarding how to assess the value added of PPPs, how to manage partnerships with the public sector and how to establish a transparent system that can track the use of public funding of PPPs and ensure their effectiveness.

Ensuring that the recent PIT reforms do not exacerbate regional and local disparities

Over the last two decades, Croatia has attempted to curb the reliance of subnational authorities on inter-governmental transfers. In 2007, for example, a higher share of Personal Income Tax (PIT) was allocated to subnational governments (from 34 to 52%), with the central government retaining the right to determine a base rate, while subnational governments could apply an additional PIT surtax (Ministry of Finance, 2024[10]). As a result, PIT (including PIT surtax) has become the primary source of own-source revenue of subnational governments, accounting for 90.1% of total subnational tax revenues in 2020. In October 2023, Croatia took additional action, amending the Income Tax Act to grant cities and municipalities flexibility in setting their PIT rates (Official Gazette of Croatia No 114/23, 2023[44]) (Box 5.5). The PIT reform can deliver important benefits to cities and municipalities, for example by strengthening their fiscal autonomy and their capacity to support local economic development. However, the reform also comes with important risks, including a possible 'race to the bottom' in which cities and municipalities could consecutively and aggressively lower PIT rates to attract investment and talent, thereby undermining their fiscal capacity.

Box 5.5. The distribution of Personal Income Tax among levels of government and the reform of PIT rates in Croatia

Since Croatian independence, subnational governments have received revenue from PIT. Since 2007, local governments retain 74% of PIT revenues, while counties retain an additional 20%. The remaining 6% is earmarked for those subnational governments tasked with additional decentralised functions, such as primary and secondary education, social care, healthcare and firefighting.

Until 2023, the national government set PIT rates, with lower and upper limits of 20% and 30% respectively. City and municipal governments—but not counties—could add a personal income surcharge on top of the nationally mandated PIT. This surtax varied depending on the size and type of city or municipality. The maximum surtax rates ranged from 10% for municipalities to 18% for Zagreb City. The introduction of the surcharge gave city and municipal governments greater fiscal autonomy. First, it enabled them to increase their own-source revenue. Second, by setting their own surtax rates within the permitted range, local governments were able to tailor their tax policies to better reflect the unique economic conditions, developmental goals, and public service requirements of their respective jurisdictions.

In October 2023, an amendment to the Law on Financing of Local and Regional Self-Government Units put an end to this regulation. As of 2024, city and municipal governments have been able to set their own PIT rates within certain limits, making PIT surtaxes no longer necessary to build local fiscal autonomy. Local governments can now choose two progressive tax rates from a range, with 15% representing the lowest possible rate and 35.4% representing the highest. However, the specific ranges available for municipalities and cities depend on their size (Table 5.2).

Table 5.2. Amended rates in the Income Tax Act as of January 2024

Entity	Pre-2024 PIT surtax rate	New lower PIT rate (2024 onwards)	New upper PIT rate (2024 onwards)
Municipalities	Up to 10%	15%—22%	25%—33%
Cities (< 30 000 inhabitants)	Up to 12%	15%—22.4%	25%—35.6%
Cities (> 30 000 inhabitants)	Up to 15%	15%—23%	25%—34.5%
Zagreb City	Up to 18%	15%—23.6%	25%—35.4%

Source: Author's elaboration, based on (Official Gazette of Croatia No 127 et al., 2017[11]; Official Gazette of Croatia No 114/23, 2023[44]; Official Gazette of Croatia No 101/17, 2017[45]; World Bank, 2021[5]).

The 2023 PIT reform could reduce city and municipal dependency on inter-governmental grants

Granting cities and municipalities the power to set PIT rates represents a significant step towards greater fiscal decentralisation and provides a number of other benefits. First, allowing cities and municipalities to set their PIT rates provides them with more control over their revenue base, potentially leading to improved financial stability and reduced dependence on central government transfers. For instance, should a city require additional funds for infrastructure projects or social services, it could elect to raise PIT rates within its jurisdiction. Second, flexibility in setting PIT rates empowers cities and municipalities to use tax policy as a tool for economic development. By adjusting tax rates, cities and municipalities can create more favourable conditions for investment, encourage business creation and expansion and attract skilled labour. This strategic use of tax policy can enhance the economic attractiveness and competitiveness of local areas, thereby driving growth and development.

A race to lower PIT rates may widen fiscal gaps between cities and municipalities

In order to reap the benefits of the new PIT system, city and municipal governments will need to strike a balance when setting local tax rates. They need to set PIT rates that are sufficiently high so as to raise the funds needed to invest in local public services and infrastructure. However, the rates also need to be sufficiently low so as to avoid placing excessive burdens on taxpayers. In this regard, the government will need to monitor the effects of the reform on local budgets closely. In particular, it should ensure that the additional powers afforded to local governments to reduce rates do not lead to excessive competition among city and municipal governments to attract and retain residents and business through aggressive and repeated reductions in the tax burden. This type of 'race to the bottom' could widen disparities in the fiscal capacity of local governments, and would be particularly damaging to the economic health of smaller cities and municipalities, given that larger cities typically enjoy greater fiscal space to absorb tax cuts (i.e. through property income or user charges and fees).

The government should also monitor the effects of the reform on county budgets. Although the PIT reform only provides additional rate-setting powers to cities and municipalities, county governments currently receive 20% of all PIT revenues that are levied in their territory. As such, any significant adjustments in PIT rates by city or municipal governments could also affect the PIT revenues that flow to county governments. Such adjustments could create revenue imbalances, thus affecting the ability of certain county governments to support investments in regional development.

A race to lower PIT rates may limit the financial resources available to smaller local governments to support local service delivery or infrastructure investment, which would increase territorial inequalities. This could also increase the need for additional equalisation transfers to ensure that similar levels of local public service access and quality can be maintained throughout all Croatian territories. As such, the government should carefully monitor the effects of the PIT reform on Croatia's two fiscal equalisation mechanisms (Box 5.6).

Box 5.6. Croatia's equalisation mechanisms

Croatia has two different equalisation mechanisms: a revenue equalisation mechanism and an expenditure equalisation mechanism. The former corresponds to the Fiscal Equalisation Fund (FEF), a non-earmarked grant that aims to mitigate revenue disparities across county, city and municipal governments respectively, and ensure they have sufficient resources to provide basic public services and infrastructure. The FEF is funded directly from the state budget and compensates counties, cities and municipalities whose fiscal capacity is determined to be below the reference value for the same level of subnational government.

The expenditure equalisation grant is the Equalisation Fund for Decentralised Functions (EFDF), through which funding is distributed to counties, cities and municipalities that are fulfilling additional responsibilities. Six percent of PIT revenues are earmarked for specific decentralised functions, such as primary and secondary education, social care, healthcare and firefighting. These revenues are transferred to the EFDF, and further supplemented by funding from the national budget where needed. The additional national budget funding is intended to cover the difference between the PIT revenues and the minimum expenditure at the subnational level that is needed to carry out each decentralised function.

Source: Author's elaboration based on (Official Gazette No 127 et al., 2017[46]).

Strengthening the Regional Development Index as a tool to encourage territorial development

The 2014 Law on Regional Development introduced the Regional Development Index (Box 5.7). The Index is used by the national government to: i) identify regional and local governments that score below the national average in terms of development (lagging regions are known as 'assisted areas') and; ii) tailor the distribution of financial support to these lagging subnational governments. In particular, the government supports various programmes (e.g. the Programme of Sustainable Social and Economic Development of Assisted Areas and the Programme for the Development of Mountainous Areas) through fiscal transfers that are based on the Index scores of Croatia's subnational governments (MRDEUF, 2022[47]; MRDEUF, 2022[48]).

Box 5.7. The Regional Development Index

The Regional Development Index is a composite weighted indicator based on an adjusted average of standardised socio-economic indicators. It is calculated every three years in order to help identify county, city and municipal governments lagging behind the national average in terms of development. In accordance with the Regulation, the following indicators are used to calculate the Regional Development Index:

- Average income per capita
- Average primary income per capita
- Average unemployment rate
- General movement of the population
- Level of education of the population (tertiary education)
- Ageing index

County governments are classified into four groups according to their Index value (two of which are above average and two of which are below), while cities and municipalities are grouped into eight categories (four of which are above average and four of which are below). All subnational governments with a below-average Index score are classified as "assisted areas". The distribution of counties was last updated at the beginning of 2024.

Table 5.3. Distribution of counties according to the Regional Development Index as of 2024

Group	Category	County
1	Below-average, lower half	Slavonski Brod-Posavina, Požega-Slavonia, Sisak-Moslavina, Virovitica-Podravina and Vukovar-Srijem
2	Below-average, upper half	Bjelovar-Bilogora, Karlovac, Koprivnica-Križevci, Lika-Senj, Osijek-Baranja and Šibenik-Knin
3	Above-average, lower half	Krapina-Zagorje, Međimurje, Primorje-Gorski Kotar, Split-Dalmatia and Varaždin
4	Above-average, upper half	Dubrovnik-Neretva, Zagreb City, Istria, Zadar and Zagreb (county)

Source: Author's elaboration, based on (Official Gazette of Croatia No 3/24, 2024[49]; Government of Croatia, 2017[50]).

The Index provides an important snapshot of county- and local-level development, which can help make timely adjustments to the reallocation of regional development funding, thereby contributing to Croatia's long-term strategic objective of balanced regional development. However, interviews with local stakeholders confirmed that some subnational governments try to 'game' their Index score in order to be eligible for 'assisted area' funding (OECD, 2023[26]). This means that the Index may inadvertently encourage county and local governments to underperform across various socio-economic indicators.

Gradually phasing out funding for subnational governments no longer considered 'assisted' could help solidify development gains

To help strengthen the Regional Development Index as a tool that can encourage subnational government to strengthen their performance, Croatia can take several actions. First, the government could consider introducing measures to gradually decrease the financial impact of transitioning out of 'assisted area' status, thereby mitigating the negative consequences associated with improving Index scores. This could involve establishing a mechanism whereby the financial support provided to county and local governments formerly considered 'assisted areas' decreases incrementally over a set period (e.g. three years). Such an approach could help to limit the incentive for local leaders to deliberately seek an 'assisted area' designation. Moreover, gradually phasing out financial support to subnational governments previously classified as 'assisted areas' could provide them with financial means to consolidate their recent developmental gains.

Second, the government could consider using the Index as a foundation to support a more performance-based funding model for regional development (i.e. one in which socio-economic progress yields certain rewards). For instance, subnational governments that perform at an above-average level might be entitled to certain concessions (e.g. tax breaks or increased investment opportunities), although such measures should be limited in scope and monitored closely so as not to unduly exacerbate territorial inequalities. Such a mechanism could serve as a vital incentive for those subnational governments that, while considered well-developed within the Croatian context, still find themselves trailing the majority of their EU peers. By recognising and rewarding their achievements, the mechanism would address concerns expressed by some RDAs that current regional development support mechanisms in Croatia predominantly favour underperforming regions (OECD, 2023[26]). Implementing performance-based incentives that are based on Index scores could help encourage all Croatian regions to strive for improvement, acknowledging the efforts of those that have made significant progress yet still have room to grow in the broader European context.

Strengthening existing co-ordination bodies to support regional development funding

To ensure that sufficient financial resources for regional development are effectively mobilised, managed and spent, it is imperative to have robust co-ordination and communication mechanisms in place. Vertical co-ordination (i.e. among levels of government) matters because it can help ensure that regional development funding mechanisms are built on identified territorial needs, as well as fiscal capacities (e.g. ability to co-fund) and human capacities (e.g. ability to respond to competitive calls for proposals). Horizontal co-ordination (across a government tier) is equally important. For instance, inter-ministerial co-ordination can help ensure coherence in how regional development funding is allocated across ministries (i.e. the MRDEUF and other line ministries). Similarly, robust horizontal co-ordination mechanisms can help to address challenges posed by territorial fragmentation, potentially enabling counties, cities and municipalities to pool resources, share expertise, and collaborate on larger scale projects that might be unfeasible for smaller entities to undertake independently.

The section identifies a number of policy options that can help Croatia to strengthen existing co-ordination mechanisms described in chapter 3 (e.g. the Prime Minister-led regional development co-ordination body[3]). In particular, it identifies measures that could foster inter-governmental debate on regional development funding sources and needs. The section also explores how macro-regional development agreements can help to address funding and financing challenges related to Croatia's territorial fragmentation.

Enabling the Prime Minister-led regional development co-ordination body to foster debate on regional development funding sources and needs

In principle, the Prime Minister-led regional development co-ordination body, which has been operating since 2016, can support both inter-ministerial and vertical co-ordination on regional development funding. However, as stated in chapter 3, this may require a number of supportive actions, including reorganising the body into two chambers: one to support inter-ministerial co-ordination of regional development policy and the other to support its vertical co-ordination among different levels of government. Second, the list of public bodies slated for mandatory participation needs to be extended, in order to include a wider set of central government bodies whose actions affect regional development.

The national-level chamber of the Prime Minister-led regional development co-ordination body could provide a platform for ministries and other central government bodies (e.g. Bureau of Statistics) to discuss the funding and financing mechanisms that could be marshalled to help achieve balanced regional development. For example, the chamber could commission an assessment of national budget funds allocated to initiatives that support regional and local development. Developing a comprehensive overview of regional development funding, which is currently not available, could serve several objectives. First, it could help to identify which ministries and other central government bodies provide funding to territorial development initiatives. This could help to determine, for example, which bodies, because of their funding for regional and local government, should be part of the Prime Minister-led regional development co-ordination body.

Second, the assessment could help the government to quantify how much is spent on regional and local development from the national budget, and how much is allocated to initiatives that target specific sectors (e.g. education, housing, SMEs, roads and transportation). Based on this information, the Prime Minister-led regional development co-ordination body could identify: i) whether the funding provided through the national budget aligns with the country's long-term development objectives; and ii) whether there are funding gaps or possible inefficiencies (e.g. due to overlap in spending). A similar exercise was conducted for Ukraine's Ministry of Communities and Territories Development, which could serve as an example for Croatia (Box 5.8).

Box 5.8. Assessment of Ukraine's state funding for regional and local development

In 2021, U-LEAD, an EU-funded programme, carried out a systematic analysis of Ukraine's government funding that had been allocated to policies and programmes supporting regional and local development between 2015 and 2019. The assessment, which was developed for Ukraine's Ministry of Communities and Territories Development, aimed to strengthen linkages between the country's regional development policy and budget planning. It also sought to provide evidence to support the high-level co-ordination of sectoral policies with an impact on regional and local development by determining which national government institutions provided funding, at what volume, and to which sectors.

The assessment identified 110 budget programmes covering 12 different policy areas that were implemented by 20 different public institutions. It also identified how much was spent on regional versus local development, on subsidies versus investment, and on sectoral versus multi-sectoral initiatives.

The assessment found that financial support for regional and local development was heavily fragmented between many public bodies. Indeed, only one-fifth of cross-government regional and local development programmes had been implemented by the ministry responsible for regional development. Moreover, spending had been heavily weighted towards a small number of large programmes in sectors such as road infrastructure or regional development.

The assessment served to highlight the need for a strategic prioritisation of the national government's financial support for regional and local development. It also drew attention to the need for stronger strategic co-ordination of regional and local development planning and budgeting at the Centre-of-Government.

Source: Author's elaboration, based on (U-LEAD, unpublished[51]).

For its part, the second chamber of the Prime Minister-led regional development co-ordination body could facilitate debate and exchange among levels of government about funding and financing needs and priorities, as well as any absorption capacity gaps that need to be addressed. Given the RDAs' role in guiding the design of the county development plans, and their support in helping to identify funding and financing opportunities for cities and municipalities, the participation of the RDAs in the Prime Minister-led regional development co-ordination body should be guaranteed.

Expanding the use of development agreements to fund and finance macro-regional projects

Croatia could also consider expanding the use of inter-regional co-operation instruments such as the macro-regional partnerships between county governments and RDAs on the one hand, and the national government on the other to help them benefit more from investment opportunities that are most efficiently delivered at scale. The main arrangements that currently exist to support macro-regional investment are development agreements and their co-ordination councils. Development agreements can be signed between at least three counties and the national government to support the management and absorption of EU and national funding and financing for regional development. They facilitate investment in strategic projects that aim to address shared development challenges and improve macro-regional competitiveness and well-being (Official Gazette of Croatia No 118/18, 2018[52]). Thereby, the development agreements and their co-ordination councils can, in principle, help address funding challenges associated with Croatia's high level of territorial fragmentation (see chapter 3). For instance, territorial fragmentation can lead to national or international funding being scattered across many small-scale projects. This can lead to inefficiencies, as the impact of investment is diluted across too many initiatives, each too small to generate significant development in the territory (OECD, 2019[53]). Moreover, managing numerous small projects increases the administrative burden on subnational governments by requiring them to oversee multiple initiatives, each with its own set of requirements and monitoring processes. This not only strains limited administrative resources but also detracts from the potential to focus on larger, more impactful projects (OECD, 2022[54]).

One development agreement that has borne witness to significant macro-regional investment has been the Slavonia, Baranja and Srijem agreement, which was signed by five counties in 2017. Under the auspices of the agreement, a co-ordination council was established that was tasked with overseeing the allocation of macro-regional development funding (OECD, 2023[26]). As of 2022, the Council had overseen the disbursement of EUR 2.6 billion worth of contracted projects. Examples of projects include the construction of a fruit and vegetable distribution centre, the building of waste management centres, the rehabilitation of railways, and the refurbishment of monuments (OECD, 2023[26]).

Despite the success of the Slavonia, Baranja and Srijem development agreement, however, there have been challenges in terms of scaling out its model of macro-regional co-ordination. While a separate development agreement was signed by five counties in Northern Croatia in 2021, implementation of related macro-regional investment projects has proceeded slowly, owing to uncertainty regarding how the development agreement will be funded (OECD, 2023[26]). For example, interviews with local stakeholders indicated that IFIs, such as the EBRD, currently do not finance development agreements, as there is no mechanism in place through which the bank could enter into a formal agreement with such macro-regional structures (OECD, 2023[26]).

To boost macro-regional co-operation, the government should explore how the success of the Council of Slavonia, Baranja, and Srijem can be replicated in other regions. In particular, macro-regional councils could provide a locus for RDAs to develop joint TL2-level development and investment strategies, which could help align objectives among regions and bridge information, capacity and financing gaps. A similar approach has been adopted in certain OECD regions. Canada's Atlantic Growth Strategy, for example, brings together four provinces—Nova Scotia, New Brunswick, Prince Edward Island as well as Newfoundland and Labrador—to collaborate on initiatives such as infrastructure development, innovation and skills training (Government of Canada, n.d.[55]). Such an approach would also build on Croatia's experiment of developing Plans for Industrial Transition at the TL2 level, which focuses on boosting innovation capacity at the macro-regional level and expanding the approach to regional development more broadly.

The Slavonia, Baranja and Srijem development agreement has been quite successful owing to the fact that when it was created, it could count on specific EU funding for macro-regional development. Providing additional certainty about the availability of such a funding stream—whether from national or EU sources—may be necessary to encourage county leaders in other parts of the country to establish similar development agreements. In relation to this, the government could explore together with IFIs, whether new support mechanisms (e.g. framework agreements) could be developed that would enable the macro-regional development councils to collectively borrow, in order to finance regional development projects. Provided the collective fiscal capacity of the counties collaborating in the macro-regional development agreements and the territorial scale they represent, they appear well-positioned to present bankable projects.

Ensuring the financial sustainability of RDAs

Croatian RDAs play a pivotal role in the design, implementation, monitoring and evaluation of the development plans at the county level. This role extends to facilitating communication between the national government on the one hand, and county, city, and municipal governments, on the other, for example in terms of funding-related information. Moreover, RDAs also help counties, cities, municipalities and non-governmental actors identify funding calls and develop project proposals. Their capacity to carry out these responsibilities, however, is curtailed by their dependence on EU Technical Assistance funding, which represents the majority of RDA revenues. Current EU Technical Assistance funding is set to end in December 2025 by which time Croatia aims to have strengthened the RDA funding model. This section explores how the current RDA funding model risks diverting critical time and resources away from their tasks and responsibilities. It also proposes several options to increase the financial capacity of the RDAs.

RDAs only receive a small share of their total revenue from their founders

To carry out their tasks and responsibilities, RDAs require staff with a diverse range of skills, such as strategic planning, project management, proposal-writing, programme budgeting, and investment planning and management. To support these functions, Croatian RDAs are funded through two main sources. RDA base funding comes from their founding counties and cities, which are charged with ensuring the RDAs have sufficient financial resources to fulfil their responsibilities. This typically represents 25% to 30% of an RDA's budget (OECD, 2023[26]). As stated in chapter 3, twenty RDAs have only one founder, namely their county government. Only the RDA of Zadar County is founded by two public bodies: the County and Zadar City. The remainder of RDA funding comes from EU Technical Assistance that is channelled through the MRDEUF.

The funding from the RDA founders is used to pay for core staff. By assigning core staff to work on EU projects, the financial resources provided by counties and cities are also used to meet the EU's co-financing requirements (i.e. core staff time is used as an in-kind contribution) (OECD, 2023[26]). Conversely, funding from EU Technical Assistance cannot be used to hire permanent staff. Instead, it enables the RDAs to contract temporary workers who collaborate with the RDAs on a project basis. In some RDAs, temporary employees represent half of total staff, who generally stay with the RDAs for less than three years (OECD, 2023[26]). Employing staff for longer would imply having to offer them a permanent contract, as per Croatian employment law. However, the core funding provided by the RDA founders often is not sufficient to retain staff hired with EU Technical Assistance funds.

Thus, while EU Technical Assistance enables the RDAs to temporarily expand their human resource capacity and hire experts with specific skills, it does not contribute to a sustainable enhancement of RDA operational capabilities. Moreover, with EU Technical Assistance only guaranteed until the end of 2025, the medium-term financial sustainability of RDAs may depend on them taking steps to mobilise additional revenue. These two aspects—the fact that a large share of RDA staff are temporarily employed, and the uncertainty of EU Technical Assistance funding post-2025—create an incentive for the RDAs to expend important time and resources on applying to EU funding calls (OECD, 2023[56]), which has two important benefits. First, it encourages the RDAs to proactively identify relevant calls to which county, city and municipal governments can apply. This increases their opportunities to obtain funding for regional and local development projects. Second, it enables RDAs to develop a high level of expertise in navigating EU funding mechanisms, thus enhancing their overall effectiveness and increasing the likelihood of securing funds for critical projects.

There are, however, notable drawbacks associated with the staffing incentive. One is the risk of RDAs diverting staff time and potentially other resources away from other tasks and responsibilities, such as tracking the implementation of the county development plan and liaising with non-governmental actors to enhance their contribution to regional development objectives. This can lead to a situation where an RDA's primary focus shifts from strategic regional development to constant search for financial resources (OECD, 2023[56]). Moreover, the need to continuously apply for competitive funding also introduces a level of uncertainty and instability in an RDA's operational planning and project implementation.

Adjusting the RDA funding model will likely affect its relationships with subnational governments and the MRDEUF

Croatia could consider various actions to boost the financial sustainability of the RDAs. First, counties could be called upon to bridge the gap left by the end of EU Technical Assistance, which is slated to end in 2025. Yet, this would severely strain county budgets and would require a roughly fourfold increase in their RDA-related expenditures (Vukovar-Srijem County, 2023[57]). RDAs and their founders could also explore the possibility of larger city and municipal governments joining the RDA, following the example of Zadar County RDA. The financial contributions from additional members could enhance RDA's financial sustainability, while also strengthening the collaborative ties among RDAs, and the cities and municipalities.

Even if counties are willing and able to increase their funding to RDAs, such a change might not necessarily benefit the implementation of Croatia's regional development policy. In particular, it could alter the relationship between the RDAs and the county administrations on the one hand, and the RDAs and the MRDEUF on the other. Should RDAs come to depend predominantly or solely on county resources, they might become more inclined to prioritise tasks assigned to them by the counties, rather than those coming from the Ministry. This could undermine the RDAs' role in supporting long-term regional development planning.

Croatia could also explore improving the financial sustainability of the RDAs by establishing them as non-governmental organisations (or possibly as co-operatives) (OECD, 2022[58]). This would allow them to generate a portion of their revenue through paid activities or services. Similar models have been adopted in OECD Member countries. For instance, some RDAs in Belgium can provide paid services to subnational governments, for example to support their strategic planning activities (IDETA, 2023[59]; IGRETEC, n.d.[60]; Wallonie Developpement, n.d.[61]). The fees and revenues they derive from these services could contribute to their operational budgets.

Allowing RDAs to once again provide paid services, however, would require Croatia to navigate different challenges. For instance, RDAs indicate that since becoming regional co-ordinators in 2018, they have lost their competitive edge to provide services in the private market (OECD, 2023[26]). Therefore, should RDAs be permitted to offer paid services again, they would need to invest substantially in outreach, for example to SMEs. They would have to clearly communicate their renewed availability and distinguish how their specific expertise can add value to private actors. Second, smaller cities and municipalities may not have the necessary financial resources to pay the RDAs, for example to help draft their local development plan or implementation programme, which would limit access to those governments most in need of technical support. Defining a series of free services that RDAs could provide (e.g. to support local strategic planning) could help to address this challenge.

In addition, the MRDEUF could provide direct funding to the RDAs through the national budget, complementing the funding provided by the county administrations (and other founders). This could have multiple benefits. First, it would help to ensure that the tasks assigned to RDAs by the MRDEUF are adequately funded. Second, it would imply that the RDA funding model better reflects the fact that, in their current setup, the RDAs carry out tasks for and are accountable to both counties and the MRDEUF, as described in chapter 3. This would give RDAs more leeway to balance requests for support made by their founders and by the MRDEUF, which may not necessarily align.

The above-mentioned options to increase the financial sustainability of the RDAs—i) additional funding by counties and other founding members, ii) possibility to provide paid services; or iii) additional core funding from the MRDEUF—are not mutually exclusive. In fact, they could, in principle, be adopted together. This would go a long way in shoring up and diversifying their funding streams, allowing them to spend less time in search of funding.

Conclusion

This chapter has laid out the way in which subnational public finances have evolved in Croatia over the past decade, outlining its implications for the country's regional development policy. The analysis has underscored a notable increase in revenues and investment at the subnational level over the past decade, driven primarily by European Union funding (e.g. to implement ITIs). This influx of funds has been instrumental for the implementation of regional and local development projects across the country, including by supporting the delivery of local public services (e.g. healthcare, education, transport).

Moreover, building on the legislative and planning framework for regional development established in 2014, Croatia has created several mechanisms through which it funds development projects that aim to meet the specific needs and capacities of its counties, cities and municipalities. These mechanisms include the MRDEUF-led Co-funding Programme, which helps subnational governments fulfil the EU's co-funding requirement for project calls, and funding for 'assisted areas' (i.e. the subnational governments whose performance on a series of development indicators sits below the national average). These funding arrangements help Croatia advance in its long-term strategic objective of supporting balanced regional development.

The chapter has also identified opportunities to improve the funding and financing arrangements for regional development. For example, enhancing existing co-ordination mechanisms (e.g. macro-regional development agreements) have been highlighted as essential steps that could improve the allocation and efficiency of funding for regional development. Additionally, the financial sustainability of RDAs and their operations has emerged as a critical concern. The government should re-evaluate the RDA funding model, in order to ensure that RDAs can continue providing vital support to the design, implementation, monitoring and evaluation of county and local development plans and programmes.

Ensuring concerted efforts are made to address the above-mentioned challenges will help equip Croatia's national and subnational governments with the necessary financial means and structures to implement regional development plans and projects. This, in turn, will help to transform the comprehensive legislative and planning framework for regional development, which has been developed since 2014, into one that can deliver even more tangible benefits for communities across the country.

References

Blöchliger, H. et al. (2010), "Sub-central Governments and the Economic Crisis: Impact and Policy Responses", *OECD Economics Department Working Papers* 752, https://doi.org/10.1787/5kml6xq5bgwc-en. [9]

Council of Europe (2007), *Local and regional democracy in Croatia: Explanatory memorandum*, https://rm.coe.int/explanatory-memorandum-on-local-and-regional-democracy-in-croatiainsti/1680718a00. [4]

Council of Slavonia, Baranja and Srijem (2024), *XVI. sjednica Savjeta za Slavoniju, Baranju i Srijem*, https://vlada.gov.hr/UserDocsImages/Vijesti/2024/Sije%C4%8Danj/12%20sije%C4%8Danj/XVI.%20sjednica%20Savjeta%20za%20Slavoniju%2C%20Baranju%20i%20Srijem.pdf. [27]

EIB (2024), *National promotional banks and institutions*, https://www.eib.org/en/about/partners/npbis/index. [30]

EIB (2023), *Presentation on "EIB Support for Regional Development" delivered in the second knowledge-sharing forum of the project "Enhanced Strategic Planning at Regional and Local Levels in Croatia"*. [28]

EIB (2017), *Croatia: Continued EIB and HBOR support for SMEs creating jobs for young people*, https://www.eib.org/en/press/all/2017-300-continued-eib-and-hbor-support-for-croatian-smes-creating-jobs-for-young-people. [29]

EIB (n.d.), *Shared management funds and financial instruments*, https://www.eib.org/en/products/mandates-partnerships/shared-management-funds/index (accessed on 15 January 2024). [31]

European Commission (2023), *Cohesion Open Data Platform - Croatia*, European Commission, https://cohesiondata.ec.europa.eu/countries/HR/14-20. [34]

European Commission (2023), *Croatia's recovery and resilience plan*, https://commission.europa.eu/business-economy-euro/economic-recovery/recovery-and-resilience-facility/country-pages/croatias-recovery-and-resilience-plan_en (accessed on 15 January 2024). [22]

European Commission (2022), *Investing in skills and jobs for the green transition in Croatia*, https://european-social-fund-plus.ec.europa.eu/en/news/skills-and-jobs-green-transition-croatia (accessed on 2023 November 12). [21]

Eurostat (2023), "Government deficit/surplus, debt and associated data", *Government finance statistics (EDP and ESA 2010)*, https://ec.europa.eu/eurostat/databrowser/product/view/gov_10dd_edpt1__custom_9654757?lang=en (accessed on 3 February 2024). [18]

Eurostat (2023), "Government revenue, expenditure and main aggregates", *Government finance statistics (EDP and ESA 2010)*, https://ec.europa.eu/eurostat/databrowser/view/GOV_10A_MAIN__custom_7657932/default/table?lang=en (accessed on 3 October 2023). [13]

Government of Canada (n.d.), *Leadership*, https://www.canada.ca/en/atlantic-canada-opportunities/atlanticgrowth/leadership.html (accessed on 2 October 2023). [55]

Government of Croatia (2017), *Index of development*, https://razvoj.gov.hr/o-ministarstvu/regionalni-razvoj/indeks-razvijenosti/112. [50]

IDETA (2023), *Nos missions [Our missions]*. [59]

IFC (2021), *The impact of the COVID-19 crisis on subnational governments in emerging markets: the outlook one year on*, https://www.ifc.org/content/dam/ifc/doc/mgrt/ifc-covid19-municipalities2021-final-web-7-28-21.pdf. [14]

IGRETEC (n.d.), *Who we are*, https://www.igretec.com/en/igretec/who-are-we/ (accessed on 2 February 2024). [60]

Ministry of Finance (2024), *Written comments provided, based on the draft "Towards Balanced Regional Development in Croatia" report*. [10]

Ministry of Finance (2023), *Subnational government accounts*, https://mfin.gov.hr/istaknute-teme/lokalna-samouprava/financijski-izvjestaji-jlp-r-s/pr-ras-i-ras-funkc-za-razdoblje-2014-2020/3173. [6]

MRDEUF (2024), *Program razvoja otoka u 2024. [Island Development Programme in 2024]*, https://razvoj.gov.hr/o-ministarstvu/djelokrug-1939/otoci/razvoj-otoka/program-razvoja-otoka-u-2024/5487 (accessed on 14 February 2024). [24]

MRDEUF (2024), *Written comments received from the Government of Croatia in March 2024*. [7]

MRDEUF (2023), *Javni poziv za sufinanciranje provedbe EU projekata na regionalnoj i lokalnoj razini u 2023. godini*. [33]

MRDEUF (2023), *Presentation on funding for assisted areas during OECD interviews*. [23]

MRDEUF (2023), *Presentation on the different funding mechanisms for regional development in Croatia during OECD interviews*. [25]

MRDEUF (2022), *Development Programme of Hilly-Mountainous Areas*, https://razvoj.gov.hr/UserDocsImages//Dokumenti/BBP%20PP//Program%20razvoja%20brdsko-planinskih%20podru%C4%8Dja.pdf (accessed on 28 November 2023). [48]

MRDEUF (2022), *Sustainable Social and Economic Development Programme of Assisted Areas*, https://razvoj.gov.hr/UserDocsImages//Dokumenti/BBP%20PP//Program%20odr%C5%BEivog%20dru%C5%A1tvenog%20i%20gospodarskog%20razvoja%20potpomognutih%20podru%C4%8Dja.pdf (accessed on 29 November 2023). [47]

MRDEUF (2022), *XIII. sjednica Savjeta za Slavoniju, Baranju i Srijem [XIII. session of the Council for Slavonia, Baranja and Srijem]*, https://vlada.gov.hr/UserDocsImages//Vijesti/2022/07%20srpanj/13%20srpnja//3.%20FIN%20Prezentacije%20SBS_Okucani.pdf (accessed on 2024 January 12). [20]

Normattiva (2023), "Legge di Bilancio 2024", *Bilancio di previsione dello Stato per l'anno finanziario 2024 e bilancio pluriennale per il triennio 2024-2026*, https://www.normattiva.it/atto/caricaDettaglioAtto?atto.dataPubblicazioneGazzetta=2023-12-30&atto.codiceRedazionale=23G00223&atto.articolo.numero=0&atto.articolo.sottoArticolo=1&atto.articolo.sottoArticolo1=0&qId=d7dcf800-fe06-4eb1-b56b-3a5e2d80cf7f&tabID. [36]

OECD (2023), *General Government Accounts - Government deficit/surplus, revenue, expenditure and main aggregates*, https://stats-3.oecd.org/index.aspx?DatasetCode=SNA_TABLE12. [2]

OECD (2023), *Interviews conducted as part of the "Enhanced Strategic Planning at the Regional and Local Levels in Croatia" project*. [56]

OECD (2023), *Interviews with local stakeholders conducted as part of the "Enhanced Strategic Planning at the Regional and Local Levels in Croatia" project*. [26]

OECD (2023), *Response the the OECD Regional Development Policy Committee Accession Background Questionnaire: Croatia*. [19]

OECD (2023), *Subnational governments in OECD countries: Key data (Brochure)*, OECD Publishing. [3]

OECD (2022), "G20-OECD Policy Toolkit to Mobilise Funding and Financing for Inclusive and Quality Infrastructure Investment in Regions and Cities". [54]

OECD (2022), *G20-OECD Policy Toolkit to Mobilise Funding and Financing for Inclusive and Quality Infrastructure Investment in Regions and Cities*, OECD Publishing, Paris, https://doi.org/10.1787/99169ac9-en. [38]

OECD (2022), *Rebuilding Ukraine by Reinforcing Regional and Municipal Governance*, OECD Multi-level Governance Studies, OECD Publishing, Paris, https://doi.org/10.1787/63a6b479-en. [42]

OECD (2022), *Response to the project questionnaire "Enhanced Strategic Planning at the Regional and Local Levels in Croatia" addressed to the Ministry of Regional Development and European Union Funds (MRDEUF)*. [58]

OECD (2022), *Results of the OECD county-level questionnaire for the "Enhanced Strategic Planning at the Regional and Local Levels in Croatia" project*. [32]

OECD (2021), *Fiscal Federalism 2022: Making Decentralisation Work*, OECD Publishing, Paris, https://doi.org/10.1787/201c75b6-en. [8]

OECD (2021), *OECD Implementation Handbook for Quality Infrastructure Investment*, https://www.oecd.org/finance/OECD-Implementation-Handbook-for-Quality-Infrastructure-Investment-EN.pdf (accessed on 21 November 2022). [43]

OECD (2021), *The territorial impact of COVID-19: Managing the crisis and recovery across levels of government*, OECD. [15]

OECD (2019), *Making decentralisation work: a handbook for policy-makers*, https://www.oecd-ilibrary.org/docserver/g2g9faa7-en.pdf?expires=1692882017&id=id&accname=ocid84004878&checksum=2980899ACFB96265DF4ECAC335994D1E (accessed on 24 August 2023). [1]

OECD (2019), *Making Decentralisation Work: A Handbook for Policy-Makers*, OECD Multi-level Governance Studies, OECD Publishing, Paris, https://doi.org/10.1787/g2g9faa7-en. [53]

OECD/UCLG (2022), *2022 Report of the World Observatory on Subnational Government Finance and Investment - Key Findings*, OECD/UCLG. [62]

OECD/UCLG (2022), *Country profiles - Croatia*, https://www.sng-wofi.org/country-profiles/ (accessed on 7 April 2023). [12]

Official Gazette No 127 et al. (2017), *Law on Financing of Local and Regional Self-Government Units*, https://www.zakon.hr/z/411/Zakon-o-financiranju-jedinica-lokalne-i-podru%C4%8Dne-%28regionalne%29-samouprave (accessed on 18 August 2023). [46]

Official Gazette of Croatia No 101/17 (2017), *Zakon o lokalnim porezima [Law on Local Taxes]*, https://www.zakon.hr/z/875/Zakon-o-lokalnim-porezima (accessed on 21 August 2023). [45]

Official Gazette of Croatia No 114/23 (2023), *Izmjene i dopune Zakona o porezu na dohodak [Amendments to the Law on Income Tax]*, https://www.zakon.hr/z/875/Zakon-o-lokalnim-porezima (accessed on 25 October 2023). [44]

Official Gazette of Croatia No 118/18 (2018), *Zakon o regionalnom razvoju Republike Hrvatske [Law on Regional Development of the Republic of Croatia]*, https://www.zakon.hr/z/239/Zakon-o-regionalnom-razvoju-Republike-Hrvatske (accessed on 2 July 2022). [52]

Official Gazette of Croatia No 127 et al. (2017), *Zakon o financiranju jedinica lokalne i područne (regionalne) samouprave [Law on Financing of Local and Regional Self-Government Units]*, https://www.zakon.hr/z/411/Zakon-o-financiranju-jedinica-lokalne-i-podru%C4%8Dne-%28regionalne%29-samouprave (accessed on 18 August 2023). [11]

Official Gazette of Croatia No 144/2021 (2021), *Zakon o proračunu [Budget Act]*, https://narodne-novine.nn.hr/clanci/sluzbeni/full/2021_12_144_2457.html (accessed on 22 August 2023). [16]

Official Gazette of Croatia No 149/23 (2023), *Zakon o izvršavanju Državnog proračuna Republike Hrvatske za 2024. godinu [Law on the Execution of the State Budget of the Republic of Croatia for 2024]*, https://www.zakon.hr/z/3634/Zakon-o-izvr%C5%A1avanju-Dr%C5%BEavnog-prora%C4%8Duna-Republike-Hrvatske-za-2024.-godinu (accessed on 27 March 2024). [17]

Official Gazette of Croatia No 16/13 (2013), *Pravilnik o ustroju i vođenju Registra ugovora o javno-privatnom partnerstvu [Ordinance on the organisation and management of the Register of PPP Contracts]*, https://narodne-novine.nn.hr/clanci/sluzbeni/2013_02_16_277.html (accessed on February January 2024). [41]

Official Gazette of Croatia No 3/24 (2024), *Odluka o razvrstavanju jedinica lokalne i područne (regionalne) samouprave prema stupnju razvijenosti [Decision on the classification of local and regional self-government units according to the level of development]*, https://narodne-novine.nn.hr/clanci/sluzbeni/2024_01_3_60.html. [49]

Official Gazette of Croatia No 78 et al. (2018), *Zakon o javno-privatnom partnerstvu [Public-Private Partnership Act]*, https://www.zakon.hr/z/198/Zakon-o-javno-privatnom-partnerstvu (accessed on 23 January 2024). [39]

Official Gazette OG No 88/12 15/15 (2015), *Regulation on Implementation of PPP Projects*. [40]

Rödl & Partner (2022), *Plastic Tax: Sweden*, https://www.roedl.com/insights/plastic-tax/sweden-eu-green-deal. [37]

Rodríguez-Pose, A. and E. Garcilazo (2015), "Quality of Government and the Returns of Investment: Examining the Impact of Cohesion Expenditure in European Regions", *https://doi.org/10.1080/00343404.2015.1007933*, Vol. 49/8, pp. 1274-1290, https://doi.org/10.1080/00343404.2015.1007933. [35]

U-LEAD (unpublished), *Funding for Regional and Local Development from the State Budget*. [51]

Vukovar-Srijem County (2023), *Proračun Vukovarsko-srijemske županije [Budget of Vukovar-Srijem County]*, https://vusz.hr/info/financije-1. [57]

Wallonie Developpement (n.d.), *Nos membres*, https://www.wallonie-developpement.be/membres/ (accessed on 2 February 2024). [61]

World Bank (2021), *Fiscal Decentralization in Croatia*, https://documents1.worldbank.org/curated/en/582501644400447803/pdf/Fiscal-Decentralization-in-Croatia.pdf (accessed on 21 August 2023). [5]

Annex 5.A. Subnational government revenue and expenditure data

Annex Figure 5.A.1. County revenue by category, as a share of total county revenue, 2014-20

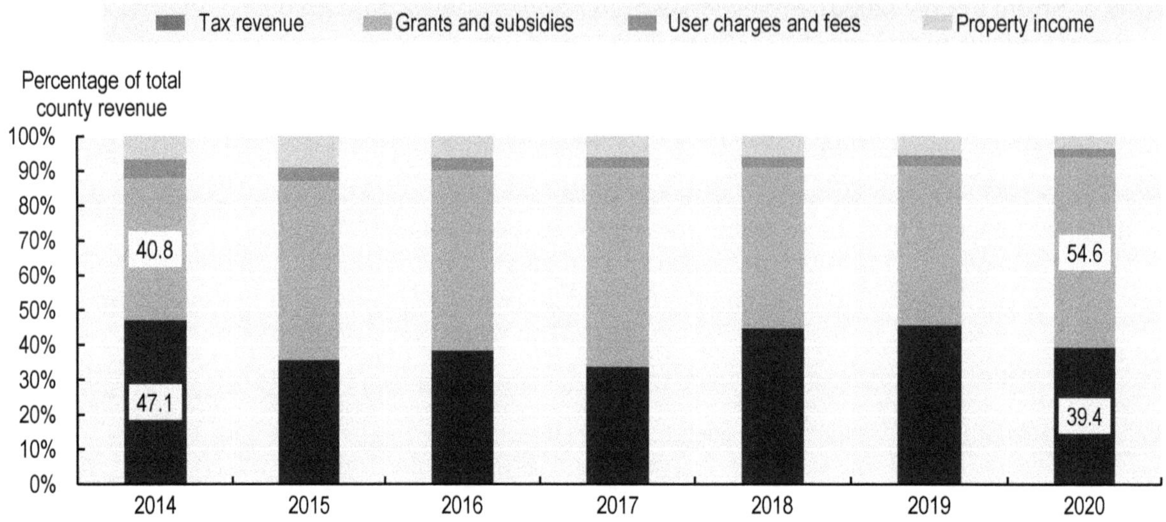

Source: Author's elaboration, based on (Ministry of Finance, 2023[6]).

Annex Figure 5.A.2. City revenue by category, as a share of total city revenue, 2014-20

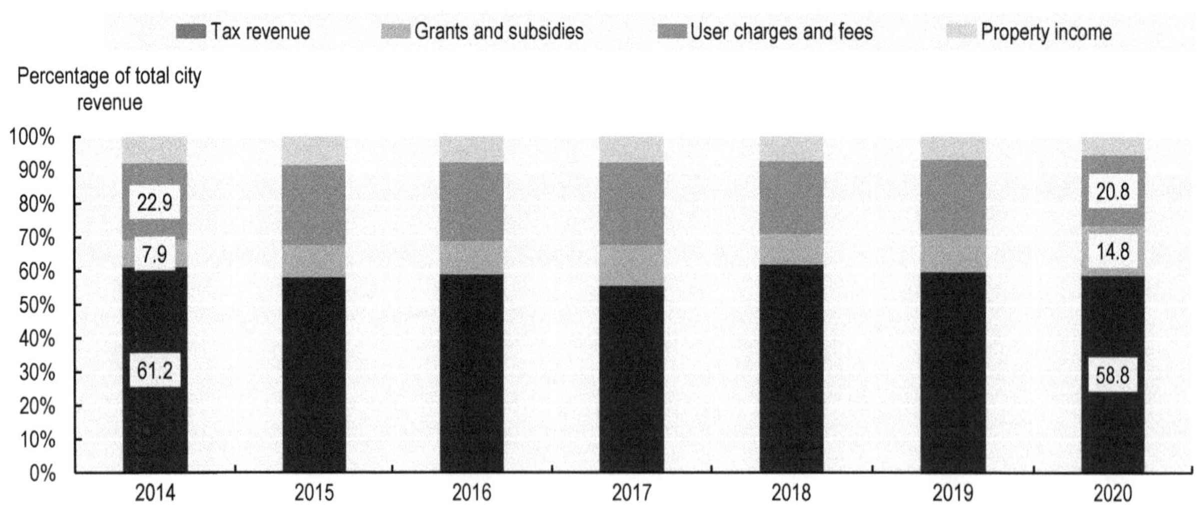

Source: Author's elaboration, based on (Ministry of Finance, 2023[6]).

Annex Figure 5.A.3. Municipal revenue by category, as a share of total municipal revenue, 2014-20

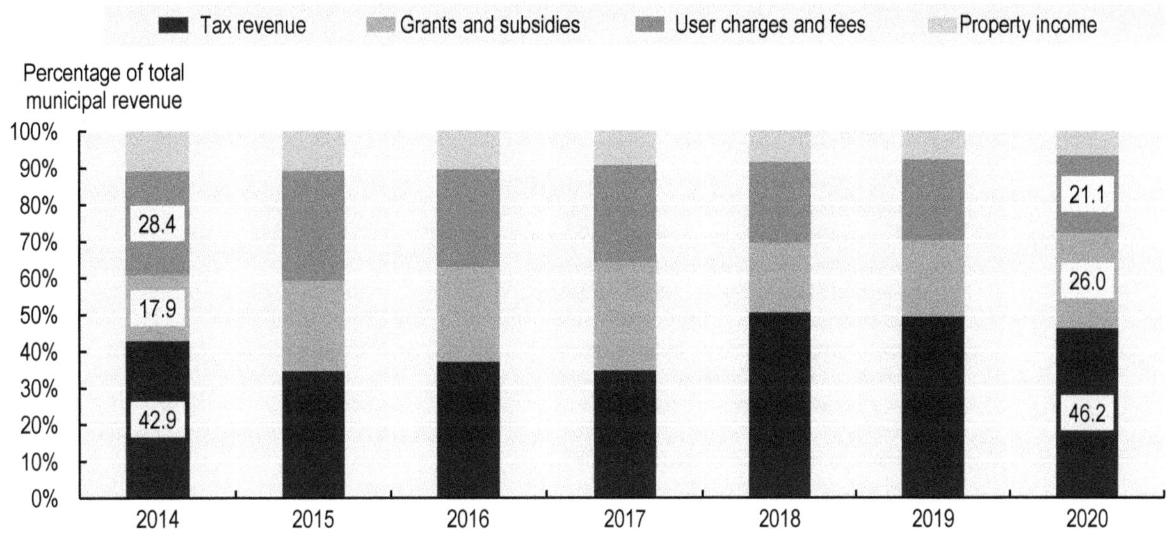

Source: Author's elaboration, based on (Ministry of Finance, 2023[6]).

Annex Figure 5.A.4. Subnational expenditure by economic classification for OECD Member countries and Croatia, latest year available

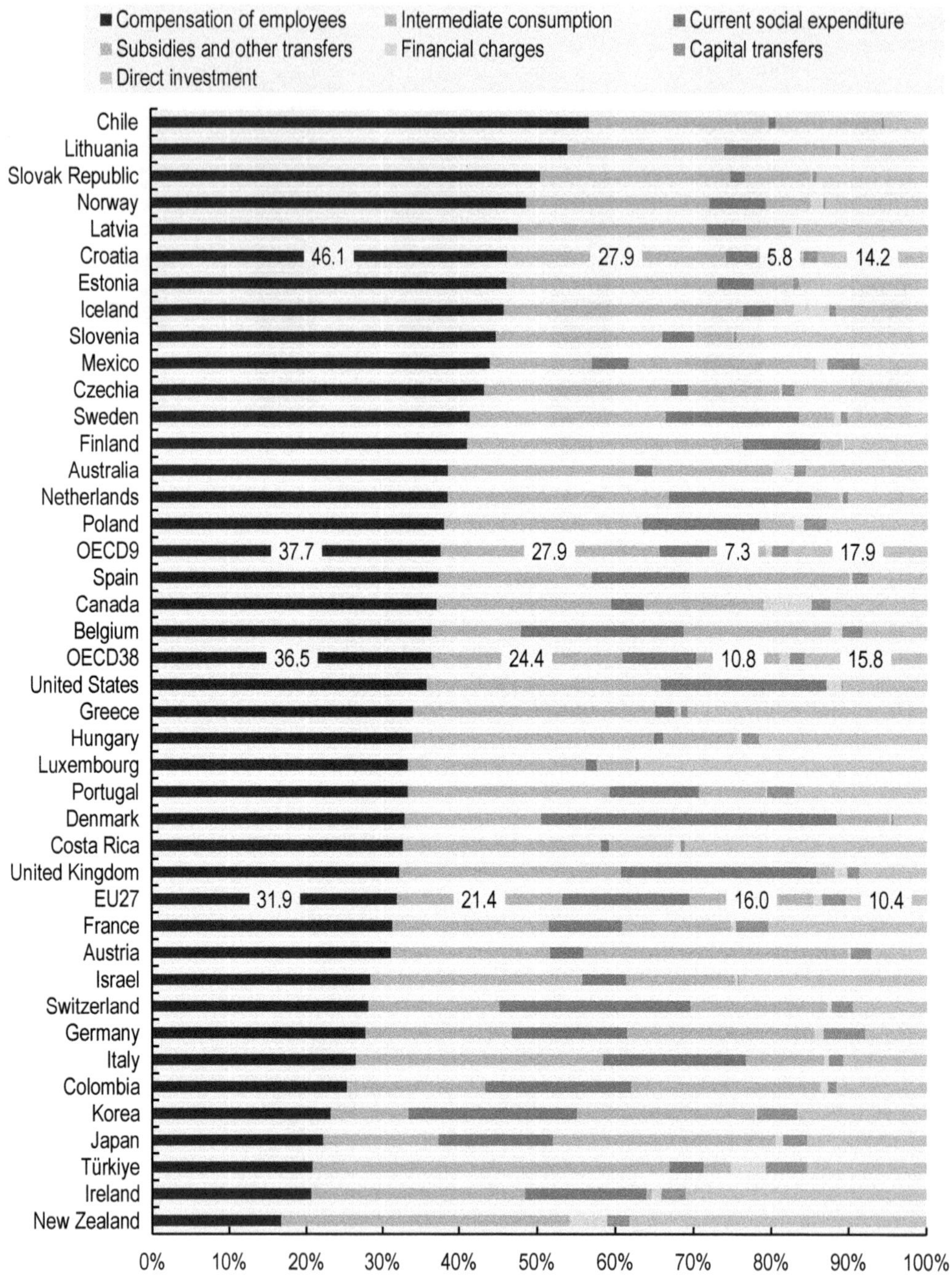

Note: Data provided here corresponds to the year 2022, with the exception of Japan, New Zealand, and the United States, where the data is from 2021, and the exception of Australia, Chile, and Türkiye, from 2020. Additionally, the data source for Australia, Colombia and Chile is (OECD/UCLG, 2022[62]), different from the general source referenced below.
Source: Author's elaboration, based on (OECD, 2023[2]).

Notes

[1] The Ministry of Finance uses the “Report on Revenues and Expenditures, Receipts and Expenses: Form PR-RAS” to provide detailed and disaggregated budgetary data categorised by the type of subnational government. While this approach provides additional granularity, the methodology employed for presenting these data remains unclear, as it appears to deviate from established international standards such as SNA 2010 or GFS 2014. The absence of a methodological note outlining data coverage and modifications to standard methodologies has hindered a comprehensive analysis of fiscal indicators by the sub-sector of subnational government. This lack of clarity has resulted in challenges in reconciling data discrepancies between the Ministry of Finance dataset and those available from OECD and Eurostat, impeding a systematic and comparative examination in this study.

[2] User charges and fees are not reported in municipal financial reports, and are instead accounted for in the reports of local utility companies, which act as service providers (Ministry of Finance, 2024[10]).

[3] The Prime Minister-led regional development co-ordination body refers to the meetings between the Prime Minister and relevant ministries, county prefects and representatives from the Croatian Association of Cities and the Croatian Union of Municipalities that have generally taken place on a biannual basis since 2016 (see chapter 3). They provide a basis for high-level political discussions on the co-ordination of territorial development between representatives from different levels of government, thereby carrying out similar tasks to those assigned to the Council for Regional Development.

www.ingramcontent.com/pod-product-compliance
Ingram Content Group UK Ltd.
Pitfield, Milton Keynes, MK11 3LW, UK
UKHW051502290926
15471UKWH00008B/1353

9 789264 767751